AN ERK'S-EY

AN ERK'S-EYE VIEW

MEMORIES OF NATIONAL SERVICE IN THE
ROYAL AIR FORCE 1952-54

TED CATON

Best wishes Tom

Ted Caton

CATON
Chelmsford, Essex

©Ted Caton, 1998
First published in Great Britain, 1998   By Ted Caton

British Library Cataloguing in Publication Data
A catalogue record for this book is available from the British Library

ISBN 0 9533030 0 4

Printed in England by Arthur H. Stockwell Ltd., Ilfracombe, Devon

To ANN
who for forty years has endured
hearing "When I was in the RAF..."
and to PETER and BARBARA
who haven't.

CONTENTS

ILLUSTRATIONS

20. USAF on the march at Camp Guynemer: colonnaded parade housing hairdresser, laundry etc. on left; equipment stores and MT sections in centre; corner of support units complex on right. [Photo: Bill Rudman]
21. Tennis courts at Camp Guynemer, near to the NAAFI building. [Photo: Bill Rudman]
22. MT Driver SAC "Scouse" Baker, POR Clerk SAC Les Goddard (before his promotion) and an unidentified LAC prior to a trip to Arromanches 1953. [Photo: via Les Goddard]
23. Snowstorm at Camp Guynemer, February 1954: French airmen and billets in background. [Photo: Bill Rudman]
24. RAF Support Unit soccer team c. 1953: From left — back, De Guyer, Crumpton, Crosthwaite, 'Jock' Fraser, LAC Hudspith, SAC Jerome; front, Cpl Evans, Chadwick, Cpl Stott, Green, Lee. [Photo: Bill Rudman]
25. AAFCE international soccer team c. 1954: RAF from left — back, fourth Sgt Fenney, fifth Cpl Tech Payne, seventh Eccles, eighth LAC Massey; front, first Cpl Stott, second SAC Griffiths; other team members were from the Belgian, French and Netherlands Air Forces. [Photo: via Les Massey]
26. LAC Brian Simpson at Camp Guynemer 1954: French airmen's billets on left and French mess in background.
27. SAC David Mollart-Rogerson (in uniform) with unidentified colleague at Camp Guynemer 1954.
28. Camp Guynemer after the author's departure: SPs on main gate duty 1955. [Photo: Tom Weatherley]
29. Ted Heath Band visit 1954: singer Kathy Lloyd with (from left) Pte J. J. C. v d Hoeven (RNAF), Cpl David Evans and AC1 Peter Prentice (RAF) and Cpl Jac Vos (RNAF). [NATO Photo]
30. The author's 'personal' pilots: Air Chief Marshal Sir Basil Embry (left) and Air Commodore Peter Wykeham-Barnes. [RCAF Photo]
31. Avro Ansons, probably Mark C19, at Melun/Villaroche, c. 1953. [Photo: Bill Rudman]
32. A De Havilland DH104 Devon similar to the one in which the author flew to Nice, at the Battle of Britain Memorial Flight, RAF Coningsby, Lincolnshire on 17 April 1997.
33. The nearest the author has been to a Pembroke since 1954: a Hunting Percival Sea Prince T1, the Royal Navy equivalent, at the Norfolk and Suffolk Aviation Museum, Flixton on 30 June 1996.
34. Le Palais de Fontainebleau, 1 May 1954.
35. A quiet scene in Fontainebleau, 1 May 1954.

36. Taking their ease outside Le Café Quartier des Suisses, Fontainebleau: AC1 Bill Rudman (right) and Pat, an unidentified erk. [Photo: via Bill Rudman]
37. Approximately half the AAFCE WRAF contingent (and one bashful erk) in the grounds of Le Palais de Fontainebleau: LACW Diane Lawson on the left. [Photo: Bill Rudman]
38. HRH The Duke of Edinburgh (left) with Air Chief Marshal Sir Basil Embry, arriving at HQ AAFCE in the summer of 1954. [Photo: Bill Rudman]
39. The author (left) and SAC Derrick Smith with one of the Duke's rhododendrons in the grounds of Fontainebleau Palace, summer 1954. [Photo: Brian Simpson]
40. Sir Basil Embry being greeted on arrival at a NATO base somewhere in Europe by a limping USAF Major General: on the left is a Général de Brigade Aérienne of the FAF and behind him, leaving Sir Basil's personal Devon aircraft in which the author enjoyed several 'gash flips', can be seen his ADC, Fg Off R. L. Lees, who contributed the foreword to this book. [NATO Photo]
41. Departing after a visit to HQ AAFCE: Admiral Radford (US Navy), Chairman of America's Joint Chiefs of Staff, with Sir Basil Embry; behind the Admiral is Fg Off R. L. Lees (RAF). [NATO Photo]
42. An apparently disinterested Sir Basil Embry being saluted left-handed by his Commander-in-Chief, Le Maréchal de France Alphonse Juin, and right-handed from the rear by an unidentified USAF officer: in fact a war wound denied Le Maréchal the full use of his right hand. [NATO Photo]
43. Signed photograph given to the author by Air Chief Marshal Sir Basil Embry on 26 October 1954. [NATO Photo]
44. Publicity photograph of the author at his desk in HQ AAFCE, feigning work on 8 October 1954. [NATO Photo]
45. Paris: NATO HQ obscuring Le Palais de Chaillot on 19 June 1954.
46. Paris: deserted Avenue des Champs Elysées on a Saturday (19 June 1954).
47. LAC Brian Simpson anxiously awaiting his lunch near La Tour Eiffel, Paris, 19 June 1954.
48. Paris: no custom for the ice-cream vendors in La Place de l'Étoile on 19 June 1954.
49. Paris: Le Pont Neuf, the subject of the author's etching, 2 October 1954.

50. With live ammunition and fixed bayonet, the author's brother Geof about to commence guard duty at Namur Camp, GHQ Middle East Land Forces, Fayid, Egypt, summer 1954.
51. Perhaps enjoying a somewhat cushier time, the author's other brother Den having apparently just emerged from WRAF billets at RAF Strubby, Lincs, 1957.
52. The author with his 'personal' Cessna 172 at Southend Airport, 20 August 1994. [Photo: Janice Harding]

Front Cover: Part of G25 Flight, 4 Wing, No 11 S of RT, RAF Hednesford, Staffordshire, December 1952.

Back Cover: Author on day of demob, 3 November 1954. [Photo: Den Caton.]

FOREWORD

by Air Vice-Marshal R. L. Lees, CB, MBE,
Head of RAF Administration Branch 1982–1986

For about a year in the early Fifties, Ted Caton and I were probably the most junior forms of Service life (as an LAC and Pilot Officer respectively) within NATO, both enormously privileged to be serving on the personal staff of one of the most senior and most charismatic RAF officers, Air Chief Marshal Sir Basil Embry, the Commander-in-Chief of Allied Air Forces Central Europe.

In those early days of the NATO alliance, we were faced with two very different challenges: the first, to put together sufficiently strong deterrent forces to counter the recently-created Warsaw Pact, which we could only do by achieving the second, which was to mould the armed forces of fifteen nations into a cohesive and integrated entity. It wasn't easy: national sensitivities were very strong and not all the fifteen nations had avoided some measure of defeat in the Second World War only ten years or so earlier; language difficulties apart, we didn't really understand each other; aircraft from one country were unable to operate, for logistic and technical reasons, from the airfields of another; inter-Service rivalry, especially between the Armies and the Air Forces, remained strong and sometimes bitter; an integrated Air Defence System was non-existent and although all the NATO nations expressed their support for the alliance, the actual delivery of commitment in terms of funding, manpower and support was very patchy to say the least.

Each nation made its contribution in its own way: for the Americans it was to 'pour concrete' and for the British it was to set high standards and underpin the staff work. How a young National Serviceman was to find himself in this rather *Alice in Wonderland* existence forms the subject of this book.

Ted Caton has done a remarkable job, without the support of detailed diary jottings or family letters, sadly destroyed, to create a real feel for the RAF of the Fifties. He must, I am sure, have retained some mementoes of his days in the Service and he has certainly taken my mind back with unerring accuracy and rekindled happy memories of events and people I thought I had forgotten, but haven't.

Had he been born forty years earlier, he might have been writing about the experiences of an eighteen-year-old in the trenches of the First World War: had he been born forty years later, it is unlikely that he would have been in the Services at all. With the strength of the Royal Air Force now approaching 50,000 all ranks, there is no room for non-regular servicemen, and more's the pity. The experiences of National Service were not universally welcomed, but there are many Captains of Industry today who chart their successful careers to those early challenges to their character and remember with gratitude the cheerful comradeship that came from facing the slings and arrows of adversity with others in the same boat.

ROBIN LEES

PREFACE

It is perhaps necessary to explain why I have thought it appropriate to place on record the story of those two years of my life during which I wore the Queen's uniform. I believe there to be a dearth of stories written by 'erks', the lowly RAF aircraftmen, and I hope the recollections of someone at the bottom will provide a refreshing alternative to the many memoirs of the men at the top, the air marshals and so on. The humble erk lives very differently and sees life from a different angle but if, as I did, he works with the commanders he has some privileges and gains some insight into what is happening at the highest levels. It was, however, one thing to work *at* the top and another to work *with* the top. Basically, therefore, the story is written from the bottom looking up and, notwithstanding that I may have been privy to a little more of what was going on than was the average erk, I could well have got hold of the wrong ends of one or two sticks; if so, I apologize.

I make no pretensions as to my ability as a writer; the reader may well not be surprised to learn that this is my first attempt at authorship. I have nevertheless gone to some lengths to tell the tale as accurately as possible, if perhaps a little tongue-in-cheek at times. I do not pretend that my story is in any way exceptional but rather that it is typical of the time served by those young men called up after World War II — even though there must be a million different stories in all. Those seeking a learned treatise should look elsewhere; they will find here no more than a not too serious account of what happened during a period of two years with perhaps a few idle thoughts along the way; opinions expressed here and there are mine alone. There is no foul language so the story is suitable for readers of a nervous disposition.

Wherever possible I have used the actual names of the persons mentioned. In a few cases, where either names have vanished into the mists of time or I would not wish to cause embarrassment, I have used fictitious names. In any event, I hope I have not caused offence. Where mentioned, Service ranks were correct at the time of which I write; some, of course, went on to greater things.

I must place on record my gratitude for the help given to me by the former Servicemen named below and, at the risk of alienating others, thank especially David Mollart-Rogerson (Moll), for his considerable assistance with the chapters dealing with my sojourn in France, Bill Rudman for the loan of many photographs and Peter Steggall for his invaluable advice and encouragement.

Former members of the Royal Air Force:

3118272	AC1	Bush, P. R.
2758413	SAC	Caton, D. G.
4097609	SAC	Goddard, L. R.

4048708	Cpl	Lake, A. B.
4061485	LAC	Massey, L.
4095043	SAC	Mollart-Rogerson, D. C.
4087041	Cpl	Prentice, P. J.
4092868	AC1	Rudman, R. W.
2589733	SAC	Shearman, J. C.
2590268	LAC	Walls, G. C.
4133375	Cpl	Weatherley, T. H.

Other former Servicemen:

S/22990279	Sgt	Caton, G. L., Royal Army Service Corps
1827444	Gunner	Steggall, P. C., Royal Artillery

David Marshall (Canada) and Jack Brackenbury have helped me greatly with information on the history of RAF Norton.

Except where otherwise stated, the photographs which I have used are my own or from my collection. I am grateful to the Air Force Adviser, Canadian Defence Liaison Staff (London); the Director of Public Relations (RAF), Ministry of Defence; and the Head of Photos and Visual Aids, NATO, for permission to use photographs; and to the Editors of the *Essex Chronicle Series Ltd.*, and the *Weekly News Series* for permission to include extracts from newspapers.

Finally, I am indebted to Air Vice-Marshal R. L. Lees, CB, MBE, for his advice and for his kindness in writing the Foreword.

Chelmsford,
Essex

CHAPTER 1

INTRODUCTION

Summer seemed a long time arriving in 1952, but by 1 July the temperature in my home County of Essex had soared to 90°F. Six days later Monday 7 July was a little less hot: it was also my eighteenth birthday. I nevertheless felt little excitement pedalling my elderly third-hand gentleman's upright bicycle into Chelmsford, the County town, in the company of my younger brother in order to start another week's mildly gainful employment. In the 1990s my spirits would undoubtedly have been high; indeed, this birthday would have been an occasion for great rejoicing, parties and general merriment. One is now deemed to come of age at eighteen, to be competent to vote at Parliamentary and local elections, to get married without parents' consent and so on: in short, to be 'grown up'.

Many young people manage to enjoy similar celebrations at the age of twenty-one also, especially if their parents happen not to be financially embarrassed. This is a throw-back to what was the situation in the 1950s when the magic age for reaching adulthood was still twenty-one. However, in those days there was one thing which you not only could do at eighteen but which in normal circumstances (and if you had chanced to be born a male) you were legally obliged to do. Whether you liked it or not you could serve for a pittance in the armed forces of the Crown and, if you were pretty unlucky, you could fight and even die for your country.

Understandably, in the 1940s and 1950s the average young man viewed the approach of his eighteenth birthday and the spectre of National Service with some trepidation. Few of us were actually anxious to undertake military service and those who were would presumably have joined one of the Services anyway. The trouble was that not enough of us were sufficiently keen (or foolish some might suggest) to want to 'join up' with the result that, following the winding down of all three Services which occurred after World War II, there were simply not enough people coming forward voluntarily to enable His or Her Majesty's Forces to meet all their commitments.

After the war and as I have already implied, only young men were selected for the doubtful honour of being conscripted. It is tempting now to wonder in this age of rampant feminism and political correctness what would be the situation in the event that compulsory service were still required. Would the young men be joined by all the women of similar age? If so, would those women be required to undertake the same training and duties as their male colleagues (the feminists would not wish to see distinctions made, presumably)?

My own view is that the answers to those two questions would probably be "yes". In this connection it is interesting to note that all three women's Services (the Women's Royal Naval Service, the Women's Royal Army

Corps and the Women's Royal Air Force) have in recent times lost their individual identities and achieved full integration into the Royal Navy, the Army and the Royal Air Force respectively.

How successful will this prove to be? As recent Courts Martial have demonstrated, problems are already surfacing following the introduction of female sailors into the crews of Royal Navy warships. I for one am not surprised: quite apart from the obvious difficulties arising with mixed crews at sea together for long periods within the restricted confines of a ship, most women simply don't possess the physical strength needed to undertake some of the required duties.

As an alternative to full integration would certain trades, for example cooks and clerks, have to be reserved for women and others, such as commandos and the infantry, for men? And if the result of conscripting all youngsters of both sexes would be to overload the Services beyond the numbers which they required or with which they could cope, how would the resultant selective conscription be fairly achieved? All in all, a potential administrative nightmare.

At the risk of departing even further from the purpose of this volume, namely, to recount my own experiences over the period of two years during which I was conscripted, I will merely quote without comment the view of a male seaman when interviewed on television during 1994, and then return to 1952 and my eighteenth birthday. He said in effect "They [the women] think they're only on board to see the world; they don't seem to realize there's a lot of hard work to be done".

By the arrival of the summer in 1952, the war in Europe had been over for seven years. Hostilities with Japan had lasted a few more months but ended abruptly following the dropping of the atomic bombs first on Hiroshima and then on Nagasaki, both in Japan itself. Little did I dream that by the summer of 1954 I would be working in an office in an international headquarters, my desk being located only a matter of yards from that occupied by the pilot of the American Superfortress which dropped the first of those weapons.

So far as World War II was concerned, 'National Service' — the term used in the United Kingdom to describe the conscription of citizens for compulsory military duty — started in 1939 almost immediately after war was declared on Germany on that fateful Sunday, 3 September. The original National Service (Armed Forces) Act applied to all men who were physically fit, not in reserved occupations such as coal mining, and aged between 18 and 41. Subsequent legislation enabled men up to the age of 51, as well as women, to be conscripted into the armed forces.

There was also provision for non-military national service, for example in the AFS (Auxiliary Fire Service) and in the ARP (Air Raid Precautions) where my own father, Leonard, served as an air raid warden for the duration of the war. Following the conscription into the Army of Chris Flatt, the neighbour and colleague with whom he had at first been able to share night-time responsibility for the streets allocated to the pair of them (Bruce Grove, Campbell Close and Stewart Road), my father then had to look after all three on his own. During periods when air raids were frequent, this could mean being on duty seven nights a week on top of his work as an accountant during five and a half days. Although not directly in the firing line as those conscripted for military service might well be, nevertheless he and his male and female colleagues across the country regularly braved falling bombs, bullets and shrapnel armed with a whistle, rattle and handbell and with only a 'tin hat' for protection. At the end of it all, my father was rewarded with a medal from the Home Secretary, the sack from his day-time employer and a letter in the following terms from the residents of Bruce Grove, the street in which we lived:

> Will you please accept the enclosed [the sum of £9/5/- or £9.25p] as a small token to show our appreciation and gratitude, for what you have done for us during the years of the war, at no doubt great sacrifice, and inconvenience to yourself.
>
> You never shirked your duty, and were always at your post, we could go to bed and shut our eyes always knowing your whistle would warn us of any danger near. May God bless you and your family and give you better health.
>
> From your ever gratefully, ...[56 families]...

By the end of the war in Europe, about five million men and women were in the three Services, the majority as one would expect being in the Army. Not all the five million were conscripts of course — many were already in the regular Services or had volunteered ahead of 'call-up' (often to get into the particular Service they preferred rather than risk being directed elsewhere) — but the figure gives some indication of the scale of the call-up which had taken place during the war. As soon as hostilities finished those who had been conscripted were naturally keen to be demobilised ('demobbed') and to return home and to civilian life at the earliest possible moment. Obviously it was quite impossible to demob everybody at once and an orderly staged release got under way as soon as the war had ended.

In 1945 Britain still had an Empire to 'rule', the international situation was deteriorating into the 'Cold War' and the now vanquished Germany had to be governed and helped back onto its feet by the victorious Allies. It quickly became clear that the country's world-wide military commitments simply could not be met by what would have remained of the Services had all the conscripts been released without further ado. Many therefore saw their release dates receding steadily into the distance and near mutinies were rumoured to have occurred in a few units as the result.

The problems led inevitably to the National Service Act 1947 which required all males between the ages of 18 and 26 to undertake twelve months compulsory military service. As from 1 January 1949 the period was increased to eighteen months full-time service followed by four years in the reserves. By 1950, with the Korean War in progress, it was considered necessary to increase the period again, to two years full-time but with only three and a half years in the reserves, i.e. still five and a half years in all. This then was the situation which continued until 31 December 1960 when compulsory call-up ended.

Post-war National Service differed from war service in that conscripts did not qualify for a gratuity at the end of it: neither did they get one of the infamous demob suits! Presumably as a sop to the pressure groups when the length of full-time service was increased from eighteen months to two years, it was announced that the final, i.e. the extra, six months would be rewarded with pay at regular service rates. My own pay increased by 3/- (15p) a day, just over £1 a week, which was actually quite a lot of money at that time.

If you wished to earn such princely sums throughout the whole of your service it was of course open to you to volunteer for the regular forces, the minimum period of engagement being three years. In other words, if you were prepared to 'sign on', as it was termed, to do half as much again, you could earn what was, with all found, quite a reasonable wage. I was to be surprised to discover what a large proportion of potential National Servicemen did in fact sign on for regular service in the Royal Air Force (RAF), especially as not one of my own work or other contemporaries did so. The only explanation for this which occurs to me is that, by volunteering in this way, one perhaps had a better prospect of getting into the preferred Service — and in my experience very few, including myself, would have preferred the Army.

Not many young men between the ages of 18 and 26 were able to avoid doing their eighteen months or two years. Obviously if you were unfit medically you were not accepted but very few would have wished this upon themselves. Rumours were current in the 1950s about ways of convincing the medical authorities that you had flat feet, which would allegedly lead automatically to exemption, but I never knew the truth of this! Needless to say the Services could not accept those with, say, severe eyesight difficulties but I think it is true to say that, overall, not many were rejected on medical grounds. In support of this assertion, one of my own work colleagues, generally felt by his peers not to be the fittest among us, was accepted and proceeded to spend about three-quarters of his service in a Royal Air Force hospital. He has since been very seriously ill.

Apart from the unwelcome possibility of being found medically unfit, there were a number of ways in which it was possible to avoid National Service. You were automatically exempt if you worked in a 'reserved occupation' such as coal mining, farming or sea-fishing or if you were, for example, a police cadet, a clergyman or working abroad for the Government. Moreover, the severe fuel shortages of the 1940s led to young men (the 'Bevin boys') being conscripted into the coal mines and so undertaking their National Service underground instead of in the armed forces.

Some fifty years later I was to encounter whilst on holiday in the Austrian Tyrol a gentleman — Fred from Macclesfield — who had actually volunteered to do his National Service in the mines. Maybe this was commonplace in certain other areas of the country but, coming from a non-mining district as I do, I had not before even realized that this course had been open to those registering for National Service. By taking this action, Fred was able to continue to live at home and cycle to and from a mine near Manchester where he worked on the day shift. He tells the story that, cycling to the mine early one morning, he noticed wisps of smoke emerging from ventilation grills on a cinema. He was faced with a dilemma: if he diverted to raise the alarm (and he couldn't be sure that all was not well anyway) he would arrive at the mine too late to catch the 'cage' when it descended to the depths and would thereby lose a day's pay. He pedalled on, completed his shift and, cycling home, observed that the cinema had burned to the ground.

Another course open to the reluctant conscript was to try to convince a Tribunal that he was a conscientious objector. I have no personal knowledge in this regard but, as I understand it, few succeeded and of those who did some at least found themselves on non-combatant duties in the Royal Army Medical Corps and elsewhere.

There was one other thing you could do: you could read the small print in the statutes and regulations and proceed to exercise all your rights of appeal, attend hearings and systematically ward off the evil day for as long as possible in the hope that conscription would cease before you reached the end of the legal road. One of my work colleagues did just this in the late 1950s. He assured his friends in the office that he would be quite prepared if necessary to do his two years in one of the Guards Regiments but that he proposed to try, using the law, to avoid call-up. He was nearing the end of the road when 31 December 1960 arrived and he had escaped. He is now a partner in a firm of solicitors. He was a little less astute on the occasion in the office when, standing with a mug of coffee in his left hand, a devious colleague enquired as to the time and he poured his elevenses down the front of his suit.

It was also possible in some circumstances to put off the evil day for a while by securing deferment of National Service. Those undergoing apprenticeships or part of the way through courses at universities and colleges could have their service deferred. In the case of some, for example those training to be doctors, the deferment could be for up to twelve or more years, although I believe the period was usually about four years.

Of course, in the 1950s there was the opportunity for only a fraction of the university and other training which exists in the 1990s and in my experience few young men sought deferment. In some ways it was better to get your service over and done with anyway. I believe eighteen-year-olds found it less onerous accepting the discipline in training camps than did those aged twenty-two or more who were themselves probably older than those enforcing that discipline.

Having been conscripted into the Services against their will, what kind of reception could the National Serviceman expect from those already there from choice? Between its inception in 1939 and its demise in 1960, well over five million men were called up for National Service. The majority

21

served in the Army, about half a million were in the Royal Navy and around one million in the Royal Air Force. Those called up during the war were conscripted for the specific purpose of fighting and winning that war. They and the regular Servicemen with whom they trained, fought, worked and (at times) played appreciated this and I think there were few, if any, problems between them, at least at the lower levels; after all, they were all on the same side.

The post-war years — with which this account is concerned — saw something of a sea-change in attitudes. To start with, those in the Services simply to get their National Service out of the way didn't want to be there anyway which inevitably coloured their attitude towards their particular arm of the Services and the people in it. On the other hand, the career regulars found themselves at times swamped by these reluctant recruits who required to be trained up to the standard needed to enable them to do something useful during the balance of their eighteen months or two years, following which they promptly disappeared back to civilian life only to be replaced by more of the same.

Training for some of the more technical jobs took a very long time and was expensive in terms of the Services' resources. For example, I understand the Royal Air Force did train a limited number of National Servicemen to be aircrew, including pilots. However, having received their 'wings' little time would presumably have remained for them to be of any use other than in the reserve after completion of full-time service.

On the other hand, the presence of the National Servicemen did at least make good what would otherwise have been a considerable shortfall in numbers and enable the Services to meet their world-wide obligations. There was considerable debate within the Services at all levels on the question of the acceptability of National Service and one of the most senior officers opposed to the whole concept of conscription in peacetime was my eventual 'boss', Air Chief Marshal Sir Basil Embry. In spite of such opposition, he did in his autobiography acknowledge what he termed the high standard of useful work and behaviour of National Service airmen. As someone who worked personally for him, I like to think that my own work and behaviour might perhaps have had just a little influence on his views!

CHAPTER 2

CHELMSFORD CHILDHOOD IN PEACE AND WAR

In 1934 the seventh hour of the seventh day of the seventh month was graced by my arrival in my parents' small three-bedroomed semi-detached house in Bruce Grove, Chelmsford. My father had paid £10 deposit to secure this £550 house new in 1932 and his mortgage with the Halifax Building Society was repaid over 25 years at the rate of £2 odd each month. Figures which appear minuscule in the 1990s resulted in strained family finances sixty years earlier, especially following the arrival in October 1935 and February 1937, respectively, of my two brothers. As was usual in those times, my mother had not worked following marriage and my father enjoyed only a modest income from his job as an accountant with a now long-defunct firm of agricultural engineers located in Chelmsford.

My parents, both from the East End of London, had set up home in the town in order to be near the job to which my father had previously been commuting in reverse (i.e. out of London rather than into it as is usual). Eventually he took lodgings in one of a row of homes in Fairfield Road, close to the railway station, which now form part of the site of the Civic Centre car park. The evils which the 'planners' and politicians have perpetrated on this once pleasant market town are beyond the scope of this story but suffice it to say that they almost defy description.

By modern day standards we three brothers had a fairly sheltered upbringing. We were not, for instance, normally permitted to join other local children in the street but required to play in the garden, resulting in the complete annihilation of a once lush lawn. We kept ourselves very much to ourselves with fairly frequent visits to and from relatives, mainly on my mother's side of the family. Such holidays as finances permitted usually involved staying with relations, almost all of whom were in the south-eastern quarter of England. Cheap-day excursions by train or bus to coastal resorts in Essex were summer highlights, the only other outings I can recall being picnics and so on at local 'beauty spots' accessible on foot: in common with most people at the time we did not have a car.

Although life was pretty simple, without any of the mechanical and electrical contrivances which govern today's existence (an ancient wireless set and a cumbersome HMV wind-up gramophone were the only concessions to modernity), I think we were happier than the majority of present-day youth would appear to be, subject as they are to the drugs, alcohol and nicotine culture, not to mention the violence, sex and general rubbish churned out by television, video and cinema. Perhaps I exaggerate somewhat as I am well aware that all shouldn't be tarred with the same brush, but nevertheless I believe the principle to be a valid one: we **were** happy. A treat was a halfpenny water ice in its triangular cardboard tube — like a miniature Toblerone — bought from Walls' "Stop Me and Buy One" tricycle. My special favourite was coloured green; I can't imagine what flavour this would have been!

At the age of five I was due to start at Moulsham County Infants' School on Monday 4 September 1939, the day following the declaration of war on Germany. In the expectation that waves of German bomber aircraft would immediately appear in the skies, my start date was postponed. As nothing happened the postponement lasted only one day and, crying my eyes out, I was taken to school by my mother on Tuesday 5 September. A well-behaved little boy who was not crying his eyes out took me by the hand and led me into the building. His name was Keith Willis. His father was to become the Borough Engineer and, as such, his name — V. J. Willis — adorned the sides of the Council's dustcarts and other vehicles. Apart from those connected with the war I have few recollections of infants' school: catching my finger in a slamming assembly hall door and, the headmistress having plunged it alternately into hot and cold water, having to wear a finger-stall for several weeks; finding the art of sewing to be beyond me and a teacher having to make up the cardboard picture frame which I was to take home supposedly as my own work; and the little girl, Sylvia Welland, who used to sit next to me. I wonder what became of her. We were not too used to girls in our family — not only did I have no sisters but most of my cousins, too, were boys.

Two or three years later I transferred across the road to Moulsham County Junior Boys' School where we were segregated from the girls at playtime by a six foot chain link fence. In the first year I received my one and only dose of corporal punishment, a whacking behind the knees in front of the class from the headmaster, burly Mr S. W. Petchey. I cannot remember what misdemeanour led to this indignity but I do recall my mother being very upset and, I believe, visiting Mr Petchey to complain about it. It's funny how some things remain in your mind: I clearly remember in the same class, at the age of seven or eight, being the only boy who knew why the Low Countries were so called and this feat of youthful brilliance being drawn to Mr Petchey's notice next time he visited the classroom; embarrassing but preferable to a beating.

I have a clear recollection also of one of the school's characters, an unkempt lad I will call Padget, who one morning arrived for school on a dilapidated old bicycle, presumably acquired by his father during the course of his trade as a rag and bone man. Young Padget was subjected by his peers to considerable ribbing, not because of the state of the machine (which was pretty catastrophic to be sure), but rather because it was a GIRL's model. Next morning he arrived with a length of string tied where the crossbar would have been.

The severe winter and fuel restrictions of 1944/45 led to the closure of the school for a time, except that the 'scholarship' class to which I then belonged continued lessons with Mr W. W. Gardiner before a coal fire in the staff room. I wasn't happy about this at the time as my brothers were at home enjoying themselves — but I expect it helped me to pass the subsequent 'scholarship' examination.

24

Thus the whole of my primary schooling fitted nicely into the period of World War II — September 1939–June 1945. The fact that the country was at war during those most formative and impressionable years not surprisingly had a profound effect on me and, I am sure, on my contemporaries. I have many vivid memories of the war, none of which I am certain will ever leave me: an anxious Mr Hudson, my teacher at the time, scanning the sky from a junior school air raid shelter worrying as to whether he dare allow his charges to set off for home without having heard the 'all clear' siren; the utter silence which followed the explosion, heard from a school shelter, when a German aircraft fully laden with bombs crashed in a field quite close to the school; the condensation trails and 'crackling' on high during the Battle of Britain, as well as the falling bullets, cartridge cases and shrapnel (jagged bits of exploded shell).

One lunch time a sudden gale caught the RAF balloon handlers in Oaklands Park by surprise and resulted in the cable tethering our local barrage balloon breaking before their frantic efforts to bring it to earth could be successful. I was walking back to the junior school carrying a pile of books tied together with string and intended for the troops when, following a loud crack, the huge balloon trailing its lethal steel cable lurched above the trees on the opposite side of the main road. I was petrified and didn't know whether to run back home or on to school. Other balloons broke away that day and Chelmsford was thus deprived of a large proportion of its airborne defences.

The town also boasted anti-aircraft guns and searchlights, the positions of which were changed at times, presumably to confuse the enemy airmen. One quiet night, the bored operators of a searchlight in Crompton Parkinson's sports field at the rear of my home lowered their light to the horizontal and swung the beam along the backs of our street of houses, thereby awakening many sleeping residents. We had to learn the hard way that ascending shells sounded much the same as descending bombs, the subsequent explosions revealing all. It might seem a little unnecessary to defend a smallish market town and agricultural centre, but Chelmsford was in those days home to a number of factories vital to the war effort and, of course, the Germans knew this. Consequently the town was the subject of a number of air attacks, major ones taking place on 15 April 1943 and, with fifty townspeople killed, on 14 May 1943. One raid in particular I remember clearly when a neighbour was killed whilst sheltering under a bridge over the nearby LNER railway line which unfortunately proved to be a target of the bombers.

The main targets were the factories of Marconi (radio), Hoffmann (ball bearings), Crompton Parkinson and Christy (both electrical) as well as the railway line and its bridges. A *Luftwaffe* (German Air Force) model of the area of the town containing the Marconi and Hoffmann works was to be on display in the Chelmsford and Essex Museum. Found by "C" Sqn, 8501 Wing of the RAF in a fire gutted photographic building at Quedlingburg airfield, Germany, on 12 June 1945, the boundaries of the factories' sites were clearly indicated by, respectively, blue and yellow colouring. The model had been made from an aerial photograph taken in May 1943 and I wonder whether use had been made of it prior to an attempt to attack Hoffmann's factory later that year, a raid notable for the shooting down of no less than three of the Dornier bombers by the fighter piloted by Fg Off Schultz (a somewhat inappropriate name in the circumstances!) A night-time raid in October 1940 killed the town's Mayor and Mayoress, Alderman and Mrs J. O. Thompson, and others of their household in New London Road. There was an unsubstantiated rumour at the time that the Mayor was ensconced in the 'smallest room' when the bomb fell. In all, 160 Chelmsfordians were killed in bombing raids on the town.

Apart from my father's whistle, rattle and handbell, my family's own defences against the bombers consisted of buckets filled with sand or water, a stirrup pump (intended to enable one to extinguish a flaming incendiary bomb without having to approach it sufficiently closely to get burnt), blackout material at all the windows (themselves adorned with strips of adhesive paper to prevent the glass shattering in the blast from explosions) and a succession of air raid shelters. My two brothers and I also had toy tin hats, literally made from tin and painted bright blue, which to our annoyance we were not permitted to wear outside the house during air raids. At the tender ages of 4, 5 and 6 we had assumed we would be able, wearing them, to accompany my father as he went about his ARP duties.

The first air raid shelter, a massive effort dug by my father and a next-door neighbour — Mr 'Postman' Smith — straddled their two rear gardens and had entrances at both ends, thereby complying nicely with the official advice that all shelters should have emergency exits. The theory at the time was that properly constructed shelters would protect you from all but direct hits and they were usually fully equipped to enable a whole family to spend a night in relative comfort, even to the extent of bunk beds being fitted. This first shelter hadn't had a lot of use before one night, fortunately when there had been no 'alert' sounded and it was therefore unoccupied, the whole edifice collapsed. I have an earlier vivid recollection of the neighbours' son, returning from his secondary school one afternoon in 1940, running down the garden path to reach this shelter while the debris from the battle being fought high above rained down around us. The strange thing is that I must have been outside the shelter myself to have seen him.

The replacement shelter, smaller and sturdier, was constructed by my father half below ground to accommodate only our family although I do recall it being shared with the wife and two children of Mr Chris Flatt, the other air raid warden (who, it may be recalled, finished up in the Army). In its turn this shelter was succeeded by an indoor Morrison shelter — initially a single-decker but converted later into a double-decker — in which the family and occasionally neighbours' children slept. This was a rectangular steel-framed structure with a sheet steel 'table' top and removable cage-like side panels, within which were positioned one or two systems of bearers for mattresses to enable it to be used permanently for sleeping. Again, it was designed to protect its occupants from all but a direct hit.

My family's 'Morrison' was located in what had been the dining room alongside the single bed upon which my mother preferred to sleep when no alert had sounded. She suffered during the war from quinsy, an inflammation of the throat resulting in large boil-like swellings and a sign, I suspect, of under-nourishment — not surprising in view of the circumstances. One night when the alert had sounded, my father out on duty as usual, she was sitting on the edge of the bed agonizing as to whether or not to join her three sons in the shelter when a severe explosion shook the house and resulted in the involuntary bursting of the current quinsy — an unpleasant experience but preferable perhaps to the usual lancing by Dr Whitley.

In the imagination of the small boy I was at the time, the German bombers overhead were sinister black and evil-sounding aircraft (it is a fact that they indeed had a distinctive engine note very different from that of our own aircraft) carrying equally sinister black-clad figures whose intent was to seek me out and drop bombs on me. No matter how my parents tried to reassure me that the true targets were factories, airfields and so on, usually many miles away, I am sure I regarded the whole affair as something personal — a one-sided conflict between myself and the *Luftwaffe*.

Writing some of these words over half a century later in the apartment of a friend on the Balearic island of Ibiza, it is difficult to believe the events really occurred. But some are so clear in my mind's eye that they could have happened yesterday. For example, the day my father took me to see the captured German bomber — a Dornier I believe — on display for a small fee, ironically on a bombed site in the town; or the day the police arrived with an Army sergeant to attempt (unsuccessfully) to billet one or more soldiers in our already well-filled home; or the night the blast from a nearby explosion caused a crashing noise within the house which could not be readily identified but which transpired to have been the sound of the trapdoor leading to the loft space being blown upwards, turned completely over and falling back neatly into its recess in the landing ceiling, upside down.

During the late afternoon of Tuesday 29 October 1940 I recall my parents being especially anxious about a nearby incident. It transpired they were aware of an aircraft crashing to earth quite near our home and were particularly unhappy that they believed it to be 'one of ours'. It turned out to have been a Supermarine Spitfire Mark II from the Fighter Command Station at Duxford, Cambridgeshire, being flown that day from the satellite airfield at RAF Fowlmere by a Royal Navy pilot, Sub-Lieutenant Anthony G. Blake of the Fleet Air Arm. On loan to the RAF, he had been attached to No.19 Squadron and had been killed prior to the crash and subsequent fire at 5.15 p.m. Known to his comrades in the squadron as "the Admiral", Blake was the highest scoring Navy pilot serving with the RAF during the Battle of Britain, credited with destroying six enemy aircraft in addition to one shared destruction and one 'possible'. I was of course entirely unaware of these details at the time: I knew simply that I had heard a sort of W - h - o - o - o - m - p.

The ARP report of the incident reveals that the road was closed at the site for a number of hours. At the time my impression was that the stricken aircraft had skimmed low over the trees in the nearby Oaklands Park before burying itself in the upstairs storey of a semi-detached house in New London Road. However, over fifty years later I was to learn a little more from an eye-witness who was eventually to undertake his own National Service in the RAF as a clerk, general duties, employed on administrative work in the orderly room at RAF Shawbury, Shropshire. He watched the Spitfire, which had appeared to be flying normally, go out of control over the town and "sort of spiral down". On another occasion he watched a lone Spitfire fly vertically through a low-flying formation of Heinkel bombers, presumably *en route* for London; one imagines the intention was to panic the German pilots into breaking formation.

The witness in question — Peter Bush, a friend and former work colleague — had the great good fortune during his National Service to fly in Avro Lancaster bombers quite by chance undertaking Friday afternoon flying training navigation exercises between Shawbury and RAF Bovingdon, Hertfordshire (concerning which Station more will be heard in Chapter 8), thereby saving time and money getting home for weekend leave with a 48 hour pass. The aircraft interiors had been gutted since the war and the flights were therefore somewhat uncomfortable but one did not turn down opportunities of this sort: they did occasionally arise — as I was to discover to my own advantage at a later date — but it was usually a matter of being in the right place at the right time.

But I digress. It wasn't all doom and gloom during the war years. On more than one occasion in junior school all the pupils were issued with large tins of powdered chocolate supplied by Canada and to be taken home to our parents. Most went home half empty as it was found that a moistened finger dipped into the tin produced a satisfactory quantity of chocolate. As the war progressed and the tide gradually turned in favour of the Allies, the seemingly never-ending Army and Air Force convoys of lorries, tanks and other vehicles, both British and American, flowed past the schools in Princes Road and on my route to and from home. I was not averse on occasion to yell the immortal request "Got any gum chum?" at American convoys, admittedly without success other than the receipt one day of a flying box of what the Americans called "candy".

D-Day (6 June 1944) I recall clearly. My father explained to me on my return home from school for lunch that Operation Overlord had been launched and that the Allies were fighting their way back into France. The excitement of the time was tempered somewhat by the arrival of Hitler's 'revenge' weapons with the terrible names which were abbreviated by the British to V1 (flying bomb or 'doodle bug') and V2 (rocket). Nothing could be done about the rockets: you didn't know one was coming until you heard the explosion. The worst incident in Chelmsford occurred at 1.30 a.m. on 19 December 1944 when a rocket fell on Hoffmann's factory, killing 40 people in all. Eleven of the victims were in properties in the neighbouring Henry Road; one was never identified. The doodle-bugs would I suppose be described in the vernacular of today as "something else". The approach of that terribly distinctive, harsh-sounding engine propelling its cargo of high explosive on a steadily expiring tank of fuel had a devastating effect on all who had the misfortune to be anywhere underneath it. They flew low enough to be clearly seen from the ground and I must confess that all of us at the time prayed that there would be sufficient fuel to carry any that arrived overhead elsewhere, to the misfortune of others. You had no option but to be selfish. In all, 28 V1s and 35 V2s fell in the Chelmsford area.

Then came VE (Victory in Europe) Day on 8 May 1945 and VJ (Victory over Japan) Day on 15 August in the same year. The former I recall vividly; everybody had been hunting out their old Union and other flags and bunting in preparation for the great day and when Churchill announced the end of the war in Europe there was an explosion of patriotism across the country. One of my neighbours adorned his home with, among others, the Red Flag. I did not understand at the time why my parents weren't too happy about this. Our 'street' party was held in the pavilion of the Crompton Parkinson Sports and Social Club, situated in their sports field to the rear of our garden (a Tesco Superstore is there now), my father was presented by the residents with the citation and cash mentioned in Chapter 1, and that was the end of my war; of VJ Day I have no recollection whatsoever.

The King wrote to me on the first anniversary of VE Day as follows:

To-day, as we celebrate victory, I send this personal message to you and all other boys and girls at school. For you have shared in the hardships and dangers of a total war and you have shared no less in the triumph of the Allied Nations.

I know you will always feel proud to belong to a country which was capable of such supreme effort; proud, too, of parents and elder brothers and sisters who by their courage, endurance and enterprise brought victory. May these qualities be yours as you grow up and join in the common effort to establish among the nations of the world unity and peace.

George R.I.

If I have dwelt at inordinate and perhaps boring length on my war, this is because I feel that my experiences in living through those six years helped accustom me to the idea that the existence of armed Services and perhaps the prospect of life therein was not necessarily abnormal or to be feared. Whilst I was not the sort of outgoing youngster who might have seemed a 'natural' for Service life — if anything I was somewhat timid at an early age — nevertheless the prospect surprisingly didn't greatly alarm me in later teenage years. Contributing also to this general attitude must have been my success at the 'scholarship' examination, my consequent arrival in September 1945 at Chelmsford King Edward VI Grammar School and, in particular, my subsequent enlistment in the Army Cadet Force corps at the school.

To be honest, I cannot admit to having enjoyed life greatly at this school — giving the lie to the old adage about school days being the happiest days of one's life — although there were some welcome factors, one in particular which has some relevance to this story and will be covered shortly. First though, the cadet corps or 'cadets' as it was termed by the boys (in those days this was a school for boys only). I cannot now recall how soon after starting at the school one joined the cadets. There was, however, little option about this: it **was** possible for one's parents to get one excused but I never discovered what sort of reasons, other than the obvious medical ones, they had to advance and very few boys didn't join. The few in question, as a sort of punishment it was generally felt, were taught German by Mr Bone ("Boney", naturally), the senior French master, on Friday afternoons while the rest of us got on with our soldiering.

We were each issued with full Army battledress uniform, including webbing belt, but without boots — we were expected to wear our own black school shoes. The uniforms were on the large size, presumably on the basis that we would grow into them. As replacements were not normally issued, most of the corps paraded in uniforms which were either too big or too small: a strange phenomenon to the interested observer. By the time I left school at the age of just sixteen, there was an embarrassing gap between my battledress top and trousers, noticeable especially on Friday mornings when it was my daily duty to post up on high before the morning assembly the number of the hymn to be sung (if that is an apt description of the noise we made) that morning. The problem arose because my form master — Mr Tom Wright — was also the music master, responsible for selecting the hymn and struggling with the hand-pumped organ accompaniment and, worse, I was to my chagrin his form prefect. I dreaded and hated those moments, especially when some bounder decided as a jape to hide the box of hymn numbers or to turn around the table in which the box reposed so that the elusive drawer was not located where it should have been. My embarrassment before hundreds of leering boys was indescribable, compounded on Fridays by the tantalising glimpse of shirt or pullover.

As cadets we drilled and marched, with and without our .303 rifles, we learned map-reading, field craft (crawled about in the normally out-of-bounds shrubbery), used radios which usually didn't work, dismantled and reassembled Bren guns and Sten guns and in fact ran the whole gamut of military training which I, and I think most of the others, thoroughly enjoyed — most of the time. I have to admit that there was a certain Company Sergeant Major Dyball, a sixth-former I believe, who incurred the wrath of many boys and parents by detaining about half of my squad — including me — after school one Friday on the grounds that the insteps of our shoes had not been polished. We had never been told that this particular area of our footwear — which were only our normal school shoes after all — needed polishing and the name Dyball became Mud in our eyes. This incident taught me one valuable military and, eventually, air force lesson: **never** assume that you are in the clear; however fireproof you may feel, remember that trouble may arrive from the most unexpected direction.

For me, the highlights of cadets were shooting and the band. For shooting we employed not our .303s but .22 rifles which, under the eagle eyes of the senior physics master, "Bruiser" Finlay, we fired on the primitive range behind the school tennis courts. To my amazement, as I had to wear John Lennon style NHS spectacles to correct short sight on such occasions, I was awarded my first class shooting badge — a rifle with a large star apparently issuing from its muzzle, which my mother sewed on to the left sleeve of my battle dress (remember I was useless at sewing at infants' school?). I have to mention the most unlikely shot of all. A certain Cadet Hayward, a brilliant musician who eventually became a Salvation Army bandmaster but who as a youngster was of a somewhat nervous and gentle disposition, in my presence once shot all his six bullets through the same hole in the centre of the target. No-one could believe this, except Cadet Hayward who was remarkably calm in the circumstances.

The band — more correctly the Corps of Drums and Bugles — was exceptional and survives to this day. During my time at the school it was pretty well unbeatable at the competitions to which it travelled and was then — and still is now — much in demand locally for parades and other occasions. For example, the band leads the annual RAFA branch Church Parade on Battle of Britain Sunday. I think some of us — rebellious schoolboys that we were really — even felt pride in marching behind this band, murmuring out of earshot of our NCOs the words attributed many years previously to the refrain of their 'signature tune' march

The rhubarb tree, the rhubarb tree;
An elephant's nest in a rhubarb tree.

The band's only real competition locally came from the Boys' Brigade. To their band's usual marching tune we supplied the lyric

Here comes the Boys' Brigade,
All covered in marmalade;
The marmalade is mouldy,
So is the Boys' Brigade.

One apocryphal story about the band. Each year all the cadets paraded, to be led by the band through the streets to Chelmsford Cathedral for the annual Founder's Day service. *En route* the parade passed under the bridge over Duke Street which carries the railway station and, in those days, three railway tracks. One of the features of the band has always been the hurling skywards of the mace by the drum major and his catching it deftly after several revolutions in the air during its passage to earth, apparently without looking at it. During five years I never saw any of the several drum majors fail in this manœuvre. Anyway, the story went that one particular drum major would hurl the mace so high on the approach to the bridge that it would somersault gracefully across the railway tracks, platforms and station buildings to enable him to catch it, without averting his gaze of course, as he emerged from the other side of the bridge. The reader will no doubt form his or her own conclusion.

I did not attend any of the cadets' annual camps, held I believe under Army auspices at training grounds near Colchester, largely because my parents were not happy about all this military behaviour and were reluctant to sign the requisite forms of consent. I was however present at a never-to-be-forgotten exercise held one Saturday morning in Blakes Wood, a few miles from the school. None of us really understood what was happening as there was no real briefing. I believe I was a member of the attacking force, dropped from the back of Army 3-ton lorries along a narrow public lane alongside the wood. No blank rounds were available for our .303 rifles. Instead we were each issued with a length of string with a loop at one end and half a dozen crackers of the type found in Christmas crackers attached thereto. The loop of string was to be placed over the foresight on the weapon and a slight tug on the other end of the string, to be held in the vicinity of the trigger, was to produce a satisfying 'crack' to represent the firing of one round of ammunition.

The section of which I was a member found itself at the rear of the rearmost platoon as we were strung along the lane, an ideal location as far as I was concerned. The lorries had by now disappeared, the sound of their engines having quite adequately given away our position to the 'enemy' in the wood without a doubt. There was, incidentally, no way to distinguish an attacker from a defender, even if you knew which you were yourself. To my horror I realized that my platoon was advancing through those in front of it and, worse, that my section was then advanced to the front of the platoon. We were at the sharp end, to enter the wood first, and were warned that the enemy might get a bit rough. We crept noisily about in the undergrowth, soon to be startled by shouting and bawling ahead, during the course of which I pulled on my string, all six crackers went off at once and somebody wearing an armband told me I was dead. With others I found a nice grassy area interspersed with sufficient bushes to enable us to spend the rest of the morning unnoticed in comparative comfort, our only concern being that we might not become aware when the farce had ended and we could go home. The noisy return of the lorries allayed our fears. As to the result of the exercise, i.e. who won, I had no idea and neither I believe had anyone else: excellent training for the Service life which lay ahead for us all.

The time arrived when I had to take the tests for what was known as Certificate A, or 'Cert A'. These consisted of a series of practical tests conducted by Army personnel and I imagine — we were never told — that the purpose was to determine which cadets were suitable for promotion. My attempt to drill a squad of cadets resulted in their eventual arrival in more or less the correct location, facing the right way but with the rear rank at the front and vice versa. Fail. The other tests necessitated marching on one's own between a succession of testers located at intervals around the school sports field, agonizing as to whether each tester required to be saluted on arrival, and, having done one's best, marching on to the next point. I think I passed the map reading test. I know I failed on the Bren because when the tester picked it up in such a way that it fell to pieces I was unable to reassemble it. Overall, I failed miserably.

But it was all good fun and at least the welcome call of the duty bugler on Friday afternoons

> Fall in A,
> Fall in B,
> Fall in all the Com - pan - eee

told us that school lessons were over for another week. And there is no doubt whatsoever in my mind that my experiences in the cadets helped tremendously to prepare me both mentally and practically for National Service and stood me in very good stead when the time arrived. I have cause to be very grateful to the school and its cadet corps.

There is in existence a historic photograph of my brother Geof (who followed me to the Grammar School and into the cadet corps) and myself standing at ease in our wretched uniforms, berets akimbo, grinning slightly.

The other aspect of school life to which I referred earlier as being of relevance to this story concerns my membership of the school's photographic society. My father had always been keen on the hobby and a camera was never far away from any family occasion. Before the war he had obtained an Ensign box camera which accepted the now no longer extant 116 film giving prints 4¼" x 2½", big enough not to require enlargement. Upon reaching the third year at school I became eligible to join the photographic society and, largely as a result of my father's encouragement and his offer to allow me to have the use of his precious camera, I did so. I never regretted this decision as the result of which photography has been a life-long hobby. (You wouldn't think so to judge from the quality of some of my photographs in this volume!)

The society met in the geography room after school each Wednesday and there cannot have been many theoretical or practical aspects of the subject which were not covered. We had the use of an excellent darkroom in which the senior chemistry master had constructed on runners reaching almost to the ceiling an enlarger which accordingly gave a huge degree of enlargement. Apart from the hobby itself and the enormous amount of pleasure it generated, I think two aspects of society life were important.

Firstly, I learned that people in authority are fallible human beings and not the distant figures of perfection I believe I had previously imagined. The society was run by a French master — Mr "Lefty" Wright (as distinct from Tom Wright mentioned earlier) — with the occasional involvement of several other masters. I discovered to my amazement that it was possible to have a perfectly normal conversation with these 'gods' who in this situation did not wish to be addressed as "Sir", did not talk down to us pupils and whose interest in the subject was on a level with ours. I learned to respect, but not to fear, those in authority and benefited in later life from this experience.

Secondly, I was asked for the first time to accept a measure of responsibility by being appointed with another member, Dennis Witham, to ensure that supplies of the various stock solutions of chemicals in the darkroom, which we mixed up from the basic 'ingredients', were always adequate for the use of members booking the facility, for which a nominal fee was charged. Our reward was one free session each week during which we usually mixed everything required and then did our own darkroom work using the freshly mixed solutions (i.e. when they were in the optimum condition!).

At this point the reader may well be wondering whether this supposed account of National Service life will ever see me into a Royal Air Force uniform. Never fear, you have only two years to wait and, having left school at sixteen, the spectre of National Service is now beginning to loom like dark clouds on the horizon. I have, however, felt that those factors and events which influenced my early life and have some relevance to my experiences and feelings when I eventually donned air force blue should be recounted in some detail.

CHAPTER 3

WORK, WORRY AND CALL-UP

From the time of leaving school, it seemed that my life was dominated by the words 'call-up' and 'National Service'. Without having been in any way brilliant, I had done reasonably well in the Midsummer 1950 University of London General School Examination (the last year before the introduction of 'O' and 'A' Levels), passing in six subjects and, having reached the required standard in five of those six, matriculating in the University as from September 1950. Mathematics had been my best subject, History my worst. Significantly perhaps, in view of what was to become of me during my National Service, I obtained a Credit in French, written and oral.

The question of going on to university simply did not arise. There were so few places available that only the very best had any chance at all of being accepted and, in any event, my family needed whatever income I could generate! The employment market was very different in the 1950s to what it is in the 1990s and only one job interview was necessary in my case. Four of us from the school — Brian Barker, Cyril Bilney and Lloyd Hardy were the others — were interviewed at County Hall, Chelmsford one hot summer's day in 1950 and all obtained positions with Essex County Council, three of us in the Office of the Clerk and Hardy in the Treasurer's Department. In those days local government was regarded as a secure career with good promotion prospects and a decent pension at the end of it, so we had all four done well.

After a family holiday with relatives at Lowestoft, Suffolk, I started work on Monday 28 August. My starting salary was £135 a year, the appointment was temporary to start with (in fact until 1 October 1951) and my exalted salary would be subject to deductions for superannuation purposes when I reached the age of eighteen. My first monthly pay slip, undated surprisingly and handwritten, reveals that my normal pay amounted to £11.5s.0d. With arrears of £1.9s.0d and a deduction of 14s.4d for insurance, my net pay for about five weeks' work was therefore £11.19s.8d (£11.98p), an undoubted fortune when compared with my pocket money. This, when my father could afford it, had amounted to a maximum of 2s.6d (12½p) a week. My salary was paid in cash and my recollection is that at least one 'white fiver' was included in the first pay packet, much to my consternation as shopkeepers and others were reluctant to accept such notes, their worth in present terms probably approaching £100 each! I kept sufficient cash to buy myself a suit for work — probably about £2–£3 as I believe it came from the Fifty Shilling Tailors — and gave nearly all the rest to my mother.

I was to work initially (until my call-up it transpired) in the Town and Country Planning Section of the Clerk's Office and my first colleagues were Peter Steggall, my immediate 'boss' to whom I owe a great deal, and John

Roulston. I must have enjoyed myself because on my second day I forgot to go home to lunch. Peter, apt to regale us with excerpts from *The Desert Song* on unexpected occasions, was a bespectacled, urbane and softly spoken man of Suffolk. As yet unmarried and nearing thirty, he was to me quite elderly. He had served through the war in the Royal Artillery where he had risen to the dizzy heights of Acting Bombardier before being demobbed as a humble Gunner. One claim to fame was that he had learned to drive in the desert "where there was nothing to hit". In fact, he drove the truck which housed the regimental office and, as regimental clerk, held the enemy at bay with a well-aimed typewriter. With our respective wives, Ann and Barbara, we still meet for lunch several times a year.

Sport-mad John, burly, prematurely balding and an Old Chelmsfordian like myself, was nearing his eighteenth birthday and becoming increasingly despondent at the prospect of call-up: no more Saturday afternoon football; no more Saturday nights in the Odeon ballroom; but at least there would be no more Monday morning arrivals in the office sporting the injuries from one or both of these activities. Destined to become a member of the Royal Army Service Corps, John was eventually to serve as a corporal on the personal office staff of the Deputy Supreme Commander (a certain Field Marshal Viscount Montgomery) at SHAPE (Supreme Headquarters Allied Powers Europe) located near Paris at Marly-le-Roi, a little to the north of Versailles. My own service career was to be similar to John's.

I soon discovered that a principal topic of conversation among the young men in the office was, not surprisingly, National Service. Had you done your two years yet? If not, when did you expect to go? Which Service would you try to get into? If you **had** done yours, which Service were you in and had you any advice? Most important from the career point of view, were you doing anything about studying for the Clerical Division examination prior to National Service? On the last point, rightly or wrongly I decided to do nothing before call-up. Allowing also for the two years away and further indecision after demob, this resulted in a delay of about five years before I eventually embarked on studies for the examinations which I was told it would be essential to pass in order to guarantee myself a worthwhile career in local government. So this was one negative effect of National Service, at least as far as I was concerned. The young ladies in the office were generally speaking able to remain aloof from the mainly male trauma going on around them; after all, a steady stream of fresh young men would continue to arrive in the office and others would be returning from two years away!

I soon taught myself to type on an ancient Imperial machine, not very well and using only about two and a half fingers — which earned me a rebuke from the typing pool supervisor who was supposed to have taught me to touch-type properly. I was also sent with nine other recent appointees on four mornings a week to the County Typewriting Office in Duke Street run by Miss Hilda Sorrell where, over a period of six months, we were taught Pitman's shorthand by Mr A. L. Loly. Blinking through tiny spectacles, small and rotund, he wielded a strange curved brush to remove stray chalk dust from his strange curved brown-suited figure but was nevertheless a very likeable man and an excellent teacher.

At the conclusion of the six months, we were required on certain evenings to attend the same Office for speedwriting classes at our own expense and, on 6 February 1952, I passed an examination at the rate of 120 words a minute, only failing by a whisker to succeed at 150. This success was to prove of some importance early in my service in the RAF. One of my fellow students was Joan, about whom more later. More later also about a certain John Shearman, known to his friends as Sheargoon, who I was first to meet during tea-making and horseplay sessions in the office kitchen. One notable morning he arrived for work on his bicycle still wearing his carpet slippers.

The period of two years between school and National Service left one in a sort of limbo: you didn't really know what you were going to do with your life and the assured prospect of a two year gap led many, including myself, to put off making decisions. I did, however, resolve to do three things: to learn to swim, to learn to dance and to learn to ride a bike. I was in my forties when I eventually learned to swim (very badly) so failed miserably with that ambition. I think I probably wanted to be able to dance because in those days it was at dances that you usually met girls. I attended a course of evening ballroom dancing classes at Chelmsford's Cathedral Hall as the result of which I could just about get by in a waltz or quickstep but could foxtrot only when pressed and then with a few trodden upon toes. I don't, however, recall attending any actual dances prior to call-up.

The third aim — the cycling one — met with more success. It may seem a little strange in the 1990s to read of a sixteen-year-old who couldn't ride a bike. However, it may be recalled that I was one of three brothers close in age and our parents invariably tried to treat us fairly, if not exactly alike. With their very restricted income there was no way they could have afforded the purchase of one bicycle, let alone three, and we therefore had to wait until we were earning money before such luxuries could be obtained. Almost as soon as I had money of my own, I purchased from the father of a friend the ancient upright machine referred to at the very beginning of this story. It was already at least second-hand and I cannot now recall whether I parted with the sum of 15s.0d (75p) or £1.10s.0d (£1.50p) but it was one or the other and it was one of the soundest investments I have ever made.

I learned to ride in a field, not a bad strategy in view of one's propensity to fall off during early attempts, and was very soon at the over-confident stage achieved by most learners. I quickly had any arrogance knocked out of me when narrowly avoiding being knocked down by a hooting coach as I shot across a main road in front of it, mounted a kerb and crashed into a close-boarded fence. Thereafter I was more circumspect. Cycling has proved to be a life-long hobby and, in my sixties, I still ride out for pleasure and exercise on what, including one I owned in France for about a year, is my fifth bicycle. It wasn't long before I had abandoned the bus and was cycling to and from the office in common with most of my colleagues. Chelmsford had a reputation in those times as a 'cycling town', awash with bicycles at certain times of the day. Sheargoon and I went through a slightly eccentric phase during which we undertook early morning cycle rides together, arriving for work dishevelled and sweat-ridden.

Towards the end of my time at school I had accepted one Saturday the offer of a lift (from the gentleman who sold me the bike) to Rayleigh Weir stadium, near Southend-on-Sea, where speedway racing took place on Saturday evenings during the summer months. I was quickly 'hooked' and became for many years an ardent fan of the Rayleigh Rockets. Eventually, with others, my brothers and I were in the habit of cycling to Rayleigh most Saturday evenings, a round and fairly hilly trip of some thirty miles. Yes, Essex does have hills. I established the record for the fastest return leg, a solo ride completed in 54 minutes. Often the speedway trips followed hard on the heels of a Saturday afternoon spent in support of Chelmsford City Football Club, in those days one of the leading lights in the semi-professional Southern League but destined never to win the FA Cup. Unbeknown to me at the time, I may well have seen playing for Hereford United the RAF sergeant with whom I was to share an office one day; he certainly played at Chelmsford on at least one occasion.

My active participation in sport prior to National Service was restricted to cricket and soccer, although I had played a little tennis at school on Saturday mornings. I played both major sports in teams representing the County Clerk's Office, where we were fairly successful, and also played 'friendly' soccer as a member of the Essex County Council Staff Third XI. These matches were usually disasters and I would say the average score was about 12 – 0 against us: we never won while I was playing. If I was any good at anything it was probably medium paced bowling. In one (admittedly post-National Service) inter-Departmental cricket match I returned bowling figures of five wickets for fifteen runs. I believe my highest batting score was eight not out, scored within the confines of Chelmsford Prison, again after my National Service. I never scored a goal, usually playing soccer as a wing-half. Most people these days wouldn't know what a wing-half was!

And so the clock ticked merrily on, 1950 became 1951, 1951 became 1952 and suddenly my eighteenth birthday neared. I've always considered that the whole business of compulsory National Service started back to front. The reluctant conscript had to make the first move. There was no waiting at home for a buff OHMS envelope to arrive with preliminary instructions. Although 'they' of course knew you existed and were waiting to prosecute you if you didn't take the required steps, nevertheless YOU had to make the first move and, it seemed at the time, thereby lumber yourself with what was to follow. Notices appeared regularly in the press giving details of the places, dates and times when it was incumbent upon those born between certain dates and with surnames commencing with relevant letters of the alphabet to present themselves for the purpose of 'registration' — even though as mentioned already 'they' knew who you were anyway.

In my case, I was required to register at the prefabricated office of the then Ministry of Labour and National Service (the so-called Labour Exchange) in Wells Street, Chelmsford, on a date several weeks **before** my birthday. This seemed a bit much at the time. This office building was demolished early in the 1990s after standing derelict and vandalised for many years. I duly presented myself at the appointed time and was surprised to find that many of the others on the same errand as myself appeared to know each other although I recognised none of them. I imagine that this occasion would have provided the opportunity for those concerned to take steps to seek exemption or deferment or to be accepted as a conscientious objector.

In addition to admitting to your name, address and date of birth, you were required to state your preference for one of the three Services. There was little point in opting for the Navy, especially if you couldn't swim, as in any event they required very few National Servicemen. Most, therefore, opted for the RAF and, rumour at the time being that you increased your chances of being accepted if you indicated a preference for aircrew rather than groundcrew, I did just that. Goodness knows what my parents would have thought; the whole prospect of National Service caused them great anxiety even though they weren't the ones required to undertake it. The clerk was a little amused at my indicated preference — he had heard it all before of course — and more or less dismissed any prospect of my flying by enquiring about my eyesight which, it may be recalled, was not all that it might be. However, I asked that my preference should be registered.

I was in fact destined to take the controls of an aircraft — albeit briefly — some forty-two years later during the course of a flying lesson from Southend Airport presented to me by my family on the occasion of my sixtieth birthday. It's not as easy as it looks! The aircraft was a four-seater Cessna 172 and my Canadian instructor, who had during his career flown United States Air Force Phantom jets from RAF Woodbridge, Suffolk, had on the previous day been in Split, in the former Yugoslavia, working as a pilot for Independent Television News. Nuggets of inconsequential information such as this are interspersed with material more relevant to this story in an endeavour to alleviate such boredom as may be experienced by the persevering reader.

It was at about the time of my registration that the quiet young man — Colin Marriott — whose place I had taken when I started work returned from two years in the RAF and, as was his right, elected to return to his former employment at County Hall. He was re-established in the Planning Section where, to me, he seemed very unsettled and unsure as to his future. I never got to know him very well and therefore had no way of knowing whether the terrible tales of Service life with which he regaled me had any truth in them. By the time I returned after my two years away, he had left this employment and was working in the offices at Hoffmann's factory, so clearly he had quite an unsettled start to his working life, not helped I suspect by National Service.

As far as I was concerned, the next stage in the inexorable journey towards call-up would be the dreaded medical examination. A few weeks after I had registered, I received instructions to present myself at an early hour on Wednesday 9 July — two days after my eighteenth birthday — to the Southend Medical Board at 52–58 Milton Street, Southend-on-Sea. This necessitated catching a very early and almost empty bus from Chelmsford, on the top deck of which I encountered a young man who I recognised as working in the emporium of a local seedsman. Name of Lilywhite, he was on the same mission as I was and I felt a little happier after gaining his company.

I cannot now remember whether we knew before arrival at the medical centre that all those to be examined that day had opted for the RAF or, indeed, from which Service or Services the personnel there were drawn. We soon discovered that there were twenty recruits and that, in addition to being medically examined, we were to sit an intelligence test. We were told that, at the end of the day, just two of us, both of whom would need to have been placed in medical grade I or II, would be accepted for the RAF, the other eighteen unfortunates being consigned to the Army. One of the twenty wore the uniform of a flight sergeant in the Air Training Corps. Unless, therefore, he was medically unfit or a complete idiot, or both, it appeared to the rest of us that the odds had lengthened and only one of nineteen would be lucky enough to wear blue.

The intelligence test came first. We sat two to a table with screens between us to prevent 'cribbing' and were given a set period (I think it was three-quarters of an hour) to provide the answers to a list of what I would term 'progression' questions; at its simplest, for example, to complete the series of numbers 2, 4, 6, 8, ? Without wishing in any way to boast, I found the whole exercise so simple that long before the time was up I had completed my paper, checked through it a couple of times and was surprised to observe over the screens that others were obviously struggling.

Then came the medical examination which, as might be expected, was of great thoroughness. Naked, we progressed from cubicle to cubicle while just about everything that could be examined and checked received scrutiny. To this day I do not know why it was necessary to be naked in order to have one's hearing tested. Positioned by an open first floor window I was required to discern above the noise of the Warrior Square traffic words and phrases — "Piccadilly Circus" was one I recall — whispered by the medical gentleman standing in the far corner of the room.

At some point during the day we were despatched to the outside world for an hour. With two or three others I strolled towards the sea front where, my mother was wont to assert, the acres of glistening mud possessed wonderful health-giving properties. She didn't actually use those words but that was what she meant. Unlike the others who had seen his approach, I fell for the street photographer's standard ploy of pretending he had taken one's photo when in reality he had simply produced a 'click' from behind the camera. "Just one more to make sure it's OK sir" and almost before I knew it I was handing over the sum of, I believe, 10s.0d (50p), together with my name and address. I was subjected to a certain amount of ribbing as the result of this encounter and felt I had suffered a loss of esteem in the eyes of my peers who stood jeering on the other side of the street.

At least the man was honest. A few days later three or four postcard sized enlargements arrived through the post from Manchester featuring a sheepish looking individual wearing an unbuttoned raincoat over the sports jacket and flannels (wide bottomed with turn-ups) popular at the time. It seems strange that I was wearing the raincoat (on 9 July!) rather than, as was the done thing at the time, carrying it over my arm neatly folded inside out so as to display the tartan lining. Needless to say I was hatless. Probably as a reaction to having been required to wear school caps for so many years, no self-respecting civilian male under the age of about thirty ever wore headgear regardless of the weather. In contrast, my father always sported a trilby or, in his later years, a flat cap, even to go into his garden; customs change from generation to generation.

Eventually, back at the medical centre, we appeared in turn before the Chairman of the Board, an Army officer, who handed us our Grade Cards completed and signed by himself, appropriately in blood red ink. Mine indicated that I had been placed in Grade II (Two). I enquired the reason for this and the Chairman said I was five pounds underweight. Apparently I was also 70¼ inches in height, had green-grey eyes and light brown hair. Rumour had it that the RAF didn't accept those with brown eyes (presumably because they didn't match the uniform!) so, what with the result of my medical, my confidence about the intelligence test and my heavily Brylcreemed hair — complete with artificial wave at the front induced by the fingers — I had everything going for me and could only keep my fingers crossed.

The outcome of the day was announced. As generally expected, the ATC flight sergeant was in, leaving just one of the other nineteen to be successful. And, wait for it, that one was to be me! So, if I had to go, at least I would be in my chosen Service which had to be a good thing. The ATC chap and I were sent home while the other eighteen remained, probably to be shouted at by someone in a brown uniform. I therefore travelled home on the bus without young Mr Lilywhite and it remained only to await call-up itself. It was generally reckoned that you wouldn't hear anything for two or three months and you were always given at least two weeks' notice of the actual date. The final countdown had now started; the only trouble was I didn't know for how long the clock would run!

I was not from a warlike family: as far as I am aware only four of my relatives had served in HM Forces, unfortunately with a 50% casualty rate. In World War I, as 200959 Private Pratt J. W., great-uncle Jim on my father's side of the family was a member of the 1/4th Essex Regiment and died during the attack on Gaza on 26 March 1917. Upon my father's death I took custody of memorabilia including my great-uncle's three medals, the letter from the Regiment's Record Office informing my great-grandmother of her son's death, a letter from an officer in the Regiment, Lieutenant E. Barrett, explaining the circumstances and various photographs etc.

Three brothers, half-cousins on my mother's side of the family, served in World War II. The eldest, Stephen Mundy, rose to the rank of Captain in the Royal Artillery, took part in the invasion of Sicily, was wounded by a mortar shell while on a reconnaissance at Termoli, Italy on 4 October

1943 and died of wounds in hospital in Tripoli, Libya on 27 October. His younger brothers, Hugh and Lionel, were both called up during the war. Respectively, they served as 1425110 LAC Mundy H., RAF, and Lance-bombardier Mundy L., Royal Horse Artillery. Both served abroad, Hugh in Egypt, Algeria and Italy and Lionel in India, and both survived the war.

And I was to be the next reluctant conscript. Admittedly the world was not now at war but there were still conflicts around the globe, for example the Korean War was in progress at the time, so you couldn't really be sure just what might become of you. One morning around the middle of October I came down to breakfast to find the ubiquitous buff OHMS envelope propped up on the window-ledge by the front door and my mother in the kitchen with her serious face on. She had always assured us as youngsters that we wouldn't have to do National Service. Originally she was sure that it would all be over and done with by the time we were old enough. Then when this obviously wasn't going to be the case, she was convinced there would be some means by which we could avoid it. And now she was having to say "It looks as if your call-up's come, dear"; she was much more concerned at the prospect than I was.

My Enlistment Notice informed me that, in accordance with the National Service Acts 1948 to 1950, I was called up for service in the Royal Air Force and was required to present myself on Monday 3 November 1952 between 9 a.m. and 4 p.m. to No 1 Reception Unit at RAF Padgate, Lancashire. There was no escape now; failure to comply would result in "OI, YEW ARE CUMIN' WIV US" from hairy great men wearing white-topped hats.

CHAPTER 4

PRELUDE AT PADGATE

In addition to the Enlistment Notice, I was the reluctant recipient of a travel warrant for a one-way railway ticket from Chelmsford to Warrington (the station for Padgate) together with advice that, if possible, this should be exchanged for a ticket a day or two before I was due to travel. A postal order for 4s.0d (20p), my first day's pay, was enclosed. There was advice as to what I should take with me and it was emphasised that I should carry only a **small** suitcase, the reason for which was to become clear at Padgate. In particular, I was to be sure to have with me my identity card (which I still have) and my ration book. Although clothes rationing had by now come to an end (this lasted from 1941 until 1949), some foodstuffs were still rationed in 1952. Food rationing, for certain items only, first came into force on 8 January 1940 and it was not until 1954 that the last items became freely available and rationing finally ceased.

Not surprisingly, I was told to inform my employer of the date upon which I was required to report for service. I was somewhat disillusioned by the apparent lack of interest in the office as a whole at my imminent departure. No weeping females threw themselves at my feet. As explained in the previous chapter, the person I had replaced in the Planning Section had already returned from his National Service and was ready to replace me. Office rules decreed that there were to be no cash collections or presentations when young men left on call-up: we had to wait for these until we either got married or left the office for good.

There was, however, some consolation. Joan, the young lady mentioned earlier, had anticipated my call-up by giving me a small leather travelling case containing a shaving-kit (safety razor, spare blades, shaving stick, shaving brush and comb) while Peter Steggall presented me with what he said had always been an essential during his Army days — a mirror — small, steel and contained in a blue case made from what must have been some of the earliest plastic (which is still in my possession). The two gifts went nicely together and were in daily use during my two years away. It should perhaps be explained that, in 1952, there was almost certainly no such thing as an electric shaver and, in any case, the RAF didn't provide power points in its accommodation for recruits' use. The choice lay between cut-throat and safety razors and about 95 % chose the latter.

Like most of my contemporaries I was not an experienced traveller. In particular I had never travelled on the London Underground on my own and, in order to get from Liverpool Street to Euston, the London terminus for the train to Warrington, I would need to do so. What is more, I would have to change trains. I had of course been on the Underground with my parents when younger and on one famous occasion I had, with others from the Grammar School, gone astray there during the only school outing in

43

which I was given the opportunity to participate during my entire school career — a trip to the West End to see Shakespeare's *Twelfth Night*. Contrast that with the junketing — abroad as well as in this country — which takes place these days.

To give myself some confidence I therefore decided to take my one and only day's unpaid leave during thirty-five years at work and spend a day in London on my own. It happened that the annual Motor Show was in progress at Earls Court during the last week of October. Having developed an interest in motor sport in general during the previous few years — largely as a result of visits to the former RAF and USAAF airfield at Boreham, near Chelmsford, where international car and motor-cycle events took place under the auspices of the *Daily Mail* — I braved London on Wednesday 29 October to visit the Show. I emerged unscathed in spite of alighting from a train at the wrong Underground station at one point — I can't remember the details which is perhaps just as well.

I took my leave of a largely disinterested County Hall on Friday 31 October. In those days we were required to work alternate Saturday mornings but I was not due to work on Saturday 1 November. My pay slip for the month (by now produced by some pre-computer mechanical means) reveals that my gross pay was £15.16s.8d to which were added £1.13s.4d special pay (I haven't a clue to what this refers) and 8s.6d overtime. Deductions of 10s.0d income tax, £1.3s.0d for insurance, 16s.0d for superannuation and 10d sports and social club subscription resulted in net pay of £15.8s.8d (£15.43p). Approximating to 10s.0d (50p) a day, this was two and a half times as much as I would receive in the RAF where, admittedly, 'board and lodging' would be found. I was surprised to receive also a cheque for 15s.0d (75p) representing pay for the weekend, 1 and 2 November, when, although not actually doing anything, I was technically still employed by the County Council.

Although attempting to behave nonchalantly, I was by now pretty wound up inside about my situation. I have a recollection of my youngest brother, Den, complaining during this last weekend about a forthcoming visit to the dentist and being roundly condemned by my mother for worrying about a half-hour visit to the surgery in New London Road when his eldest brother was about to embark upon the unknown for two whole years. I decided the best way to get through Monday morning would be to leave home, on my bicycle, at the usual time as if going to work and, having parked the bike in the usual place, walk to the nearby station having neatly broken my ties with home in a routine manner.

But my father had other ideas. During the weekend he dropped what was for me a minor bombshell by announcing that he had booked a day's leave for Monday and proposed to accompany me as far as Euston. He obviously had his doubts about my travelling abilities notwithstanding the previous Wednesday's excursion, and there wasn't really very much I could do about it. These days you would probably tell your father to push off if you disagreed with him, but this was not the case in 1952. We compromised. I would still leave on my bike and he would precede me on foot, carrying my **small** suitcase, and meet me at the station. One of my brothers would collect the bike later in the day and pedal it home.

We journeyed together to Euston, not saying much. He did, however, give me a few 2½d (1p) postage stamps and ask me to write when I could, as well as a ready-addressed postcard, stamped 2d, with the entreaty that I should write a few words on it and send it as soon as possible "so that Mum will know that you have got there all right". This actually meant "so that Dad will know that you have got there all right". It has to be appreciated that the age of universal telephones had not yet dawned and, even if I had been able to gain access to one at Padgate — which was highly unlikely — my home didn't boast one anyway. A telephone had been a necessity during my father's ARP service but, certain of the neighbours having tended to use our home as a phone box, it had been removed amid a certain amount of acrimony after the cessation of hostilities. One neighbour in particular was most upset!

I left my father standing somewhat forlornly at the end of the departure platform at Euston and found myself a corner seat on the 10.20 'Padgate Express'. I had to convince myself that I was already a member of the Royal Air Force and this was no time to show emotion. Even though no change of train was involved, the journey seemed painfully slow and it was well into the afternoon and, inevitably, drizzling slightly when we pulled into Warrington station. In the meantime I had consumed the sandwiches my mother had added to the contents of my **small** suitcase and, although I had spotted a number of others of like age to myself — who I decided were to share the same fate as I was — I don't recall speaking to anyone on the train. I certainly wasn't prepared for the numbers who alighted at Warrington — there must have been well over a hundred — to be met by RAF personnel on the platform directing us to a fleet of the sturdy Bedford 3-ton lorries which were to become so familiar to us during our service.

I cannot remember very much of the journey by road to RAF Padgate or, indeed, of our arrival at No.1 Reception Unit but I do recall that we were treated perfectly fairly; there was none of the hectoring or bawling which some might have anticipated (and which might well have occurred had we been arriving at Aldershot to join the Army!) and my only complaint was the increasing rain. After we had registered our presence by telling a clerk who we were, the first thing I recall happening was being required to queue at an open hatch at the equipment stores. Through this hatch we each collected an initial issue of kit comprising a pint mug, a set of 'irons' (knife, fork and spoon) and an abomination known in the RAF as a groundsheet. This was an olive-green L-shaped piece of allegedly waterproof material, of the sort used for some cycling capes, which in theory could be wrapped around oneself, a couple of buttons fastened and, hey presto, you have a means of keeping dry when it rains. In practice, you seemed inevitably to finish up rather wetter than you would have been without the thing, one corner of which always conspired to drag along behind you in the mud — even when you are 70¼ inches in height.

A number of us recruits then 'marched' to the airmen's mess for our first RAF meal — tea — having been told to which barrack hut to report after eating. The meal, taken at long tables with benches seating about six on either side, included something cooked which might have been fritters followed by bread and jam, all washed down with tea from our huge mugs. We quickly learned that bread (ready sliced), butter (one large dollop in the middle of a dinner plate on each table) and jam (ditto) were strictly limited and that, if you didn't grab what you wanted while it was still available, you went without. There was very little finesse; no "May I pass you the jam, Cecil?" "Oh, thank you so much, Claud".

About two dozen recruits repaired after tea to the standard RAF type wooden barrack hut to which I had been assigned. There we found ourselves in the charge of an airman who, although we didn't realize it at the time, was of the same rank as ourselves, i.e. the lowest of the low — an aircraftman second class (AC2) — a humble erk. In the trade of admin orderly, he was unqualified like his charges and, in the RAF in general, could find himself undertaking the most menial of tasks. He had in fact fallen on soft ground in his present job, which involved general responsibility for our hut and its occupants and, in particular, 'marching' us as a flight around the camp as and when required to meet our various commitments during the few days we were to be there. He treated us with every civility and our introduction to the RAF and discipline could not have been more gentle.

Our tasks on the first evening consisted of little more than lighting one or both of the coke stoves which would be the only source of heat in the hut and making ourselves comfortable in our temporary abode. One piece of advice we were given at the outset: don't write letters home giving RAF Padgate as the address simply because, by the time replies were received, we would almost certainly have moved elsewhere and the RAF postal service would not be too happy trying to establish the whereabouts of what could well be hundreds of new recruits at any given time. At the time of my enlistment, every National Service airman reported initially to Padgate; those who had signed on for regular service went to No.2 Reception Unit at RAF Cardington, Bedfordshire. We were not therefore given the details of our present postal address. I wrote a few lines on the stamped postcard given to me by my father. Others were also scribbling and doubtless we found somewhere to post what we had written.

Steel framed beds with mattresses, not the military style 'biscuits' of old, lined both sides of the hut and each recruit was provided with one pillow, two sheets, three or four blankets, a wooden wardrobe and a separate locker. I discovered to my amazement that the person occupying the bed on my right hailed from Braintree, a small town about ten or twelve miles from Chelmsford, and, incredibly, that he was also a keen supporter of the Rayleigh Rockets. It was nice to learn that, quite apart from the predicament in which we now found ourselves, we had something very much in common with which to console ourselves.

I cannot remember whether 'lights out' was at 10 or 10.30. However, it was a chilly and damp evening, the hut didn't warm up too well and we had nowhere to go and nothing much to do. I think we were all trying to make ourselves comfortable in our unaccustomed beds long before the face of our guardian erk appeared around the door to check that lights were going out as required. We were all pretty miserable. My attempt to lighten the gloom by reminding those within earshot that we had already done one day and there were only 729 more to do didn't go down at all well. I didn't sleep much and nor, I suspect, did many of the others. I have a clear recollection of lying awake during that fateful night agonizing as to what sort of dreadful future might be in store for us all — myself in particular!

An awful lot happened during the next four days. It is quite impossible now to remember the sequence of events but I have a reasonable recollection of many of them and of the order in which they probably occurred. Obviously at an early stage our erk taught us the rudiments of drill, simply to enable him to move us as a body around the camp between barrack hut, airmen's mess, clothing store, various offices and everywhere else we were required to go. Most of the time it was raining so those wretched capes were very much in evidence, both initially when we were still dressed in our 'civvies' and later in uniform.

One of our first calls was at an office where documentation, including the issuing of Service numbers, was undertaken. One of the clerks wielded a hefty rubber stamp which automatically advanced by one the seven-figure number printed each time he thumped it on some poor erk's papers. By this means — a bit like using a child's printing set — I became 2576583 AC2 Caton E.

Every RAF document is identified by a form number. Rumour had it during my service that even toilet paper was blessed with such a number and certain unprintable suggestions were made as to what that number might be. One of the first documents we encountered was the RAF identity card — otherwise RAF Form 1250 universally known as your 'twelve-fifty'. Having been issued with it, you were required to carry it with you at all times in order to be able to produce it whenever required to do so. My twelve-fifty was serially numbered 887629 and was issued to me on Wednesday 5 November. As it bore my photograph (prison-style, with my Service number underneath my dejected image) and as I was wearing uniform for the photo, there's no doubt that our visit to the clothing stores must have been on the Tuesday, 4 November.

Humorous tales of the issue of Service clothing are legion: they are all true! There was not even pretence of measurement. Separating the major, rack-lined portion of the clothing store from the smaller area into which we recruits were in turn projected ran a long counter behind which a succession of equipment clerks added to one's personal pile of goodies as it progressed along the counter items of such size as the NCOs in charge considered appropriate and bellowed instructions accordingly. This procedure was carried out at breakneck speed and, at the far end of the counter, the bewildered recruit was supposed to cram his entire bundle into the kitbag which had been one of the items issued. This proved to be a physical impossibility and the 'flight' (the term by now used to describe us as a whole) returned to the billet in some disarray, various items of uniform and equipment spraying around us as we staggered through the drizzle.

Sorting things out in the relative comfort of the hut, we found that we had each been issued with a greatcoat, two uniforms (No.1 Home Dress or 'best blue' and No.2 Dress or 'working blue'), two berets — the forage cap or fore-and-aft so beloved of our predecessors having quite recently been withdrawn from use — with two hat badges, one pair of boots, one pair of shoes, one pair of plimsolls, one pair of woollen gloves, a pullover, two black ties, two vests and pairs of underpants, four pairs of woollen socks, two pairs of blue and white striped pyjamas, two towels, three shirts, six collars, one pair of braces, one PT vest, one pair of voluminous navy-blue shorts of the Stanley Matthews variety (NAVY-blue? — had someone blundered?), two shoe brushes, a button-stick, a housewife, a mess tin and, of course, the kitbag.

We had been advised in the papers accompanying our Enlistment Notices to take collar studs with us as these were not issued: I had never worn shirts with separate collars and it had therefore been necessary to buy studs. Reference before collecting our kit to the issue of a 'housewife' had led to certain ribaldry and some mystification but we lost interest when the item in question turned out to be a small mending and darning kit, complete with needles, cottons and wools of appropriate colours, relevant buttons and a thimble. I finally disposed of the remains of my housewife during the summer of 1994.

Instances of mutual support among the members of our flight now occurred. Every item of kit was required to be adorned in one way or another with one's Service number. With the advice of our guardian erk and the loan of necessary equipment, for example a hammer and metal punches to indent our numbers into the sides of shoe brushes, we set to work with marking ink, needle and thread and so on. Some recruits proved less adept at certain tasks than others and it was gratifying to see the extent to which help was freely given to those seen to be struggling. I still have the larger of my shoe brushes, the number clearly but erratically punched therein.

During the course of the long-drawn out marking operation it came to light that, whilst the rest of us had numbers commencing 2576, my Braintree friend's number was 2567562. Upon hearing of this our guardian erk was near to panic, instructed my unfortunate friend to cease his marking activities and disappeared at high speed. The eventual determination by higher authority was that the stage had been reached when the number couldn't be changed, and so it came to pass that two RAF National Servicemen bore the number 2567562.

It might be worth noting here that all who signed on as 'regulars' in 1952, and who reported initially to RAF Cardington, were issued with numbers commencing other than with a '2'; they were therefore readily distinguishable, on paper at any rate, from National Servicemen. Of far greater importance, it was impressed upon us that we must immediately learn our 'last three', the final three digits of our Service numbers, as it was by this means that we would be identifiable, especially at pay parades. The digits 583 have been impressed on my mind since those days at Padgate. Kit marking completed, tunics and trousers belonging to some of us were removed to the tailors for alterations deemed necessary at the time of issue and all our boots went to the cobblers. Upon the return of these items a day or so later, the uniforms didn't appear to have changed much but the boots had all been equipped with steel tips at the toes and heels, resulting in satisfying noises when worn in anger. At some stage, narrow strips of black leather were sewn inside trouser bottoms to prevent fraying but I cannot remember when this was done. The exhortations about small suitcases were soon to be explained.

By about the Thursday, 6 November, almost all the week's intake were fully kitted out and no longer wearing any of their civilian clothing. There were one or two unusually shaped exceptions still awaiting replacement or altered garments. We were accordingly told to pack all civilian gear in our suitcases and, using standard sized sheets of brown wrapping paper and lengths of string with which we were each issued, parcel up the suitcases and address them to our respective parents. Needless to say, in many cases the paper or string was insufficient and some weird and wonderful efforts left for the GPO. I just about coped with my parcel and I was to hear later from my mother that it arrived home in good order.

My ex-RAF friend Peter Bush, when similarly occupied at Padgate during the late 1940s, with the rest of his flight received detailed instruction from no less than a sergeant as to how to pack a suitcase and prepare it for the post. By good fortune Peter's case and gear were chosen for a demonstration, leaving him merely to address the finished result. When he arrived home for his first leave some weeks later his mother complimented him on how well he had packed his case!

Resplendent in vivid blue we at least now gave the appearance of being airmen. The uniform item causing the most aggravation was probably the beret. Everybody's seemed too large and few were able to make theirs look even sensible. Some protruded sideways giving the appearance of flying saucers, others ballooned upwards; indeed, no two looked alike. We knew the badge had to be over the left eye and the band one inch above the eyes. After that it became difficult. Leaving one's beret to soak in water overnight was rumoured to be a worthwhile exercise, the shrunken result being easier to control, but doing so was apparently a chargeable offence. The charge sheet was RAF Form 252, a number not easily forgotten.

At least we didn't have the problem of too much hair to hide beneath the beret — we had virtually none left. Although most had heeded the advice to arrive with recently cut hair, we had all been shorn fairly drastically at the RAF's expense. In future, however, haircuts would cost us one shilling (5p) and we were always to have such a sum about our person. It was apparently also a chargeable offence to be told to "GIT YER 'AIR CUT" and not have the means to do so immediately.

During the week we each received one £1 note, the balance of our first week's pay, following which we were marched forthwith to the NAAFI (Navy, Army and Air Force Institutes) where we were obliged, whether we already had them or not, to purchase such items as boot polish, Brasso and dusters. The NAAFI ladies knew what we would require and that we wouldn't have the correct change but we found that they had everything organized prior to our arrival. At least we didn't need to buy Blanco (webbing cleaner) which had been the scourge of my time in the cadets at school. Luckily, we had been issued with no webbing (belt, gaiters, small or large packs) and so we were at least spared one military evil. Neither had we been issued with what were termed 'denims', all-in-one overalls of dirty olive-green hue worn for work by those in certain trades, for example aircraft fitters.

Identity discs (dog tags I believe our American friends call them) and pay books were not issued. The latter, more correctly termed the Airman's Service and Pay Book — RAF Form 64, was only issued if and when one was posted overseas. I cannot remember the circumstances of the pound notes mentioned earlier being issued to us. Certainly we attended no formal pay parade. I do however recall our being advised to record the serial numbers of such banknotes as might come into our possession, advice which may appear somewhat eccentric in the 1990s but which I acted upon as will become apparent in the next chapter. I recall also being more or less obliged to open RAF Post Office Savings Bank Account number 239245 and giving authority for the sum of 6d (2½p) a day — the minimum possible — to be transferred from my meagre pay into that account.

What else did we do during our week at Padgate? Not a lot that I can remember. With the advice of our guardian erk we made a start on trying to smooth the toecaps of our boots and produce the requisite shine. One dangerous way to do this was to insert the handle of a spoon into the lighted stove in the billet and, when red hot, apply it to the leather. Some did this but ran the risk of setting fire to the boot or destroying the stitching with equally disastrous results. The official method was 'spit and polish', literally spitting and polishing with liberal applications of Cherry Blossom or similar, and this is basically what I did although I recall making some use of a spoon handle. The use of the button-stick to prevent Brasso getting on to one's 'best blue' jacket, greatcoat or beret when polishing buttons and badge was impressed upon us.

Discipline was fairly relaxed. We were naturally required to keep the billet clean and tidy and had also to attempt to fold our sheets and blankets for display during the day in the precise manner to assume such earth-shattering importance during the eight weeks basic training ('square-bashing') soon to come. Perhaps because we made a decent attempt to march properly and gave him no cause for complaint in the billet, our guardian erk appeared happy to treat us perfectly fairly and he and the flight got on well enough. We realized that he could not be too lax with us: whilst marching through the camp on one occasion we heard one of his fellow guardian erks threatened by a superior with losing his flight if he couldn't keep better control of it.

As the week progressed I think our sense of insecurity increased along with foreboding as to what was soon to be in store for us. What had perhaps started as a bit of an adventure was now being seen in a different and unhappy light. Homesickness was soon rife: in my case the sight from one of the camp roads on the evening of Wednesday 5 November of early bonfires and fireworks in the gardens of nearby houses had a devastating effect. Whereas previously I had succeeded in relegating thoughts of home to somewhere in the back of my mind, I now found myself dwelling on the many happy Guy Fawkes nights spent with my family and neighbours and experienced a profound unhappiness.

As, basically, a somewhat shy and introverted individual, I now found it necessary in order to try to overcome my feelings to push myself to the forefront of whatever was occurring among the members of my flight, in particular in the evening in the billet. Hence, for example, when after lights out tuneless choruses of "I belong to Glasgow", "She's a Lassie from Lancashire" and others were rendered by erks from the areas concerned, I led a terrible version of "Maybe it's because I'm a Londoner" even though I'm not. I became an undoubted pain and was eventually told in no uncertain terms to shut up.

As the week drew to a close, there was inevitably speculation as to where we would be sent to do our 'square-bashing'. There were a number of Schools of Recruit Training, including one (No.3) here at Padgate. Schools were also located at Wilmslow near Manchester (No.4), West Kirby in Lancashire (No.5), Bridgenorth in Shropshire (No.7), Melksham in Wiltshire (No.10) and Hednesford in Staffordshire (No.11). None was anywhere near Essex! Bridgenorth had the reputation of being the one to avoid as a posting there was reckoned to be at least as bad as being in the Army.

Although it could not necessarily be assumed that we would all be sent to the same training camp, our guardian erk thought that this would in fact probably be the case and his guess was that we would all go to Hednesford. He told us a little of what we could expect in the way of discipline but, perhaps deliberately, he didn't really prepare us for what was in store. Up to now we had really enjoyed a fairly leisurely time with three cooked meals a day, no real work and little to concern us in our day-to-day existence.

All this was set to change: word reached us that we would all depart for No.11 S of RT, Hednesford on Monday 10 November.

CHAPTER 5

HELL AT HEDNESFORD

It was just as well that it was winter and cold to boot. We were therefore able to wear our greatcoats for the journey to the Midlands. There was no way we could have crammed them into our kitbags which were already proving too small for the rest of our gear. One tip we soon learned about packing a kitbag: ensure that your mug and irons, the essential items often required soon after arrival at your destination, are near the top.

The ubiquitous 3-tonners returned the previous Monday's vast intake to Warrington station (and perhaps waited to collect the next instalment of unhappy arrivals) whence we were taken by special train to Rugeley in Staffordshire. The journey of not much more than about fifty miles seemed interminable and, although I think we must have eaten *en route*, I now have no recollection of doing so.

Thankfully the afternoon was dry when we eventually arrived at Rugeley station. The town, situated between Stafford and Lichfield, is about twenty miles north of the centre of Birmingham. Another convoy of 3-tonners conveyed us up winding roads through extensive autumn-tinted areas of forest to the beautiful but bleak expanses of Cannock Chase whereon the former prisoner of war camp for which we were bound was situated. The scenery might have been idyllic but our prospects certainly weren't!

From the open backs of our lorries passing the small police post at the barbed-wire topped and double-gated entrance to the camp ("camp" was the term usually used to describe an RAF station) we glimpsed the grim-faced Service Police (SPs) resplendent with knife-edge creases, white webbing and white-topped, vertical-peaked caps. Not a glimmer of a smile here and, when we thought about it afterwards, the Motor Transport (MT) drivers had been strangely reticent too. I think it was all part of the carefully orchestrated 'welcome' prepared for the arrival of intakes of new recruits, I would guess either weekly or fortnightly at this vast camp.

Clearly by prior arrangement the 3-tonners came to a halt in line abreast across a parade ground. Some distance to the rear of the lorries stood groups of Non-Commissioned Officers (NCOs) who, we were soon to learn, were the Drill Instructors (DIs) about to impose a considerable degree of misery upon our very existence. All the lorries having stopped, with engines silenced and drivers remaining in their cabs, for about five seconds there was utter silence while we looked at the DIs and the DIs looked at us. Then, obviously at some pre-arranged signal, all hell broke loose.

En masse, the most dreadful cacophony of screaming, bawling and swearing emanated from the pace-stick and baton wielding DIs. The gist of their message was "What do you lazy chaps think you are doing hanging about in those lorries and don't you think you ought to disembark and run over to join us?" but they didn't actually use those words. As if by magic the tailboards dropped — the drivers having suddenly materialized — and erks and kitbags cascaded to the ground.

Has the reader ever tried to run with a fully laden kitbag? Does one place it on one's shoulder, under one's arm, cradle it in both arms, hold it by the top with either one hand or two, or what? There was quite a long way to run and the resultant shambles, so patently engineered, helped reduce us to the required level of jibbering idiocy. In all directions erks were falling over their own and other men's kitbags in their panic to reach the screeching DIs. We were required to form up in pairs in line astern, the composition of the resulting hut-sized groups separating, quite deliberately, friendships made at Padgate. It may seem far-fetched to say this but, from the way this exercise was carried out, I was convinced at the time that what happened was intentional. Certainly my Braintree friend and I, although we tried to stick together, finished up in different huts and, I believe, different flights and I rarely set eyes on him again.

Amid further induced chaos my party of twenty or so, with the corporal DI who was to be our particular pain-in-the-neck for the next few weeks, doubled (i.e. ran) to what was to be 'our hut'. We had been advised in no uncertain terms that we would be doubling everywhere for the next eight weeks. If we had been given the time to think about it we would have realized that this would not in fact be the case, if for no other reason simply because the DIs who would have to accompany us would not be happy about running around all day and, had they not done so to keep pace with us, we would have disappeared over the horizon.

To set the scene RAF Hednesford formed part of the RAF's Technical Training Command and housed No.11 School of Recruit Training. There were, I believe, four training wings on the camp and I found myself in No.4 Wing. I'm not sure how many flights comprised a wing. Mine was G25 Flight, housed in five wooden huts each home to about twenty recruits and, in a separate room in one corner, one DI. There were four corporals and, in the centre hut and in overall charge of the flight, the fearsome figure of a sergeant. The separate ablutions hut was sufficiently far away to be a nuisance in the wintry weather we were to endure. Each hut, or billet, was heated by two coke stoves although the severity of fuel rationing meant that usually only one was lit. The billet warmed up just in time for lights out, by which hour the stove would have become red-hot and occasionally appear incandescent. In the opposite corner at the DI's end of the hut was an ironing room, wherein was also housed a locked rack of .303 rifles for our use when suffering arms drill.

Although we of course weren't aware of this, 'our' corporal DI (who I will call Monk) was soon for demob and was not to be replaced following his departure a few weeks' later. That he was not as severe on the inmates of his hut as were I believe some of his colleagues was probably attributable to his consequent demob-happy condition.

Each standing by a bed in our new quarters, we were in turn subjected to Monk's critical inspection. Then: "ONE PACE FORWARD ANYONE WHO HAS BEEN A MEMBER OF THE ATC". No response. "WELL

THEN, HAS ANYONE BEEN IN THE ARMY CADETS?" I and one other moved one pace forward. To me: "WHAT RANK WERE YOU?" "Cadet, corporal". "DID YOU GET YOUR CERT A?" "No, corporal". To the erk on my right: "AND WHAT RANK WERE YOU?" "Company sergeant-major, corporal". To the other erk (who, I was to learn later, hailed from Colchester, a mere twenty-five miles from my home): "RIGHT, YOU WILL BE HUT ORDERLY. MOVE YOUR KIT TO THE END BED NEXT TO MY ROOM AND THEN REPORT TO ME". Then to me: "YOU WILL BE HIS DEPUTY. MOVE YOUR KIT TO A BED AT THE FAR END OF THE HUT". To all of us: "GET YOURSELVES SORTED OUT — M O V E!"; all the foregoing bellowed at the top of Corporal Monk's voice.

Subjugation, demoralization, degradation, humiliation, intimidation: words the meanings of which would probably not be understood by the average DI, despite his ability to put them into practice with great effect. They were all present during the next nine weeks. It is not possible after more than forty years to give a detailed account of what followed but merely to refer to bits and pieces, not in any particular sequence, in order to attempt to convey an impression of square-bashing, RAF style, during the fifties.

We had been instructed at a very early stage that, upon the entry of an officer or NCO into the hut, the nearest erk would immediately shout "OFFICER IN THE BILLET" or "NCO IN THE BILLET" at the top of his voice whereupon all recruits, regardless of what they were doing or where they happened to be at the time, would immediately stand to attention. This imposed a worrying obligation upon erks, like me, occupying beds closest to the hut doors as failure to notice the arrival of the grandee and respond immediately could have severe repercussions. It also resulted in some strange spectacles when recruits happened, for example, to be half in and half out of their trousers or perched on some article of furniture in order to clean, say, a lampshade on a 'bull night'. In practice it was almost unheard of for an officer to venture into a billet and the NCO's next order would hopefully be "OK, CARRY ON" or, if you were unlucky, "STAND BY YER BEDS!" followed by some idiocy or other.

Recruit training, to use the correct term, normally lasted for eight weeks. In my case Christmas intervened and the period stretched to nine weeks. After four weeks the recruit could expect to go home for the weekend on a 'forty-eight', a pass which in theory allowed 48 hours leave but which in practice enabled him to be absent from after duty on the Friday to 2359 hours (one minute to midnight) on the Sunday. One such pass could normally be expected during each month of RAF service and, on some camps at least, it was possible for return to be delayed as late as 0745 on the Monday morning. Incidentally, midnight doesn't exist in the Services and time apparently jumps from 2359 to 0001 hours.

Every recruit was expected to attain a satisfactory level of proficiency in each of a number of activities prior to taking part at the conclusion of the eight weeks training in a passing-out parade. He then went home for about a week's leave, at the conclusion of which he went direct to the RAF station to which he had been posted either as a member of the permanent staff or, if appropriate, for trade training. He could find himself stationed anywhere from the UK to the Far East.

There were continual threats of 're-flighting', being relegated to an incoming flight and re-starting recruit training from the beginning. Again, if we had thought about this we would have realized that, with the number of recruits passing through Padgate and the organization involved in processing and filtering them out to training stations such as Hednesford on a continuing basis, re-flighting was simply not a feasible proposition other than perhaps in very exceptional circumstances. I have heard of this occurring only in rare instances of illness when the recruit was patently incapable of completing the required training. In practice, as will be seen later, every effort was made by the DIs and other training staff to ensure that nobody failed anything, even to the extent of unlawful assistance!

On the Tuesday, Armistice Day, the whole of the previous day's intake assembled in the camp cinema where just about everyone of importance from the Commanding Officer (CO) downwards was either on the platform or lurking on the sidelines. Although other matters were dealt with, the principal object of the exercise seemed to be to identify such professional or other top-level sportsmen as might be in our midst, presumably to ensure that Command and RAF teams were aware of their existence.

It had by now become clear that one of our number was cutting a bit of a dash in a brown civilian suit. A short, round and bespectacled Scot, he was not unlike a 1950s Harry Secombe and it had to be assumed that it had still not been possible to locate a suitable uniform for him. During the course of the proceedings in the cinema he, perhaps unwisely, saw fit to question the platform about his lack of uniform and, in particular, to address the CO by his rank (Group Captain) instead of using the correct term, "Sir". "How did you know I was a group captain?" he was asked. "Because my father is a group captain" was his even more unwise reply. The DIs were ecstatic. One of the two ground-rules in the Services is to remain inconspicuous — not to draw attention to oneself. And here was someone not only making a fuss but having a senior officer as a father and, to cap it all, still wearing civvies. He couldn't have made himself more conspicuous if he had tried and accordingly spent a miserable nine weeks in his brown suit or, occasionally, in a pair of oversize denims, the butt of everybody with the slightest bit of authority. I cannot believe that it was impossible to find him a suitable uniform in a couple of months and remain convinced that, as a result of his own actions, he was the subject of a terrible conspiracy.

The second ground-rule is, of course, never to volunteer for anything. This I was to prove wrong during the summer of 1953.

We hadn't been at Hednesford many days before we were required to hand in one of our berets in exchange for a cap SD (Service Dress). This universally disliked abomination, usually known as one's big 'at or bus conductor's helmet, proved especially adept at blowing off in a wind or getting in the way of one's rifle during drill. It was impressed upon us that we were under no circumstances either to change the shape of the hat by bending the rim or to cut the ends of the peak and bend it to the vertical. One law for the SPs, who did both these things, and one for the erks.

Our day started with reveille blasting through the Tannoy speaker at, I believe, 0700 — at least, it should have done. We soon discovered that there was enough hot water in the ablutions for only a couple of dozen washes and shaves and blokes from all five huts were getting up earlier and earlier until the whole thing became ridiculous. As early as 0400, having been roused by the unfortunate recruits on fire picket duty, erks with greatcoats over their pyjamas were groping their way through darkness and anything from drizzle to a blizzard for a share of the precious hot water before returning to bed. A danger was that, if you had your shave too early, by the time of the first parade you could look to be in need of another one, with possible dire consequences at the hands of the DIs.

Breakfast, the first of the day's three cooked meals, was at 0800. I cannot now remember whether we marched to the mess as a flight or, more likely, made our way there independently. Dinner and tea were at 1200 and 1600, respectively, and I believe we marched to those meals. We were required to rinse our mugs and irons after use in huge tanks of water which was invariably either scalding hot or freezing cold. If the former, a dropped iron couldn't possibly be recovered and a replacement had to be sought from the equipment stores with an appropriate deduction from one's pay.

Between meals we trained. Drill occupied the greatest proportion of our time and will be discussed later. We marched around the camp as a flight between various training locations. "Left, left, left right left" when Corporal Wiseman was in control became "yofts, yofts, yofts yights yofts". He was probably the oldest of the four corporals and appeared to assume command when the sergeant wasn't around — which was virtually the whole time. When the camp roads were icy or snowbound, and especially when we were going up or downhill, the accompanying DI tended to walk on the grass verge if there was one. This ensured that anyone falling base over apex would be an erk.

After tea most of the evening was spent cleaning, polishing and pressing uniforms as well as looking after the hut. Wednesday night was 'bull night' when the entire evening had to be spent polishing, cleaning and dusting everything which could be polished, cleaned or dusted in preparation for an inspection next morning. If you were really unlucky there would also be a kit inspection. Every item of kit was required to be laid out on one's bed in a prescribed and, frankly, ridiculous fashion and woe betide the unfortunate erk found to have anything missing, dirty or improperly displayed. I remember going through this performance only once and recall at the time being concerned that, notwithstanding that all items were marked with one's Service number, the practice surely provided the perfect opportunity for anyone with access to the hut before we returned to it at Thursday dinner-time to purloin perhaps the odd sock or two. It was bad enough to discover that one's kit had, on some pretext or other, been hurled around the hut by the inspecting officer or NCOs.

Saturday afternoons and Sundays were much more relaxed and there was time for letter writing, reading and so on. On Sunday morning a local newsagent appeared in the mess with newspapers. For sale were a few copies each of such titles as the *Sunday Times* and the *Sunday Express*, as well as a three feet high pile of copies of the *News of the World*. I don't recall reading much, if at all, but I corresponded regularly with my mother and my friend Joan and also received the occasional letter from a couple of other young ladies in the office in Chelmsford.

One early Sunday, in the queue for breakfast, it suddenly dawned on me that I was the only airman among hundreds in the mess wearing his best blue. Don't ask me why I had it on: I can only surmise that on a previous Sunday we had perhaps been on a church parade and I had somehow got it into my head that best blue was the Sunday order of the day. About as conspicuous as I could get, what with polished brass buttons and belt buckle shining in the gloom, I anticipated at any moment the bellowed "OI YEW, AIRMAN, WOT ARE YEW DEWING WEARIN' YOUR BEST BLEW?" Luckily all was well while, shrinking into my shoes, I gobbled my rude repast and scurried off back to the billet to get changed.

Weekends and, to a lesser extent, evenings provided the opportunity for visits to the NAAFI canteen. I went there on few occasions but clearly recall my hut orderly sitting alone, opened bottle of Worthington ale and partly filled glass on the table in front of him, staring blankly into space and looking utterly dejected. Facilities for relaxation and refreshment were provided elsewhere on the camp by the Church Army and, I believe, the Women's Voluntary Service (WVS). I couldn't possibly have foreseen in 1952 that, in the 1980s and 90s, I was to spend many years as a member of what had by then become the Women's Royal Voluntary Service (WRVS) helping with the organization of the meals-on-wheels service in my home town. Yes, they do accept men as members of what is fundamentally a women's organization!

The camp as a whole was not much to write home about, as many an unhappy recruit who struggled up 'kitbag hill' to reach it from the main road will confirm. It had apparently been used to house enemy prisoners during the Second World War and had, allegedly, been condemned as unfit. I believe all the buildings were of wooden construction and, the ground sloping away to the south-west, most barrack huts were raised on brick pillars. Certainly during the appalling weather conditions prevailing most of the time I was there, it was almost impossible to feel warm and dry. Beyond the perimeter fence the bleak moorland of Cannock Chase seemed to stretch interminably. Vacated by the RAF in about 1956, the site of the camp is now included in Cannock Chase Country Park and a picnic site and visitor centre are nearby.

I had hoped to ease my general feeling of despair in one respect but was to be disappointed. I had become a devotee of *The Goon Show* and looked forward on Tuesday 11 November to the first programme in a new series, due to be broadcast on the Home Service at 1930. BBC programmes were available over the Tannoy during the evenings. However, when Andrew Timothy announced the evening's show, *Fred of the Islands*, the nearest erk promptly switched it off. Next week *The Egg of the Great Auk* met the same fate and my faith in human nature evaporated somewhat. I don't think I was to hear a single show during the whole of my National Service. Television was in its infancy and I don't recall a set on the camp, even in the NAAFI.

None of the occupants of my hut was married and, with one exception, all were aged eighteen. The odd man out, a cheerful cherubic looking erk from Hayes in Middlesex, aged about twenty-two, had completed an apprenticeship before embarking on his service. I couldn't help but feel sorry for a tall, gangling individual with a hang-dog expression, Prince Charles ears and a terrible Geordie accent who had been issued with Aertex underpants reaching to his knees. I couldn't understand a word he said but I realized he suffered considerable embarrassment.

We were required to sleep 'head to tail', i.e. with heads in adjoining beds alternating between the wall and the centre of the hut. The luck of the draw found me, in the end bed as deputy hut orderly, with my head to the centre. All erks were required to use the door at my end of the hut which meant that it was upon the end of my bed, adjacent to my head, that the fire picket rained blows with their truncheon when making 'early calls'.

Being deputy hut orderly possessed only disadvantages as it turned out. The hut orderly was required to maintain a list of recruits awarded 'fatigues' (for such minor sins as being last on parade, for example) and, when a 'fatigue wallah' was required for some unpleasant duty, to instruct whoever had risen to the top of his list to do whatever was required. At the outset, before any of us had had an opportunity to earn 'fatigues', the hut orderly was told by Cpl Monk simply to draw up a rota, omitting his own name but putting mine at the top. As the result, I spent much of an early Sunday in the cookhouse peeling and coring apples. I cut a finger quite badly and, although they didn't know it, the recruits enjoyed apple and blood pie that day. Very few others in the hut were imposed upon in this way; the ultimate indignity if you were not there as a result of some misdeed would have been the tinroom in the cookhouse, cleaning the receptacles used for the previous meal.

Another disadvantage of my position. One Saturday afternoon Cpl Monk was entertaining a fellow DI from another flight in his room and told me to light the small coke fire therein. Fire lighting has never been a strong point of mine and, after several abortive attempts, I was instructed to drop dead by numbers — several times — until the two NCOs had enjoyed their bit of fun and were satisfied that I had been humiliated adequately, before being dismissed.

We were told at an early stage that G25 Flight was a POM flight. This meant we had previously been selected as potential officer material and were all expected to apply for the Queen's commission. The fact that only one occupant of my hut did so incurred the displeasure of the powers-that-be. The exception was Keith Benn, tall and bespectacled and from somewhere in Middlesex, who was eventually accepted for officer cadet training and duly commissioned into the Accounts Branch. How do I know this? Because the best part of ten years later I was to meet Benn on a coach in Innsbruck, in the Austrian Tyrol, and on a subsequent humid and thundery evening to be photographed with him and our respective wives in a gondola on the canals of Venice. A far cry from the wilds of Staffordshire!

On the wall to the left of the hut door referred to earlier was a full-length mirror. On the right was displayed a chain of command detailing the names and ranks of everybody from the hut corporal upwards. We were supposed to memorize the whole of this although it didn't really mean anything to us so early in our Service 'careers'. If the top name was that of HM The Queen I expect we might have remembered her but, as for the rest, not a chance. Fortunately, we were never quizzed about this.

A couple of weekends into our training and after the threats to the contrary to which we had by now become accustomed, we were permitted to leave the camp on the Saturday afternoon. Having passed the scrutiny of the SPs at the gates some of us, resplendent in best blues and big 'ats, went by bus into the small town of Lichfield where we at last felt we could relax for a while along the rainy streets, in a cinema and, perhaps best of all, with a modest civilian meal in a café. The fact that the only waitress in the crowded upstairs room was rushed off her feet and we had to wait some while for our egg, chips and whatever, worried us not one jot: I think I felt happy for the first time in weeks.

To revert to less pleasant matters, square-bashing proved something of a misnomer in my case. G25 Flight actually bashed the square on very few occasions: I can recall only the passing-out parade and the rehearsal on the preceding day. Our foot and rifle drill was undertaken on the roadway running past our huts (there was no traffic to disturb us) and marching about the camp — "yofts yights yofts yights" — between various locations. Some found the drill onerous and even difficult but my experience in the cadets stood me in good stead. The drill was identical and my only problem lay with timing: all the various movements had been faster in the cadets and, until I had attuned myself to the slower pace, I was in grave danger of making myself conspicuous!

In an attempt to get the whole flight moving in unison, we were required to yell out the timing as we drilled. For example "ONE (pause) two, three (pause) ONE (pause) two, three (pause) ONE!" while sloping arms. During one such session the DI sergeant appeared in the doorway of his hut. "WOT'S THE MATTER WITH YEW LOT — CAN'T YOU MAKE MORE NOISE THAN THAT?" he roared, emphasising his words with his pace-stick on the adjacent woodwork, "I COULD MAKE MORE NOISE BANGIN' MY KNOB ON THE END OF THIS HUT!".

During most of our training we were under the control of only one or perhaps two corporal DIs at any time — never the sergeant who, one has to assume, enjoyed a fairly easy life. We set eyes on him on very few occasions. My only real conversation with him took place in the ablutions and was of an obscene and somewhat one-sided nature. My principal contribution consisted of a nervous laugh. I also suffered a chance encounter with him on a pathway alongside, I believe, No.4 Wing's HQ when I had the misfortune in my anxiety to please to refer to him as "corporal". This produced a tirade of invective and much jabbing of fingers on his 'tapes'. Happily, the location meant that my discomfiture was suffered more or less in private but I think my two-year long paranoia about ranks in general and saluting in particular, about which I write in a later chapter, originated in this incident as much as any other.

DI humour on parade was legendary and we soon discovered that it was best not to laugh but to keep a straight face, gaze into the distance and avoid eye-contact with your tormentor. It should be emphasized that the best way to avoid being on the receiving end of these well-rehearsed 'jokes' was, again, to avoid being conspicuous. Don't turn left when the flight turns right; try not to march with the left arm and leg swinging forward together (DIs really appreciate this!); don't become a victim of the 'only man in step' syndrome; just try to be one of the crowd, so to speak.

Two examples of what we had to put up with. DI, mouth about one inch from recruit's face upon which he has noticed some slight blemish (e.g. shaving cream) and onto which he is now spraying germs and remains of breakfast: "AIRMAN, DID YEW 'AVE A SHAVE THIS MORNIN'?" "Yes, corporal". "AND DID YEW USE A MIRROR WHEN YEW 'AD A SHAVE THIS MORNIN'?" "Yes, corporal" (knowing full well what was coming but powerless to stop it). "WELL, AIRMAN, TRY USIN' A RAZOR TERMORRER!" Or how about this one? DI, standing about one inch behind erk who doesn't know he is there and accordingly jumps about three feet in the air at the voice spraying the back of his neck: "AIRMAN, AM I 'URTIN' YEW?" "No, corporal." "ARE YOU SURE I'M NOT 'URTIN' YEW, AIRMAN?" "Yes, corporal". "WELL, I SHOULD BE BECAWSE I'M STANDIN' ON YER 'AIR — GET IT CUT!"

The DIs didn't always win. One bitterly cold but beautifully sunny morning the flight was out on the road in the charge of one corporal, his colleagues presumably tucked away somewhere in the warm. He had on his greatcoat and gloves while his rifle lay on the grass verge. We were without greatcoats or gloves and were engaged in rifle drill — difficult and painful in the freezing conditions. Out of the corner of my left eye I noticed an RAF chaplain walking along the main camp road which ran at right angles to that on which we drilled. He paused to observe us, seemed to hesitate, but then approached the flight. After the usual salutes (all chaplains were commissioned officers): "Are you in charge of these men, corporal?" "YES, SIR". "Well, either you will send them into their billets for their greatcoats and gloves or you will remove your own and pick up your rifle. Carry on, corporal". Sheepishly the DI removed the offending garments and picked up the rifle. The chaplain watched us for a few minutes before proceeding on his way. Drilling ended soon after his disappearance and we regained the warmth of our huts in relatively good humour.

I almost felt sorry for the DI. He was the only one ever to crack his face with a smile and appeared generally too cheerful for his job. To start with I wasn't sure whether he was good-natured or disguising a sadistic streak but the former turned out to be the case. The fourth corporal DI, not mentioned specifically so far, was of a cheerless disposition and gave the impression he would rather be somewhere else. Perhaps he was a National Serviceman!

On Thursday 13 November and again on Wednesday 10 December we were lined up, outdoors, for 'jabs' — TABT inoculations and, on the first occasion, smallpox vaccination as well. Strangely, it was the big strapping types who fainted, sometimes just at the sight of the needle, while ordinary mortals like myself were troubled only by standing around in the cold and the prolonged bout of rifle drill which followed on each occasion. This did, however, have the effect of banishing any stiffness which might otherwise have been experienced in the left arm!

Again, it was the allegedly tough guys who required assistance from the medical orderlies when we were shown films featuring the symptoms of certain communicable diseases which we were exhorted to avoid at all costs. I think, though, that we managed without the medics after we had been marched, "yofts yights yofts yights", to one of the DIs' delights, the gas chamber. This turned out to be a scruffy little wooden hut from around the door of which wisps of something smokey-looking were emerging. Parties donned gas masks and entered the hut to walk around the evil contrivance in the centre producing gas before, at a signal, removing the masks and running round a couple of times. Having burst from the hut coughing and spluttering with eyes streaming, most ended up horizontal on the grass outside. Why on earth were we made to do this?

Other delights about which the DIs had been gloating since our arrival were the assault course and the rifle range. The thought of having to attempt the former did worry me. I have never claimed to be one of the fittest people around and I was pretty concerned at the prospect. I needn't have bothered: on the due day the assault course was frozen solid and deemed too dangerous for use. We were too close to the end of our training period for fresh arrangements to be made so I assume we were all recorded as having passed the test on the basis that we hadn't failed it.

The rifle range held no terrors for me. Although I had never fired a .303 my experiences with .22s in the cadets gave me every confidence and, what was more, I had thankfully thought to pack my John Lennon specs in my **small** suitcase all those weeks, which by now seemed like years, ago. I knew that, unlike .22s, .303s produced a pretty hefty 'kick' and that, if you didn't pull the butt tightly into your shoulder, a broken collarbone or worse was possible. I must confess I disobeyed orders and set off for the range — by lorry as it was located some distance from the camp — with a pad of folded handkerchiefs under my shirt. I'm no hero!

Others were pretty scared and it was difficult to reassure them. In small groups we fired from the prone position at targets set up in front of a wall of soft sand. As I anticipated I had no problem meeting the required standard (it wasn't often I was as confident as this at Hednesford) although others were missing their targets completely. It was easy to see where their bullets were disturbing the neatly smoothed sand. Then I realized that DIs

61

were standing over us, firing from the shoulder at the targets which were being missed. So nobody failed on the range. I had the dubious privilege of ensuring that all the spent cartridge cases were safely removed in an ammunition box. The only snag was that the box was locked and each individual cartridge case had to be inserted via a precisely shaped slot in the lid so designed that if it still contained a bullet it would not pass through.

As far as I can recall the training course involved no written work. We were, however, marched "yofts yights yofts yights" to lectures, usually given by officers, on various aspects of RAF life. I quite enjoyed these talks if for no other reason because we were sitting down in the warm at the time.

I did not enjoy our visits to the gym which, fortunately, were pretty infrequent. In the first place we doubled to the gym ("yofts yights yofts yights" twice as fast) in our PT kit which wasn't a lot of fun in the freezing conditions. Moreover, I am not the world's best gymnast and, in particular, have never been able to perform a forward roll satisfactorily. Backward, yes, but forward, no. I had to put up with a stream of abuse from the Physical Training Instructors (PTIs) when they discovered this and on one occasion was required to run twenty times round the gym. I didn't object to this because it was well within my capabilities and, while so engaged, I couldn't of course be expected to do anything else.

In addition to the assault course two DIs' delights which did NOT materialize in the case of G25 Flight were the route march and the cross-country run. Whether this was also a result of the atrocious weather conditions we never knew. I think I could have coped with a route march but I'm not so sure about the cross-country.

A recurring nightmare for me was the weekly pay parade. On the face of it this seems a trifle eccentric when the object is to receive money. A large body of airmen parades in front of a long table behind which are ranged accounts officers and pay clerks. One or more NCOs lurk behind, presumably to prevent any possible theft of the cash, which comprises a pile of £1 notes, a pile of 10s.0d notes and mountains of florins (2s.0d pieces), arranged neatly in front of the paying officer. From the long list in front of him a pay clerk calls names in alphabetical order. When you hear your name you come to attention, yell "Sir" and your last three, march up to the paying officer, salute, take your pittance in your left hand, salute again, right turn and march away.

Well, what's so bad about that, the reader might ask? I'll tell you. Pay clerks all seem to have quiet voices, I always finished up in a rear row on the parade where I couldn't properly hear what was being said and, to make matters worse, my surname is slightly unusual and was invariably pronounced incorrectly by pay clerks. The result was that, at Hednesford at any rate, I either didn't hear my name or, on more than one occasion, misheard another erk's name with the result that two of us yelled "Sir" and last threes. In any event I and perhaps one or two others with similar difficulties remained on parade in splendid isolation when everybody else had been paid and gone. Inevitably there would be abuse and shouting before I and any others received our miserable pay and were allowed to go. I endured all that each week for the grand sum of £1.

Gross pay at the rate of 4s.0d a day totalled £1.8s.0d a week. From this was deducted 3s.6d (6d a day) for my newly-opened Post Office Savings Bank account and a sum — 3s.0d I believe — in respect of National Insurance, leaving £1.1s.6d net. As we were paid only in multiples of 2s.0d my actual pay amounted to £1 with 1s.6d added to my 'credits'. One could ask for credits to be paid, less any debts, before going on leave. As advised at Padgate, I conscientiously noted the serial number of the £1 note collected each week and had occasion to make use of this detail a few weeks later.

I had been feeling unwell for a couple of days and one Wednesday evening, having undertaken my share of bull-night labours, including using the heavy 'bumper' to polish the brown lino of my bed-space (following which one had to slide around on pads of old blanket material or incur the wrath of all and sundry) I went to bed early. During the night I had a vivid dream wherein I was sick over my bed-space. I awoke in the morning, feeling dreadful, to find it hadn't been a dream. With my 'small kit' (overnight gear) I joined the morning sick parade outside the station sick quarters. After an examination by a Medical Officer (MO) I was admitted and spent two days in the luxury of a warm room with meals in a comfortable bed. I was given no medication and nobody told me what might have caused the sickness.

During the Thursday I was befriended by an airman who spent much of the day chatting at my bedside. I didn't know whether he was a patient or a member of the staff but, from his age and the colour of his uniform, he clearly wasn't a recruit undergoing basic training. Naturally I had with me my entire wealth, which at the time consisted of two £1 notes and a few coins, and before going to sleep I ensured that this fortune was safely tucked away in my bedside locker. Next morning the two £1 notes were not there. My 'friend' had also vanished and I never saw him again. I reported the loss and, several hours later, a pretty disinterested SP turned up to take details. I was of course able to give him the serial numbers of the notes — at which he was somewhat taken aback — but I don't recall daring to mention my suspicions about my 'friend'. I heard no more of this matter and, paranoid that I might have been at the time, I couldn't but feel from the attitude of those involved that I was the victim of a conspiracy. Two pounds might not seem much now but it amounted then to two weeks' pay: why, I wonder, was I not seen by the Provost Police, the equivalent (I believe) of the civilian CID? I wasn't exactly overjoyed when I returned to my billet on the Saturday afternoon.

Two highlights of my time at Hednesford, both threatened with cancellation by the DIs of course, were the 48 hour pass after four weeks' training and the Christmas break two or three weeks later. We should have realized, had we thought logically, that neither would be cancelled because surely the DIs wanted their breaks just as much as we did. The '48' was of a somewhat eventful nature on account of the weather. The country was in the grip of severe fog, the resulting 'smog', especially in the cities, killing thousands during the very weekend of our leave. After duty on Friday 5 December, and with the magic RAF Form 295 (Leave and Pass Form) safely in my pocket, I travelled by coach from the camp to Euston station, London, arriving later than expected because of the fog. By the time I reached Liverpool Street station the last train to Chelmsford had gone and I could only reach Shenfield — some eight or nine miles distant — by rail. We had been required to take all our kit home and so, lugging my kitbag, I made my lonely way — it was by now well past midnight — to the A12 road with the idea of hitch-hiking. Have you ever tried to hitch in thick fog, in darkness? There was no traffic anyway. I eventually trudged back to Shenfield station and succeeded in calling up a taxi which cost me two or three weeks' pay. It was a hard life being an airman!

My home appeared to have shrunk since I left it. In particular my room, which was only a 6ft by 6ft boxroom anyway, seemed minute — but the feather bed was luxurious! Saturday evening I went with Joan to the Regent cinema in Chelmsford. She lived in a village several miles away and had braved the fog to come into the town by bus. I met her outside the cinema wearing my best blue and big 'at. I can only assume that either I was proud of the uniform or I was an idiot — either way I must have looked a proper prune.

The weekend passed very quickly. For some reason which now escapes me I was in danger on the Sunday of missing the train which I needed to catch to Liverpool Street in order to reach Euston in time for the return coach. I therefore ran through thick fog to Chelmsford station accompanied by my brothers on their bicycles, one with my kitbag balanced between his crossbar and handlebars. Remarkably, in view of the conditions, the local train ran to time. Outside Euston station, however, the fog was so dense that it is no exaggeration to say that I walked along the pavement running my hand along the wall of the station building so as not to lose my direction. In doing so I actually bumped into an elderly man coming the other way. Needless to say no coaches had arrived from Hednesford to convey back the crowds of erks now milling around in the murk and we were told to return early next morning and try again.

I was concerned about having to go back home but had the good fortune to encounter one of my hutmates who invited me to spend the night at his home in Ealing. His mother was a little startled to find two erks on her doorstep when she had not long before waved farewell to only one but nevertheless made me welcome. Next morning the conditions had improved just sufficiently for the journey to Hednesford which we regained in the early afternoon. Needless to say we were told we would all be charged for failing to be back in camp by the due time — the usual idle threat of course. Hundreds from different parts of the country were arriving late and there was obviously no question of taking action against all of them in view of the prevailing weather conditions. But the DIs did delight in putting the wind up their charges at every opportunity.

Generally speaking DIs were a law unto themselves, although they did occasionally get their comeuppance. Two contrasting tales before I leave them. One snowy night I found myself on fire picket duty. My colleague and I, armed with one torch and one truncheon between us, spotted a light long after midnight. One of our duties being to enforce 'lights out', with some trepidation we entered what turned out to be a smoke-ridden billet occupied by a number of corporals playing cards. In no uncertain terms we were told to clear off and keep our traps shut — which we did. Between duty turns, we rested on beds — without mattresses — in a freezing hut with only tea and sausages for sustenance.

The other tale concerns a DI corporal known to me by sight but allocated to another flight. I was to hear later via the 'grapevine' that, shortly after I had left Hednesford, this NCO ordered all the recruits in his hut outside during the night, wearing pyjamas, to search in the snow for a white dog which, it transpired, did not exist. One of the erks wrote to his Member of Parliament and the DI, no longer a corporal, was last observed digging a trench on the camp.

To return to my leave, Christmas was a re-run of the 48 without any of the problems. I believe we went home on Christmas Eve and returned on Sunday 28 December; in those days New Year's Day was not a bank holiday. I cannot now remember anything of the holiday but I'm sure I enjoyed myself. Around this time a group photograph of the flight was taken by a gentleman from Liverpool. This panoramic picture, of which I still have a copy, features 91 miserable erks (from which number I deduce that some must have been absent), Cpls Wiseman, 'Smiler' and 'Cheerless', and three electricity poles. The sergeant missed the occasion of course and presumably Cpl Monk had by now been demobbed. We never saw his going. One afternoon we returned from tea to find a small table set up in the billet bearing such valuable articles as pens, pencils, rubbers etc which he was graciously prepared to sell to us, following which episode we didn't see him again.

Recruits were not issued with a training programme or timetable of any sort and consequently rarely knew from one hour to the next what delights were in store. "OUT ON THE ROAD IN TEW MINITS IN (e.g.) WORKIN' BLEWS, LARS WUN OUT'S ON FERTEEGS" followed either by drill on the road or "yofts yights yofts yights" to some as yet unknown destination on the camp was the usual routine.

The end of our training was in sight and, "yofts yights yofts yights", we found ourselves at the trade selection centre to discuss our respective futures in the RAF. Having had a brief look at information on the various trades available, I enquired as to the possibility of becoming a photographer. "You would need to sign on for eight years" I was told. "If I were to do so, would this guarantee my becoming a photographer?" "No, it would not", so that was the end of that. It was suggested, possibly because of my height (70¼ inches it will be recalled!), that I might become an SP. Me? An SP? Not likely! I demurred politely. The fact that I was a qualified shorthand writer and a competent typist led to the suggestion that I might care to go to RAF Credenhill, Hereford to be trade tested. If successful no trade training would be required before a posting, as a shorthand typist, direct to a permanent station.

Back in 1949, on Saturday 7 May to be precise, when I had attended my first speedway meeting, Rayleigh Rockets' opponents (defeated 45–37) were Tamworth Hounds. Nobody to whom I spoke at the time seemed to have any idea as to the whereabouts of Tamworth. I found out one Sunday lunchtime in January 1953 when I spent an hour or more sitting on the town's deserted railway station waiting for a connection to Hereford. Administrative and clerical trade training was undertaken at RAF Credenhill and it was not therefore surprising that the camp appeared to be awash with WRAFs (Women's Royal Air Force personnel).

It had been two months since I last touched a typewriter or wrote shorthand but I had no difficulty when tested on the Monday morning in reaching the modest standards required for promotion to leading aircraftman (LAC), namely 50 words a minute shorthand and 32 typing, despite the typewriter being a bit of an old wreck. Because the RAF would not need to train me, it transpired that when the administrative wheels had turned I would become an LAC as from the day I was called up, with a retrospective increase in pay to 6s.6d a day, and consequently miss out the rank of aircraftman first class (AC1). I returned to Hednesford the same day feeling slightly pleased with myself.

I think our passing out parade was on or about Friday 9 January. Band playing we marched and counter-marched in incessant drizzle, a few hardy relatives of recruits sitting under blankets and umbrellas on the edge of the parade ground. We were inspected by an officer with scrambled egg on his cap who then saluted us when we marched past staring at him — at least that's how it seemed. Thereafter, having in theory been given details of our postings either for trade training or to permanent stations, we all went home for a week's leave. In practice there was no posting for a few of us, including me, and we were instructed to return to Hednesford where we would join 'Pool Flight' for a temporary period.

Although I could not for one moment pretend to have enjoyed my square-bashing, I had experienced the comradeship of others in the flight. They were a pretty resilient and cheerful group of blokes who, I would say, were of above average intelligence and undoubtedly honest. Lack of marmalade at breakfast time had prompted me to return after our '48' with a jar of Robertsons Silver Shred. Nobody even asked for a share, let alone helped himself when I wasn't looking: what more can I say?!

My friend Peter Steggall was aware of my interest in motor sport and, during the course of my leave, he asked me to act as navigator to his cousin, John, who would be taking part in a car rally organized by the Thames Estuary Automobile Club on the night of Saturday 31 January. I declined, partly in view of the uncertainty as to my RAF future but also because I have never travelled well by car, especially if trying to read on the move — something which a navigator would need to be doing constantly. More of this in the next chapter.

I returned to RAF Hednesford on about Sunday 18 January. Pool Flight was a doddle as long as we kept the billet and our noses clean. There was virtually no discipline although we were allocated certain not too onerous tasks to keep us occupied between visits to the orderly room to enquire as to whether postings had materialized. I was put in charge of the coke compound, a part-time job as the gates were unlocked for only an hour or two each day. Armed with a clip-board and a list of hut numbers my task was to stand in the falling snow ticking off the numbers as recruits from each hut collected their daily ration of one bucket of coke and a few lumps of coal to get their fire started. Many were the ruses employed to get a second bucketful and I turned a blind eye to all of them. Why not? After all, I had been a 'sprog' (term used to describe airman under training — u/t — or with less service than oneself) only a week or two earlier!

Apart from regular visits to the orderly room and to the camp post office (where I searched through hundreds of incoming letters in the mistaken belief that I might find some for me) I did what I found it best to do on any RAF station: maintain a low profile and never go anywhere you don't have to. This avoids the bellowed "OI YEW, AIRMAN, WOT ARE YEW DEWIN' 'ERE?", with unlimited potential for trouble.

Some questions remained unanswered. Had our tea in the mess been laced with bromide? If so, was our cherubic friend from Hayes being honest when he said he had overcome the effects while off camp one Sunday afternoon? Was it a fact that you couldn't be charged (with being 'idle in bed'?) if when so apprehended you had one foot flat on the floor? Why was it forbidden to sleep on one's uniform trousers in an effort to induce creases therein? I invariably slept not only on my trousers but on most of the rest of my uniform as well. The modicum of warmth thus achieved provided a little comfort when the freezing morning arrived. In common with many others I rubbed soap on the inside of my creases. When pressed with a not too-hot iron, knife-like results were anticipated but not always achieved. A too-hot iron resulting in soap showing on the outside of the trouser was to be avoided at all costs.

I believe it was early in the week beginning Monday 26 January that the orderly room clerk surprised me with "Yes, your posting's arrived. You're going to RAF Norton as shorthand typist." Could he tell me where Norton happened to be located? No, he couldn't and nor could anyone else. One thing I did know was that it wasn't anywhere near Essex and that my hopes of a posting near home were dashed. On the other hand it wasn't in one of the overseas trouble spots so I supposed it could have been worse.

When I called back later to see what further information was available I was handed a railway warrant for Sheffield. Oh no, not Sheffield!

CHAPTER 6

MONOTONY AT NORTON

With all due respect to Yorkshire and its people — and one of my greatest friends, the late Bill Hunt, had been a Yorkshireman — I just didn't want to spend the best part of the next two years there. It was too far from home for me to be able to return as often as I would have liked. Moreover, although I believe it is very different these days, Sheffield in the 1950s was a pretty grimy and unprepossessing place of factory chimneys belching forth vast quantities of smoke which often remained suspended rather like a lid over the saucer in which the city seemed to lie. [Nothing to do with my RAF story, but Bill Hunt was a lawyer whose secretary, preparing the Will which he had drafted for me in later years, referred to him as "my **fiend** and solicitor", a Freudian typing slip if ever there was one!]

So, in the last week of January 1953, it was with heavy heart and feet that I made my way from Sheffield Midland station to find initially that nobody seemed to have heard of RAF Norton — not surprising as a fair bit of the RAF hadn't either. Eventually, kitbag tucked under the stairs, I found myself on the rearmost seat of a double-decker bus on which the conductor had a pretty good idea where the camp might be. The bus climbed southwards out of the saucer, through the lid and up via Gleadless to the very outskirts of Sheffield. At about the point where the housing ended I was put off the bus and told to keep walking until I found the camp on my left.

"Are you a credit to the Royal Air Force?" I wasn't too certain how to answer the question posed above the full-length mirror by the door of the guardroom: one never looks one's best after travelling half the day with a loaded kitbag. I was booked in and directed to SHQ (Station Headquarters) by a surprisingly civil SP: at this stage I did not of course appreciate the differing attitudes adopted by those in authority at permanent stations as compared to those at training camps. A pale-faced and somewhat frightened looking LAC orderly room clerk, who happily had been anticipating my arrival, relieved me of the large brown envelope containing my 'documents' which I had conveyed from Hednesford, said he supposed I would be working in SHQ when I had 'arrived' and told me where to draw bedding and find a vacant bed.

He also issued the RAF form (in fact a large coloured card) which I required in order formally to 'arrive' at the station and, eventually, to 'clear' from it when posted elsewhere. This form listed various locations on the camp, for example the equipment stores and sick quarters, at which it was necessary in effect to check-in and was dual-purpose in that it not only notified those who needed to know that you had arrived but also ensured that you very soon learned the whereabouts of most things on the camp that mattered.

The billets were a revelation. At first glance hut 22 appeared to be a standard wooden barrack block of the type to which I had by now become accustomed. However, investigation revealed two rows of seven parallel huts, connected internally to an extensive central ablution block. The huts themselves were not only brick-built but, incredibly, centrally heated! I was told later that the camp had been constructed for use during World War II by Women's Auxiliary Air Force (WAAF) personnel, the standard of the accommodation and the nature of the facilities provided in the ablution block lending support to this suggestion. General opinion among erks was that the station had served as a headquarters for the barrage balloon defences of Sheffield and that balloons had been flown from the site. I have since learned that No. 16 Balloon Centre, responsible for 72 balloons and forming part of No. 33 (Balloon Barrage) Group of Balloon Command, occupied the site from 1939 until it was re-named RAF Norton on 1 July 1943; WAAFs had replaced male trainees after the outbreak of war. From 1942 the station housed an Aircrew Refresher Centre. Servicing of radio and radar equipment was also undertaken during the war.

Perhaps I may employ the time which I spent 'arriving' at RAF Norton to refer back to the previous chapter and to the request that I should act as a navigator in the car rally to be held on the night of 31 January, my first Saturday at Norton. I had hardly set foot on the station before I received first a letter and then a telegram from John Steggall trying to persuade me to change my mind and travel to Essex for the event. However, for the reasons already mentioned I didn't feel able to do so. And how glad I was that I had stuck to my guns. 31 January/1 February turned out to be the night of the catastrophic east coast flooding in which hundreds of unfortunate people lost their lives in coastal counties from Yorkshire to Kent. Essex was very badly affected and, although the rally started near Southend-on-Sea, by good fortune the route took the cars inland — in fact westwards out of Essex — and the competitors suffered a wild night without being in any danger. In the event my friend Peter navigated for his cousin. Thousands of Servicemen were drafted to the east coast to assist with repairs to the battered and destroyed sea defences but I was not aware that RAF Norton contributed any personnel.

In addition to Norton's location in Yorkshire, I was disappointed to find that it was not a flying station. As a reluctant member of Britain's military flying Service I had hoped that I would at least be able to practice my trade as a shorthand typist within sight and sound of its aircraft but this was not to be so. In fact RAF Norton was a comparatively small station which served as the parent unit, and to provide a base, for No.3 Ground Radio Servicing Squadron (GRSS) commanded by Sqn Ldr A. Singer. As its title implies, the GRSS serviced ground radio (and radar) installations and it consisted largely of specialist and other vehicles travelling in convoy to various sites in the United Kingdom and Germany.

Interestingly, the RAF had to cope with the arrival of my younger brother Den about two and a half years after my own enlistment and, after training him at RAF Locking, Somerset, dumped him in the wilds of

Lincolnshire. As a radar mechanic his job was to service and maintain the radar installation at RAF Skendleby — precisely the function of a GRSS as I understood it — and he assures me that no such unit ever visited his station; indeed, he had never heard of them until I posed the question in recent years. One has to assume either that the servicing procedure had changed or that the GRSS convoys were an elaborate hoax with the corollary that RAF Norton didn't need to exist. Could we all have gone home?

RAF Skendleby was a top secret Fighter Command station at which cameras and photography were prohibited. I have nevertheless seen photographs of my brother on the site, including one of him perched on the rotating radar equipment atop the (now demolished) 250ft tower which he had to ascend in order to ply his trade. I think 25ft would have been about my limit and I'm sure my parents would have been horrified!

But to return to RAF Norton and my arrival there for work. Not surprisingly, the frightened orderly room clerk was correct in assuming that I would be based in SHQ, a single-storey E-shaped wooden building quite close to the camp entrance. My desk and elderly Imperial typewriter were located in a corner of the registry — the office wherein were located clerks carrying out filing and mail handling duties. As well as undertaking general typing along with an LAC typist I was, as the only shorthand writer, also to act as the CO's secretary.

Norton fell within No.90 (Signals) Group, the only group not forming part of one of the RAF's Commands. In 1953 these comprised Bomber, Coastal, Fighter, Flying Training, Home, Maintenance, Technical Training and Transport Commands. 90 Group was in fact to achieve command status as Signals Command for ten years from 1958 before reverting to its earlier status. So, in 1953, the chain of command stretching from a humble erk in the corner of a registry, via his CO and the Air Officer commanding (AOC) 90 Group to the Assistant Chief of Air Staff for Signals in the Air Ministry in London (to whom the AOC reported directly), seemed surprisingly short!

Wing Commander Kenneth A. Mummery had only recently arrived to command the station and I viewed our initial encounter with some trepidation, notwithstanding that it would be of a working rather than disciplinary nature. As a non-flying technical officer he had, as I understood it, reached the highest rank possible. Whilst he didn't suffer fools gladly and, when necessary, could be a strict disciplinarian, I nevertheless enjoyed working with and for him. I needn't have been apprehensive: he always treated me fairly and, as will be seen, accorded me a measure of responsibility in our day-to-day work.

To me the CO, a slightly tubby and balding figure of perhaps less than average height, appeared pretty elderly although in fact he was probably not much more than about forty. From a conversation with him about the depressing panorama of the East End of London as viewed from trains into and out of Liverpool Street station, it became apparent that he was familiar with my East Anglian part of the world. Many years later I was to discover why: he had between 1948 and 1950 been the CO of RAF Bawdsey,

Suffolk, birthplace of radar which had played so vital a part in the Battle of Britain. In earlier years he had also served as an NCO at RAF Hornchurch, Essex, one of the nearest stations to my home.

Needless to say I knew little of the foregoing at the time of my arrival at Norton. What I did know was that I had ended up in an office, in a headquarters, in a station, swamped by Yorkshiremen, many of whom emanated from Sheffield and its environs and had received permission from the CO to 'live out' at their homes. There was thus a mass exodus from the camp after work each day, a long queue forming at the guardroom to book out after what was almost always only a cursory inspection by the SPs on duty. I couldn't make up my mind whether these fortunate individuals were part-time National Servicemen or part-time civilians!

To start with I was baffled by the preponderance of 'locals' on the camp but soon discovered that it was open to an airman to seek his CO's permission to exchange postings with another of the same rank and in the same trade if he could locate such an airman at the RAF station of his choice. Not surprisingly, the men concerned were required to pay the costs of the exchange. The LAC typist with whom I was to work initially — Jon Crewe from Oxfordshire — a few months later was to accept an opportunity to switch to RAF Mountbatten, a Coastal Command station near Plymouth, to enable a homesick typist from Leeds to replace him at Norton.

The other three erks in the registry all came from Hull — or Kingston-upon-Hull as one of them insisted on the city being called. Both occupants of the adjoining office — responsible for the promulgation of SROs and PORs — were from Sheffield, the non-identical twin brother of one of them working in the orderly room. Severe penalties were likely to befall those failing to read and understand the Station Routine Orders and Personnel Occurrence Reports which they produced. The purpose of SROs is presumably self-explanatory; in PORs were published miscellaneous notices affecting individuals, for example, promotions, permissions to 'live out' or consents to keep specific items — in my own case a camera — on camp.

I soon settled into a routine at Norton. LAC Crewe and I maintained a common 'In' tray, each typing whatever happened to reach the top of the pile next. As far as I can recall only the CO ever dictated anything and, as the sole shorthand writer, it obviously fell to me to undertake this work and, in effect, to act as his secretary. Crewe and I aimed to empty the 'In' tray by tea-time each day and both typewriters, together with occasional outstanding work, were locked away overnight in a four-drawer filing cabinet. As far as I can recall there were only two or three other typewriters: one in the SRO and POR office, one in an entirely separate office maintained by the GRSS elsewhere on the camp and there may have been one in the orderly room.

A fair proportion of the CO's dictation related to the RAF Table Tennis Association, of which he happened to be Chairman at the time. One element of the work was just up my street. As mentioned earlier the CO had not long been at Norton and, a week or two prior to my own arrival, he had instituted a weekly 'CO's Conference'. Most, if not all, of the station's officers were to attend, along with the Station Warrant Officer (SWO, responsible for discipline) and a civilian representative of the Air Ministry Works Directorate (AMWD — known as 'Works and Bricks'), and matters pertaining to the running of the station would be discussed. A shorthand writer having now descended upon the station, this humble erk would also be present to take a note of the proceedings of his elders and betters every Wednesday morning.

I was thrown in at the deep end, my attendance being required at a meeting in the SHQ conference room only a day or so after my arrival. Apart from the CO I did not of course know anybody and felt, especially in view of my status *vis-à-vis* all those concerned, that I would find myself somewhat at a disadvantage at the meeting, to say the least. I had no doubts as to my ability to take the necessary notes but considered that a bit of background would be helpful at this early stage. I therefore asked to see the minutes of the one or two meetings which had taken place prior to my arrival. Having spent in excess of two years in the Clerk's Department at County Hall, Chelmsford, at that time probably one of the finest offices in the country in which to learn from the bottom up how to go about calling, holding and recording meetings, I was appalled at what I saw at Norton. There is no need to go into detail here but the 'minutes' were a shambles. I tried to convey this to the CO as gently as possible because I had no idea who had drafted them but suspected it might have been the CO himself and I was sure he meant well! He was after all a technical expert, not a committee administrator. The upshot was that, notwithstanding that I was an unknown newcomer, I was given *carte blanche* even at that early stage to prepare the agenda and minutes for future meetings in whatever form I thought fit.

Henceforth during my service at Norton, every Tuesday the CO handed me a note of the matters he wished to be discussed on the morrow from which I was able to concoct a formal agenda. The conference usually occupied most of Wednesday morning and it was my task during the afternoon to produce a set of minutes to be handed to the CO first thing on the Thursday. Any reader who has served in the RAF will realize that Wednesday afternoon on most stations is 'sports afternoon' and that, on the face of it, I therefore found myself somewhat at a disadvantage. Not so! There were no sports facilities at Norton. However, the CO being of an innovative and enterprising nature (as we shall continue to see), an area of unused grassland within the camp boundaries was to be transformed into a sports field and Wednesday afternoons were spent not in the enjoyment of sporting activities but in clearing the area in question of stones and generally making it fit for sport. Wednesday afternoons were therefore dreaded by all who couldn't 'skive off' this activity but not by me. I was able to sit quietly in the near-deserted SHQ drafting my minutes and never once did I spend the afternoon picking up stones.

My typewriter being the only one with a carriage long enough to accommodate foolscap paper horizontally, it regularly fell to me to complete the RAF form listing the forthcoming week's menu in the airmen's mess.

Seven columns wide and four deep, precise details of what we erks could expect for breakfast, dinner, tea and supper were included. Although I completed dozens of these forms, it didn't occur to me to question why we never received 'supper' at Norton. In practice, those feeling peckish during the evening took themselves to the NAAFI and, provided they could afford them and after the statutory chatting up of the NAAFI 'bints', got themselves around egg, chips and beans or similar, perhaps with a small bottle of brown or light ale. I did, however, realize that the mess menu as typed was a work of pure fiction. Almost none of the succulent goodies listed thereon actually appeared on our plates when the relevant meals were taken. Would this perhaps explain why only those at least six feet six inches tall were able to read the copy of the document displayed at a great height in the mess?

From time to time I was asked to type details onto RAF Form 252, the charge sheet. These small buff forms were in fact required to be completed by hand but I didn't really have much choice in the matter when the senior SP, Cpl Simmons (as far as I knew the only substantive corporal SP and a surprisingly affable individual), sidled into the registry and asked me to perform this small service for him. Thus, not for the last time during my service, as will be seen, I found myself in a situation where SPs were seeking favours from me. The remainder of the SPs, all acting corporals I believe, kept themselves very much to themselves and only occasionally seemed to go out of their way to be thoroughly unpleasant. At least one of them ensured that his trouser legs crisply overhung his white gaiters by a judicious helping of chains or ball bearings, crashing and rattling his way about the camp like some demented robot. Apart from that of Cpl Simmons, all the SPs' big 'ats were bent and cut in precisely the fashion ordinary erks were forbidden to treat theirs.

Needless to say the most important element of my work was the weekly CO's conference. At the head of the table I sat on the CO's right, the Senior Administration Officer (SAdO — Sqn Ldr J. G. McCathie) on his left. Others present included the Adjutant (Adj — Fg Off A. Terry), the Accounts Officer (Flt Lt Wilson), the Senior Technical Officer (Sqn Ldr S. E. Craig, MBE), the Education Officer (a pilot officer) and, as already mentioned, the SWO and the AMWD representative. In order of seniority, commissioned ranks up to that of the CO were as follows:

> Wing Commander
> Squadron Leader
> Flight Lieutenant
> Flying Officer
> Pilot Officer

The SAdO, a Scot of ruddy complexion and occasional short temper, was the only possessor of pilot's wings on the station. During the war he flew as a navigator in Fairey Battle light bomber aircraft in France, his squadron withdrawing after bitter fighting. In order to maintain his flying qualification, he was obliged to put in a minimum number of hours at the controls each year. One morning during his absence from SHQ the station was 'buzzed' on a number of occasions by an elderly training aircraft — an Airspeed Oxford I believe. It transpired that the SAdO had taken this old kite up from RAF Finningley (near Doncaster and the closest flying station to Norton) to get in some flying hours. When, later, he appeared in the registry, flushed with success and obviously wanting to talk about his adventures, we all feigned ignorance and pretended not to have noticed. Finningley is still a flying station in the 1990s although I chanced to learn only recently that, like so many others of its famous contemporaries, it will have closed by the turn of the century.

Of the other officers, only the burly and, to me, somewhat intimidating Adj boasted even an aircrew brevet — that of an air-gunner (AG). A cockney by the sound of him, he had been a London bus driver prior to the 1939–45 war. The Education Officer deserves a mention. A National Serviceman like many of us on the station, he was however a little older than most as he had secured deferment in order to pursue a university course. Always conspicuous on formal parades, he was not only very tall but had moreover exercised his right as a National Serviceman not to spend a small fortune on an officer's 'best blue' (a superior version of that issued free to erks) and so paraded as the only man wearing 'working blue'.

Seemingly like all those of his ilk the SWO was a big man. Usually known as the SWOman, he shared a small office in SHQ with his sidekick, a mustachioed and considerably less frightening sergeant. Responsible for discipline on the station as a whole, I suppose the RAF SWOman was somewhat akin to the Army's Regimental Sergeant Major (RSM). He was not a man to be crossed; conversely in times of trouble, as personnel on stations the subject of attacks by the *Luftwaffe* during the war will testify, there was no braver or more staunch ally.

My attendance at the CO's conference put me in the privileged position of knowing much more than my fellow erks about the affairs of the station — in particular about what was likely to occur in the future — although I had of course to respect the confidentiality of what I learned. I recall only one hiccup: a day or two after a discussion as to precisely what time-off would be allowed on the occasion of the August Bank Holiday in 1953, it became apparent that station personnel in general were in possession of this information prior to its publication in SROs. There was of course a witch-hunt and, whilst I couldn't recall divulging information to anyone, I felt I was bound to be the prime suspect. In fact blame was accorded to (and reluctantly accepted by) the LAC PBX (telephone switchboard) operator in SHQ whose repertoire extended also to the Telex and the Gestetner duplicating machine, giving him the opportunity to read the results of my Wednesday afternoon labours each week.

The LAC in question, whose name unfortunately has vanished into the mists of time, deserves a paragraph of his own. From somewhere in the London area, possessed of a nonchalant gait and topped by lank dark hair and cherubic face-splitting grin, he had the unique ability to wear a beret almost vertically on the side of his head. His job placed him in the enviable position of being the only erk on the station with ready access to a telephone, in the evening as well as during the day. Accordingly he achieved considerable popularity by acting as the link between the young ladies of Sheffield and such of his peers as might seek his services. He features briefly in my personal story, as will be seen shortly.

Those of us working in the registry were able, mid-morning and mid-afternoon, to catch a first glimpse of the NAAFI wagon emerging from behind the nearby NAAFI with its cargo of tea, food and NAAFI birds. First call on its journey around the camp was SHQ and we were usually able, via the window behind my desk and the surrounding lawn upon which it was forbidden to walk (but we ran), to be first in the queue. There were no WRAF personnel at Norton and the NAAFI ladies (women, girls, birds, bints, whichever you prefer) were the only females on the station. Airmen are notoriously bad at dancing backwards and chaos at the regular station dances, held in the NAAFI, was avoided by the despatch of RAF buses to Sheffield's City General Hospital and their return filled with nurses. I didn't play a very active part in these dances. I did however smoke about half my lifetime total of cigarettes (ten or a dozen) during these functions.

One evening during the summer, an invitation having been extended to Norton's airmen by the nurses, I was one of a busload who travelled to the hospital to attend a dance at the nurses' home. To this day I'm not sure why I went: I was never much of a dancer. Perhaps I was by now experiencing the boredom about which I will write later. I had no idea at the time but it transpired that, during the evening, one of the nurses decided she liked the look of me. As the result I was shortly to be informed that arrangements had been made by intermediaries, including inevitably our grinning friend with the vertical beret, for me to rendezvous with said nurse (Kathryn) outside a certain cinema in Sheffield — the Gaumont I believe — a couple of evenings later. Whether I liked it or not I had no alternative but to turn up. There was no way I could get in touch with the girl (I didn't even know her surname) and only a cad would have stood her up.

Gentleman that I am I arrived outside the cinema in good time and surveyed the busy scene. Obviously she would recognize me from the nurses' home dance but I hadn't a clue who from the milling throng would approach me. Eventually Kathryn made herself known: she had a wooden leg; well, artificial anyway, and suddenly I had a recollection of dancing with someone so afflicted. At least if I trod on her foot, which was more than likely, it wouldn't have hurt. We saw the film, shared a bag of sweets and that was the end of that. Nothing to do with the artificial leg but I really don't think blind dates are a very good idea.

Most RAF stations boasted a cinema — the Astra, run by the RAF's own cinema organization — but unfortunately Norton was too small for such a luxury. I don't think I had the pleasure of attending any Astra during my entire service. So, those of us at Norton who wanted to go to the pictures had to take the bus down through the lid and into the dirty saucer. As a keen cinema-goer in those days, I did so about once a week.

Harking back to the CO's conference but still on the subject of entertainment, at one of the meetings I gleaned the item of fairly useless information that, whilst the postal address of the station was just 'Sheffield 8', nevertheless almost the entire camp was situated within the County of Derbyshire, only a relatively narrow strip along the north-western boundary falling within what was then the County Borough of Sheffield. Of little importance one may think? Not when the licensing hours differ as between the two local authorities' areas and it is obviously of the utmost importance to ensure that the bar in the NAAFI remains open as long as legally possible, especially on the occasions of the station dances! At one stage it was even suspected that the relevant boundary passed through the NAAFI building itself. I don't think this was so and believe the NAAFI to have been in Derbyshire. An interesting one for the lawyers, perhaps.

The persevering reader may have realized by now that Norton wasn't exactly the most thrilling or stimulating posting in the RAF. Apart from the dances — monthly I believe — nothing more exciting than weekly tombola sessions took place on the camp. "THERE WILL BE TOMBOLA IN THE NAAFI — T O N I G H T!" yelled an intruding mustachioed corporal after hammering, and often bending, some unfortunate's spoon on a table in the airmen's mess during tea each Tuesday. The procedure soon changed: the moustache would enter, a spoon would bend and a hundred or more voices would roar "T H E R E   W I L L   B E   T O M B O L A   I N   T H E   N A A F I — T O O N I I G H H T T !" One afternoon he of the moustache had the last laugh, correcting our mass offering with "THERE WILL **NOT** BE TOMBOLA IN THE NAAFI — TONIGHT!" Exit one corporal left, grinning. Tombola cards (slips of paper in fact) cost threepence (just over 1p) a game and, if you were lucky, you might win one shilling (5p). Today it's called bingo!

The other mess occurrence — not only at Norton but throughout the RAF — guaranteed to move the inmates to a noisy reaction, thunderous cheering even, was the dropping of a plate or mug — preferably one well loaded. A cook would usually appear bearing a filthy cloth and matching smirk, leaving the unfortunate airman to clear up the mess. If it was a mug which bit the dust (a fate which in fact befell mine), means of quenching one's thirst until such time as it was possible to get a replacement from the equipment stores posed a problem.

Many of the station's personnel wore the 'sparks' badge, denoting radio or radar specialist, but how exactly they all occupied their time I hadn't a clue. One, with whom I became quite friendly, I knew looked after pigs. Not radio-controlled pigs, just ordinary pigs. As he had done at RAF Bawdsey our ever-enterprising CO had established a mini-farm and sought out someone with the necessary experience to look after it. My agricultural friend, who had been hauled into the RAF straight from farm work at Bures on the Essex/Suffolk border, was just the man and henceforth wallowed around in denims and gumboots. Possibly the only man on the station with his own motor vehicle — a 500cc Norton motor-cycle with the (to me) welcome Essex registration letters UPU — his quiet, rural North

Essex/Suffolk dialect was music to my ears amidst the loud and abrasive South Yorkshire voices which assailed them most of the time.

Although I had a number of pals at Norton, there were no close friendships. Until he left for RAF Mountbatten, I suppose Jon Crewe would have been my closest friend; others were the cousin of Geof Duke (the racing motor-cyclist) from Newcastle-upon-Tyne; John, a keen cyclist from Birmingham who obtained permission to keep a bicycle on camp; and, of course, the pigman. My cyclist chum infuriated the SPs by getting permission to leave camp for early-morning training rides long before anyone else stirred. SPs can't stand anything which they interpret as somebody getting away with something. Naturally they saw these rides in that light but, after one or two mornings' aggravation to start with, there was nothing they could do to interfere as long as John was back on camp by the due time. The bike was stored in the ironing room within hut 22 and John rode it home to Birmingham each weekend, a round trip of about 120 miles. One Sunday evening John and bike were conspicuous by their absence. We were to learn later that he had left the road and hit a tree with no recollection of the incident. No other vehicle had been involved and it was assumed that he had either blacked out or fallen asleep. It was a somewhat bruised and chastened John who soon resumed his RAF 'career' minus bicycle.

Another bruised inmate of hut 22 was the curly-haired giant who went off to play Rugby league football for Huddersfield on Saturdays during the season. Each Sunday evening he returned resplendent with fresh bruises, black eyes, cuts, everything but broken bones! Also resident in hut 22 was the first example of a married airman encountered during my service. Short and dark, bespectacled and anxious, he was a 'sparks' from Leeds who talked a lot about getting home to his wife.

I made a point of cultivating a modest friendship with the pay clerk in the orderly room. A softly spoken Scot, he was the only man from north of the border with whom I established the slightest rapport during my service. It's always as well to be 'in' with the pay clerk anyway but I was anxious also to be able to put behind me the nightmares of the Hednesford pay parades by ensuring that those at Norton who mattered knew how to pronounce my name and were sufficiently sympathetic to yell it again if I didn't catch it the first time. As the result I was even able to enjoy pay parades in the hangar at Norton. They were as good a way of passing half an hour as any other, there was money at the end and a certain amount of entertainment could be derived by observing some of the crazy salutes offered when discipline was relaxed — as it usually was. Salutes would end up over heads, behind heads or, a favourite, scratching ears. Cpl Simmons' approach to collecting his (considerable) pay was novel. Lots of smart stamping and saluting of course followed by the removal of big 'at with the left hand, scooping up of banknotes and florins with the right hand, cash into the big 'at, big 'at onto head, more smart saluting and stamping, right turn and away. Great stuff!

My own pay as an LAC at the rate of 6s.6d a day now totalled £2.5s.6d a week. Deductions of 3s.6d (6d a day) for my Post Office Savings Bank account and 3s.0d for National Insurance left £1.19s.0d net. I therefore received £1.18s.0d on pay parade, 1s.0d being added to my 'credits'. As from 1 August 1953 I tripled my daily savings to 1s.6d, resulting in net and actual weekly pay of £1.12s.0d (£1.60p).

In the orderly room, the flight sergeant (accounts) from the west country sported what must have been just about the greatest girth in the RAF. We reckoned he obtained his uniforms from a tent-maker. A replacement orderly room sergeant was posted in not so long after my own arrival. Short, scruffy, wild-haired and gap-toothed, fag ash littered his working 'grey' — you couldn't really call it 'blue'. He used to boast to us in the registry of extra-marital conquests in his native Liverpool. We could only assume that either the women in that city were a funny lot or his non-athletic appearance belied an ability to run faster than they could.

What is the connection between physical jerks, military bands and CO's parades? At Norton the common denominator was our innovative CO who, following upon his triumphs with the budding sports field and mini-farming, introduced all three activities during the first half of 1953. The PT and CO's parades weren't too popular with those 'living out' because they took place before work and therefore necessitated earlier arrivals on camp. The PT took place daily to start with, either inside or immediately in front of the pay parade hangar depending on the weather. All ranks were to attend and it was therefore of interest to observe, for example, the wing commander being required to jump up and down by an acting corporal PTI — not to mention the undoubted strain imposed upon the poor old heavyweight flight sergeant (accounts). We didn't change into PT kit but merely removed jackets and hats, resulting in somewhat sweat-ridden arrivals for work until such time as this activity had — very gradually — fizzled out.

The band was a great idea which proved surprisingly successful on so small a station. The CO's initial enquiries revealed that there was on camp an airman who in civilian life had played the trumpet in a dance band. Hauled before the CO, this airman was given the task of rooting out anybody who either had played, or would like to play, a musical instrument. For his part the CO undertook to procure the necessary equipment: where on earth everything came from it is perhaps best not to enquire but arrive it all did! Incredibly soon a small but enthusiastic band was in being and able to produce a very satisfactory noise — and it's so much easier to march well behind a decent band.

CO's parades were held weekly before work, on Wednesdays I believe. Everybody who couldn't find some way of skiving off paraded in front of SHQ; the CO, who lived off camp, was driven through the nearby main gate at just the right moment; there was a suitable amount of shouting, stamping and saluting; the RAF flag was raised; the CO disappeared into SHQ via his personal entrance; the rest of us were dismissed and mooched off to work. One morning it all went horribly wrong. I was duty clerk on the day in question which, among other things, necessitated my being in SHQ from an early hour. One of my duties was to 'bull' the lino in the corridors and, having made a good job of the area just inside the CO's personal entrance, I locked the door from the inside to prevent its illegal use with consequent detriment to my handiwork. Unfortunately I retired to the registry during the parade having omitted first to unlock said door. Shouting, stamping and saluting completed, the CO turned his back on the parade, now silent and standing to attention, and marched up to his personal entrance only to find that he couldn't open the door. He therefore suffered the indignity of walking around the building to gain entry by the other ranks' entrance. The parade, still standing to attention, was by now not quite so silent and definitely showing signs of interest. Needless to say I knew none of this but detected a certain air of levity when my office colleagues trundled in for work.

"Charge the duty clerk" instructed the CO and, having identified me as the culprit, the SWOman soon had the necessary formalities in hand. Informed that I was the guilty party the CO detected a problem. If the charge proceeded and he awarded me a period of 'jankers', then during the days and part nights I was marching to and fro between my billet and the guardroom, burdened down by full packs and webbing, nobody would be available to undertake his secretarial work; more important, no shorthand writer to attend the CO's conference! If, on the other hand, the CO was minded simply to issue a reprimand it seemed a bit silly when I was in and out of his office several times each day anyway during the normal course of work to have me marched in, hatless, between an escort of two of my comrades, wearing their hats, while the SWOman bellowed in the background. So, the charge was dropped and I was called in and delivered of a suitable rocket, in response to which I submitted profuse and genuine apologies. The last thing I would have wanted to do was embarrass the CO in the way I had. I think he realized this only too well and the whole incident was a matter of great regret for both of us.

My privileged position in attendance at CO's conferences not only gave me early intimation of his various initiatives but also enabled me to hear such gems as the discussion as to whether the civilian barber who set up his emporium on camp one day a week should be permitted to offer for sale what were euphemistically termed 'gentlemen's requisites'. The SAdO was especially illuminating on this question. Another noteworthy discussion concerned the sales tactics of SPs faced with the disposal of a bundle of copies of the 'Royal Air Force Flying Review' (costing 1s.0d monthly and published with the co-operation of the Air Ministry). No doubt this was an excellent publication and one which many of us would have been happy to purchase. However, pressure to do so was applied and, in the manner of things, this naturally increased sales resistance. In particular, those 'living out' were on occasions prevented by the SPs on duty from leaving camp to travel home unless and until they had purchased a copy. One evening there was still a long queue of recalcitrant airmen some hours after work finished. I heard what the CO had to say about this and he wasn't best pleased.

Fire picket duty lasted a week, during which the two men so lumbered were required to remain on camp wearing uniform and a red armband. The main bind was having to get up sufficiently early to wake others, cooks for example, requiring early calls. During my week's duty I once drew the short straw and had perforce to make the long walk to the officers' mess and awaken the heavily perfumed and green-haired slumbering batman/waiter. The two RAF firemen on camp emerged from their 'fire station' (a garage housing one small fire appliance) on occasion to instruct the fire picket in the use of a hose. During my week's duty they did so but declined to permit the use of any water, perhaps because they didn't want the trouble of drying the hose afterwards. My instruction was therefore somewhat academic in nature, unlike that of a couple of blokes a few weeks earlier who had been allowed to squirt water and chose to do so in such a manner that it descended vertically upon the corner of SHQ wherein was located the CO's office. It happened to be dinner-time on a beautifully clear and sunny day and the CO, having heard and observed the 'rain' on his office window, shortly emerged to be driven home wearing his uniform raincoat with collar upturned.

One morning AC1 Brocklesby, a clerk in the POR office who 'lived out' in Sheffield, failed to arrive for work. He apparently shared a room at home with a younger brother. We were to learn later that his brother had awakened during the night to observe our hero departing via the bedroom window, as befits a member of the Royal Air Force in an upward direction. He was sleepwalking and duly ascended the roof to halt on the ridge-tiles by the chimney-stack. A sudden awakening could have resulted in a catastrophe and the local fire brigade were summoned to effect a delicate rescue. He made the headlines in one of the tabloid national papers and, somewhat subdued, returned to camp a few days' later.

Another airman of note was to be found in the GRSS office elsewhere on the camp. A ginger-haired Jack-the-lad cockney corporal, he seemed the most unlikely character to have the ability to type at the incredible speed of 90 words a minute whilst gazing vertically at the ceiling. I know this to be the case because I gave him a test — giving some idea of the pressure of work in the registry, where we even found time to set ourselves up as a sort of multi-brained Leslie Welch (the 'memory man' of wireless fame) with the ability to answer such sporting questions as "Which country won the hockey event at the 1920 Olympic Games?" (Answer: Great Britain.) My own speciality was speedway, a sport upon which even my undoubted modesty does not preclude me from saying that I was something of an expert in 1953. I could, for example, have described the team colours of the St Austell Gulls (blue and white), said who was No.2 in the 1952/53 world rankings ('Split' Waterman of England) or specified the length of the Swindon Robins' track (410 yards). Others were capable of reeling off with equal brilliance similar trivia relating to other sports.

There were, however, more anxious times as, for example, the morning I was ordered at short notice to present myself at a meeting of technical officers in the SHQ conference room and to take a detailed note of the proceedings. Apart from the Senior Technical Officer (who attended CO's conferences) I knew none of those attending and I barely understood a word

1. *The author's father in ARP uniform c1940*

2. *The author (left) and brother Geof in Army Cadet uniform c1948*

3. *Great-uncle Jim (Private J. W. Pratt, 1/4th Essex Regiment), died on active service 26th March 1917*

4. *The author's friend Peter (Gunner P.C. Steggall, Royal Artillery) in Damascus, spring 1943 [Photo: via Peter Steggall]*

5. *V1 flying bomb photographed by a British soldier at Kraak, Germany, in June 1945 [Photo: via Peter Steggall]*

6. *Captured by street photographer at Southend-on-Sea, 9th July 1952*

7. *The author's medical grade card*

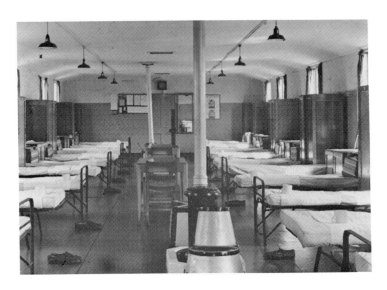

8. *Typical barrack hut: this one at RAF Hednesford, c1951*
[Photo: Orbit Photographic Productions Ltd]

9. *Typical kit layout: this example at*
RAF Locking, 1955 [Photo: Den Caton]

10. Gateway to 'hell': entrance to RAF Hednesford in 1951......
[Photo: Orbit Photographic Productions Ltd]

11. ...... and forty-five years later!

12. AOC's inspection guard of honour at RAF Norton 1953, the author second from left in rear rank [Photo: ©CROWN COPYRIGHT/MOD]

13. AOC's inspection march past, CO of RAF Norton (Wg Cdr Mummery) nearest camera [Photo: ©CROWN COPYRIGHT/MOD]

14. A Norton at Norton: from left; Geof Duke's cousin, married 'Sparks' from Leeds, and the author, not making much progress on the pigman's machine behind the barrack blocks

15. The site of RAF Norton looking very sorry for itself on 12th July 1996

*16. RAF barrack block 12M at Camp Guynemer,
Fontainebleau — compare with typical blocks at
RAF Norton shown on opposite page [Photo: Bill Rudman]*

*17. AAFCE Headquarters building, Fontainebleau
[Photo: Bill Rudman]*

*18. Nice: the author on La Promenade des Anglais on 5th March 1954
[Photo: Brian Simpson]*

*19. NAAFI building at Camp Guynemer, Fontainebleau
[Photo: Bill Rudman]*

20. *USAF on the march at Camp Guynemer: colonnaded parade housing hairdresser, laundry etc on left; equipment stores and MT sections in centre; corner of support units complex on right [Photo: Bill Rudman]*

21. *Tennis courts at Camp Guynemer, near to the NAAFI building [Photo: Bill Rudman]*

*22. MT Driver SAC 'Scouse' Baker, POR Clerk SAC Les Goddard
(before his promotion) and an unidentified LAC prior to
a trip to Arromanches 1953 [Photo: via Les Goddard]*

*23. Snowstorm at Camp Guynemer, February 1954: French airmen
and billets in background [Photo: Bill Rudman]*

24. RAF Support Unit soccer team c1953: from left — back; De Guyer, Crumpton, Crosthwaite, 'Jock' Fraser, LAC Hudspith, SAC Jerome: front; Cpl Evans, Chadwick, Cpl Stott, Green, Lee [Photo: Bill Rudman]

25. AAFCE international soccer team c1954: RAF from left — back; fourth Sgt Fenney, fifth Cpl Tech Payne, seventh Eccles, eighth LAC Massey: front; first Cpl Stott, second SAC Griffiths; other team members were from the Belgian, French and Netherlands Air Forces [Photo: via Les Massey]

26. LAC Brian Simpson
at Camp Guynemer 1954:
French airmen's billets on left
and French mess in background

27. SAC David Mollart-Rogerson
(in uniform) with
unidentified colleague at
Camp Guynemer 1954

28. Camp Guynemer after the author's departure:
SPs on main gate duty 1955 [Photo: Tom Weatherley]

*29. Ted Heath Band visit 1954: singer Kathy Lloyd with (from left)
Pte J.J.C. v d Hoeven (RNAF), Cpl David Evans and
AC1 Peter Prentice (RAF) and Cpl Jac Vos (RNAF) [NATO Photo]*

30. The author's 'personal' pilots: Air Chief Marshal Sir Basil Embry (left) and Air Commodore Peter Wykeham-Barnes [RCAF Photo]

31. Avro Ansons, probably Mark C19, at Melun/Villaroche, c1953 [Photo: Bill Rudman]

*32. A De Havilland DH104 Devon similar to the one in which the author flew to Nice, at the **Battle of** Britain Memorial Flight, RAF Coningsby, Lincolnshire on 17th April 1997*

33. The nearest the author has been to a Pembroke since 1954: a Hunting Percival Sea Prince T1, the Royal Navy equivalent, at the Norfolk and Suffolk Aviation Museum, Flixton on 30th June 1996

34. Le Palais de Fontainebleau, 1st May 1954

35. A quiet scene in Fontainebleau, 1st May 1954

36. Taking their ease outside Le Café Quartier des Suisses, Fontainebleau: AC1 Bill Rudman (right) and Pat, an unidentified erk [Photo: via Bill Rudman]

37. Approximately half the AAFCE WRAF contingent (and one bashful erk) in the grounds of Le Palais de Fontainebleau: LACW Diane Lawson on the left [Photo: Bill Rudman]

38. HRH The Duke of Edinburgh (left) with Air Chief Marshal Sir Basil Embry, arriving at HQ AAFCE in the summer of 1954 [Photo: Bill Rudman]

39. The author (left) and SAC Derrick Smith with one of the Duke's rhododendrons in the grounds of Fontainebleau Palace, summer 1954 [Photo: Brian Simpson]

40. Sir Basil Embry being greeted on arrival at a NATO base somewhere in Europe by a limping USAF Major General: on the left is a Général de Brigade Aérienne of the FAF and behind him, leaving Sir Basil's personal Devon aircraft in which the author enjoyed several 'gash flips', can be seen his ADC, Fg Off R.L. Lees, who contributed the foreword to this book [NATO Photo]

41. Departing after a visit to HQ AAFCE: Admiral Radford (US Navy), Chairman of America's Joint Chiefs of Staff, with Sir Basil Embry; behind the Admiral is Fg Off R.L. Lees (RAF) [NATO Photo]

42. An apparently disinterested Sir Basil Embry being saluted left-handed by his Commander-in-Chief, Le Maréchal de France Alphonse Juin, and right-handed from the rear by an unidentified USAF officer: in fact a war wound denied Le Maréchal the full use of his right hand [NATO Photo]

*43. Signed photograph given to the author by Air Chief Marshal
Sir Basil Embry on 26th October 1954 [NATO Photo]*

*44. Publicity photograph of the author at his desk in HQ AAFCE,
feigning work on 8th October 1954 [NATO Photo]*

45. Paris: NATO HQ obscuring Le Palais de Chaillot on 19th June 1954

46. Paris: deserted Avenue des Champs Elysées on a Saturday (19th June 1954)

47. LAC Brian Simpson anxiously awaiting his lunch near La Tour Eiffel, Paris, 19th June 1954

48. Paris: no custom for the ice-cream vendors in La Place de l'Étoile on 19th June 1954

49. Paris: Le Pont Neuf, the subject of the author's etching, 2nd October 1954

50. With live ammunition and fixed bayonet, the author's brother Geof about to commence guard duty at Namur Camp, GHQ Middle East Land Forces, Fayid, Egypt, summer 1954

51. Perhaps enjoying a somewhat cushier time, the author's other brother Den, having apparently just emerged from WRAF billets at RAF Strubby, Lincs, 1957

52. The author with his 'personal' Cessna 172 at Southend Airport, 20th August 1994 [Photo: Janice Harding]

of the highly technical matters which were discussed. I could do no more than take down as much as possible of what was said — at least my shorthand was pretty good — and hope my typed version of events didn't contain too many idiocies — spelling or otherwise. In the event I was congratulated a few days later on the excellence of my notes. This was all very well but the snag about such an outcome is likely to be that you get lumbered with repeating the performance. The trick is to do what I did and get posted first!

Needless to say it was my practice to return home at weekends as often as circumstances and finances permitted. In addition to monthly '48s', it was possible to obtain a '36' for other weekends (except, for example, when on fire picket) and those who could afford to do so went home most Fridays or Saturdays. The camp was therefore pretty sparsely populated at weekends. I have already said that my net weekly pay was £1.18s.0d, reducing to £1.12s.0d in August. As a 'service return' ticket from Sheffield to Chelmsford cost in the order of 15s.0d or 16s.0d, to which had to be added bus fares at each end and London Underground fares if you got caught (there were no automatic barriers in those days!), it will be seen that finances were pretty stretched. My parents had made it clear from the outset that I was never to allow lack of cash to prevent my returning home as they would always help as necessary. However, being only too well aware of their own financial problems, I never accepted a single penny from them. In any case, my father to his everlasting credit was continuing to pay on my behalf monthly contributions into the Essex County Council's superannuation fund. Employed as he then was on the administration of the superannuation scheme at Crompton Parkinson's factory, he understood only too well the importance to one's eventual pension of maintaining payments: I was able to reap the benefit of his actions when obliged to take early retirement some thirty-two years later.

Of my own volition I had been contributing further to my cash shortages right from the start of my service. I had decided that my elderly third-hand gentleman's upright bicycle needed replacing by something a little more racy and had an arrangement with my two brothers that, whenever I could afford to do so, I would send money home in the form of a Postal Order and they would use these funds to buy the bits to construct what turned out to be a purple-framed machine of some distinction. Each time I arrived home the bike had grown — a wheel here, a brake lever there — and, by Saturday 2 May, it was sufficiently complete to convey me to Rayleigh to see the Rockets defeat St Austell 59-25.

My first weekend home — I suspect on a '48' rather than a '36' — was that of 7/8 February 1953 and I returned to Sheffield on the Sunday evening wearing (or possibly carrying in my small suitcase — I can't now be certain) the alternative uniform of neat shirt and tie, Fair Isle pullover, sports jacket, grey flannels, raincoat and sensible shoes, but definitely no hat, known as one's civvies. (I also had with me a one pound jar of Robertsons Silver Shred marmalade.) In normal circumstances once you had the opportunity to wear civvies you wouldn't be seen dead in public in uniform — which of necessity meant best blue and big 'at — and my reason for wondering whether I might in fact have been so attired on the Sunday evening is that my small suitcase would quite simply have been too small to accommodate all of my uniform, including greatcoat and big 'at. The important thing was to get some civilian clothes on to the camp as soon as possible so as never again to leave it in uniform when not on duty.

I managed to get home on at least one weekend each month. I invariably returned on the train leaving St Pancras for Sheffield Midland at about 9 o'clock on Sunday evenings, carrying many National Servicemen back to RAF and Army camps after their weekends at home. There were usually enough airmen for Norton to fill two taxis, which arrived at the camp some while after the 2359 deadline. There were, however, no problems with the SPs as long as they were satisfied that groups such as ours arriving from various parts of the country had travelled on the anticipated trains and that everybody was in good time for Monday mornings's parade or work. It was the practice of the London contingent (awfully good-natured lot that we were!) to make a reasonably silent entry into the billets without putting on the lights and get into bed with the minimum disturbance to those already in residence. Why we bothered goodness only knows: just as we settled down to sleep — C R A S H — door thrown open, all lights on, drunken Geordies shouting, everybody awake. The Newcastle train was in! And so the pattern continued through the remainder of the night as groups arrived from other areas of the country. Only the drunks got any sleep. One Sunday night I conveyed from home with great care a nightcap in the form of a vacuum flask lovingly filled by my mother with milky coffee. In the darkness of the billet I placed it carefully on my locker while I undressed and then, just as carefully, knocked it to the floor. When retrieved it rattled.

On one of my early weekend leaves, having first established that my retrospective promotion to Leading Aircraftman had been duly POR'd and then obtained the requisite badges of rank from the stores, I took my uniform jackets and greatcoat home so as to accord to my long-suffering mother the privilege of "putting my props up" as the act of affixing the one to the other was termed. The badges featured two-bladed propellers and it may be recalled that from infancy I hadn't been too dexterous with needle and thread.

I was able during the summer to cycle to six further speedway meetings at Rayleigh, three of them during a period of leave in early August. The momentous events of later that month, to be recounted shortly, were to prevent any further attendance. I did, however, have the good fortune on Saturday 27 June to attend the 836th speedway meeting at Belle Vue, Manchester, travelling pillion (and hatless!) on the pigman's Norton. Belle Vue Aces were defeated 46–38 by the Wembley Lions. Conveyed by the same means a few weeks later, I was present at a motor-cycle scramble in Derbyshire where near vertical sections of the course were an eye-opener to lads from Essex and Suffolk used to comparatively flat terrain.

What else was there to provide excitement for young men dumped far from home in what seemed alien territory and with little funds? Not a lot really. I didn't write many letters. My correspondence with Joan had petered out; I didn't write home very often as fairly frequent visits rendered this less necessary than previously and no more cash was needed for the bike; I did, however, conduct a somewhat lunatic exchange of letters with my friend Sheargoon (he of the cycling carpet slippers) who, after square-bashing at Hednesford, went to Credenhill for trade training and ended up at the Headquarters of the RAF's Coastal Command. By a stroke of genius this coastal HQ was established at RAF Northwood in the landlocked County of Middlesex. Sheargoon recalls that one of my letters to him was written with alternate lines upside-down, leading to disorientation whilst reading. His reprisal was a letter so elaborately entwined amongst Sellotape that there was some doubt as to whether I would ever succeed in disentangling it. Gosh — those were heady days.

Minimal excitement was generated one early Saturday afternoon when I decided to take the tram (yes, tram) to the Hillsborough ground along with thousands of fag-ridden ee-bye-gooms and flat caps to see Sheffield Wednesday play Manchester United. It was a miserable afternoon and I found myself high up on the exposed banking at one end of the ground from whence, without my NHS specs, I couldn't see an awful lot. The match resulted in a goalless draw; it was only my second visit to a Football League ground (Upton Park to see West Ham play Blackpool, with Stanley Matthews, had been the first — also by tram!) and I felt such disappointment that the best part of ten years were to elapse before I attended another.

I was invited by one of the three Hull lads in the registry (I will call him Roger) to spend a '36' with him at his parents' home. Slim, pale and fair-haired, he was something of an extrovert and I thought the weekend would at least make a change. The four of us travelled together. We changed to the Hull train at Pontefract whereupon one of our number — quiet and introverted — was immediately pushed out of the 'wrong' side of the train and made to wait on the track until the very last moment before the train departed. Apparently this was a weekly ritual of which I didn't think too much and which led quite appropriately into a strange weekend. After tea at his home Roger announced that he was going out to meet his pals, didn't invite me to go with him and left me to spend the evening chatting to his parents — who I had of course only just met for the first time — and listening to their wireless. Roger returned rather late and somewhat the worse for wear, waking me up in the process, and as a consequence arose late on Sunday morning. My only outing was a short stroll during the afternoon and I eventually returned to the billet as one of the party from Hull disturbing those already abed. The funny thing was that Roger kept going on afterwards about what a great weekend it had been.

Not a lot more worthy of note occurred during my sojourn at Norton. I suppose the principal non-event followed upon the rumour which swept the station one afternoon to the effect that a contingent of WRAF would be arriving to spend that night on the camp. Needless to say in view of the all-male nature of the place speculation was rife as to where they would be billeted. They solved the problem by not turning up. Another non-event was the death of Joseph Stalin on Thursday 5 March: those of us who might have thought his passing would herald an immediate end to the 'Cold War' proved mistaken and we weren't allowed to forget about National Service and push off home!

Early summer saw the inspection of the station by the Air Officer Commanding (AOC), an annual event heralded by a prolonged period of 'bull' which in turn provides the basis for the assertion in the RAF that "if it moves salute it, if it doesn't move paint it". Although my duties enabled me to avoid the general 'bulling' of the station — undertaken largely on sports afternoons — I couldn't escape being a member of the 36-strong guard of honour: apparently 70¼ inches was the right height. Resplendent in best blue and big 'ats, bearing rifles with fixed bayonets and sporting white webbing belts and rifle slings, commanded by a 'technical' flight lieutenant and led by the disciplinary sergeant, we did the honours in front of SHQ when the AOC arrived. We later led the march past of the entire complement of the station while the AOC took the salute. Unfortunately the infant band had not yet reached the stage when we could all benefit from its services. I never discovered who had the misfortune to blanco our webbing belts and rifle slings. It certainly wasn't the members of the guard of honour and I supposed it might have been some unfortunate 'janker wallah'. An official RAF photographer attended and I ordered copies of three of his photographs, one of which featured the AOC (Air Vice-Marshal W. E. Theak, CB, CBE) and myself glaring at each other during his inspection of the guard of honour. Curiously, although copies of the others were later supplied, I never received this photograph.

Barnsley — home to a certain SAC 'Dingle' Smith yet to feature in this story; gem of the North and a name to conjure up visions of golden beaches and swaying palms. No? Was my geography somewhat awry? In any case why on earth was I, and everybody else who couldn't get out of it, marching best blue'd and big 'atted behind our band through the streets of Barnsley on a dull, rain-threatening Thursday morning? The explanation for this somewhat bizarre behaviour was that this was not just any old Thursday morning, but Thursday 2 June 1953 and RAF Norton had been accorded the doubtful honour of leading that fair city's Coronation Day parade. The fact that a Salvation Army band was also within earshot somewhere to the rear didn't help, but we triumphed over adversity (*Per Ardua Ad Astra* and all that) and subsequently lined the pathway to the city's main church during the entry of the local bigwigs. We sat at the rear during the service so as to beat a hasty retreat in time to repeat our route-lining when the knobs emerged. A bun-fight had been laid on at the town hall for all the participants in the parade. It goes without saying that the RAF got there first, only to find to our horror that all doors were locked. We eventually received some sustenance before being bussed back to camp and bed, the afternoon having turned wet. We arose temporarily for tea. Her Majesty The Queen probably had a somewhat better day, on the whole. For a start, she wasn't in Barnsley.

Although, as mentioned earlier, I had obtained permission to keep a camera on camp (a modest eight exposures on a 120 film Hawkeye folding camera which my ex-Army friend Peter Steggall felt must be of Scots origin — think about it!), only seven photos were taken at Norton. I believe the eighth shot, at the start of the film, is one of myself while on my first '48' in February 1953, probably taken by one of my brothers. In the countryside not too far from Chelmsford I am pictured leaning nonchalantly on railings surrounding a (now long-vanished) pond wearing, strangely, a pin-stripe suit with collar and tie set off by my blue and gold Rayleigh Rockets supporters scarf. Eccentric garb for a country walk — or, more likely, cycle ride.

At Norton the general level of 'bull' was not too high. There was a weekly 'bull' night which, I believe, coincided with tombola in the NAAFI — not one of the most brilliant feats of organizational genius. However, most weeks there was no evidence that an inspection of any sort had taken place the next morning and I cannot recall any instance of an occupant of hut 22 being in trouble as the result of an inspection. In other words, the mere threat of inspections was enough to keep us in line. So far as our uniforms were concerned, I have mentioned that the hut had an ironing room and certainly most of us took care to keep our uniforms properly pressed. An SP or the SWOman would be quick to spot anyone not taking sufficient care over his appearance. There was only one electric iron in hut 22, the custodian of which went home every weekend. His normal practice was to leave the iron available for those of us still on camp to see to our ironing at weekends. One Saturday, in a fit of pique, he went off on a '36' leaving the iron locked in his locker. Unless by chance he reads these words he will probably never know that, once he was clear of the camp, we borrowed a screwdriver from the pigman's toolkit, removed the back from the locker, retrieved the iron, saw to our domestic chores and reinstated his property. As a result of this incident, I made it my business to obtain my own iron which thereafter I made available to others when required.

Certainly one aspect of working life at Norton was an improvement on what had gone before. Almost non-existent was that most infuriating practice in the Services whereby anyone entering the domain of an individual of higher rank who considered himself important was completely ignored and required, like some idiot, to stand at attention for several minutes while the great man pretended to be busy. The length of time one had to wait varied and, roughly, was in inverse proportion to the rank and genuine importance of the tormentor who, at some stage, might well temporarily fix one with a vacant stare before returning to his pools coupon or love-letter. It was all an absurd game — only too prevalent at RAF Hednesford — designed to reduce one to the status of something which had just crawled out from under one's boot. I often wondered what the reaction would have been if, after a couple of minutes of this treatment, one had marched out without having said a word.

This seems an appropriate point to list the RAF's non-commissioned ranks in order of seniority, omitting the technician ranks — the wearers of upside-down stripes — as they don't feature in this story:

Warrant Officer
Flight Sergeant
Sergeant
Corporal
Senior Aircraftman
Leading Aircraftman
Aircraftman First Class
Aircraftman Second Class

I think I have said enough about life at Norton to have made it clear that we led a pretty humdrum existence. The trivial nature of much of what I have described serves only to reinforce my feeling that there didn't seem to be a lot of purpose about our lives. Although I don't think I felt this way at the time, I now see the station as a sort of self-perpetuating entity which we airmen were employed to keep ticking over simply to give us something to do. True, the GRSS convoy arrived occasionally and was with us for a few days during which its personnel required housing, feeding and, I suppose, re-equipment, but this didn't seem to happen very often and they had their own unit office and other base personnel anyway. What I did know at the time was that I was pretty fed up: fed up with being so far from home and leading what seemed a fairly pointless existence; fed up also (sorry to have to admit this) with the relentless battering from that harsh South Yorkshire accent. Made worse by the fact that the station was so small, there was almost nothing in the way of entertainment without the bus ride into Sheffield and back.

Could there be no escape for me before demob in November 1954?

CHAPTER 7

NEVER VOLUNTEER — UNLESS!

Relief might be at hand! In July, not so long after my nineteenth birthday, a signal arrived from Group. The message was not POR'd as it could only concern two airmen. Was there a typist on the station in the rank of LAC who would be interested in a posting to SHAPE (Supreme Headquarters Allied Powers Europe) located at Versailles, near Paris? My typist colleague in the registry had only recently transferred to Norton to be near his home in Leeds and so, not surprisingly, he was not interested. As for me, in chapter 3 I explained that my County Hall office chum John Roulston had in his Army capacity been posted to that very Headquarters where, until his demob a few months earlier, he had worked on the office staff of a chap called Montgomery. I was aware from correspondence with John that he had thoroughly enjoyed life both in and out of the HQ and, notwithstanding that I knew him to be somewhat more of an extrovert than myself, I was, as already explained, so unhappy with my present lot that I did something really quite out of character (as well as contrary to all the old soldiers' advice about not volunteering for anything) and said, yes, I was interested. Strictly I wasn't in the running as the request was for a typist and I was a shorthand typist but the message went forward to Group anyway.

My parents would have been horrified had they known. No member of my immediate family had ever ventured abroad and, of the four not so immediate relatives who had (all in the Services as explained earlier), two had not returned. Notwithstanding that I had offered to be posted only to France, a country with whom we were in theory at any rate at peace, at this stage I decided, knowing full well how my parents would worry, not to tell them what I had done. A week or so later another message from Group: sorry, no posting this time; would he still be interested if anything else comes up? Again I said, yes.

My recollection of events now becomes a little confused. The end of July was approaching and, in fact, after work on Friday 31 July I was due to leave camp for a period of leave, to include the August Bank Holiday weekend the subject of the earlier witch-hunt. At about this time an instruction arrived from Group. I was to report at pretty short notice to RAF Kenley, Surrey for interviews in connection with a posting to one of SHAPE's subordinate HQs, namely, that of Allied Air Forces Central Europe (AAFCE). I cannot now recall whether I went to Kenley before, during or after my leave. I do however remember the Accounts Officer doing his best to dissuade me from pursuing a move to France. For some reason he spent time emphasizing the international nature of the HQ — as if, perhaps, it would be a terrible wrench to throw away the comfort and security of an ordinary RAF station — and finally delivered the *coup de grâce*: "Of course, you realize you would have to speak French". 'Well' I thought to myself 'if John Roulston can manage, why shouldn't I who went to the same school and took the same exams'. Out loud: "That shouldn't be a problem, Sir, I achieved a Credit in French, written and oral, in my School Certificate examinations". From the fact that he didn't try to test my knowledge of the language, I inferred that Flight Lieutenant Wilson didn't speak French!

I was on leave until Wednesday 12 August, having in the meantime cycled to Rayleigh for three speedway meetings, and the more I think about it the more convinced I am that I must have travelled to Kenley from Chelmsford during that leave. Certainly I arrived there at an hour during the morning which would not have allowed me to have travelled all the way from Sheffield without an exceptionally early start and I have no recollection of being the unhappy recipient of an early call. Whyteleafe was the station for RAF Kenley. A nearly empty Southern Region third-rail electric conveyed me out of London on a glorious summer morning and, as I sat alone in my non-corridor compartment just behind that of the driver, the sunlit woodlands of leafy Surrey seemingly engulfing the train at times, I began to have doubts as to whether I was doing the right thing. Should I perhaps have heeded the universal advice never to volunteer for anything? Despite my unhappiness at Norton, would I have been better advised to make the best of the 'devil I knew' and see out the remainder of my time there? After all, things weren't really *that* bad were they? On the other hand, who knew what sort of a place this AAFCE might turn out to be? Would it be sensible to throw up the chance of what might be the experience of a lifetime? My mind was still in turmoil when I walked through the gates of what had been one of the key fighter stations during the Battle of Britain.

As one of the Fighter Command airfields closest to London, RAF Kenley, a Sector Station in No.11 Group, was quite obviously heavily involved in the Battle. The other station in the sector was at Croydon and each was home to two squadrons of fighters, changing from time to time as the Battle progressed and individual squadrons required to be withdrawn from the front line to less onerous duties or to re-form. Kenley, for instance, on 1 July 1940 housed Nos.64 (Spitfire) and 615 (Hurricane) Squadrons. By 7 September Nos.66 (Spitfire) and 253 (Hurricane) were in residence, the first two having by then retired to the quieter skies of the north of England and south-west Scotland, respectively. Kenley received the unwelcome attentions of the *Luftwaffe* on a number of occasions, the most intensive raid being that of 18 August 1940 when, along with nearby Biggin Hill, the station was singled out for special treatment and badly damaged. As the result of, first, low-level and then high-level bombing the station became non-operational for a time. On this day 615 Squadron lost four Hurricanes in the air and six on the ground; hence its transfer to Scotland. Among those killed on the ground was the station's MO.

My own arrival at Kenley was somewhat less momentous! All seemed very quiet — almost too quiet — as the station basked in warm sunshine. I don't recall much about the interviews for which I had been summoned but I think they centred largely around my background and general, as opposed to trade-specific, suitability for the posting. I don't think shorthand and typing were even mentioned and I certainly wasn't tested. As to my background, I think the main interest was politics: in particular, did I have extreme left-wing leanings? I think at that time NATO in general and the United States in particular were pretty paranoid about the USSR and Communism — reds under the bed and all that — and my interviewers had to be assured that I posed no risk in that direction. Generally, I think there was probably a desire to ensure that complete idiots were not sent, in effect, to represent the UK at an international HQ. I was sufficiently conceited to consider that I did not fall within that category. Certainly I was quizzed in some detail about my family, what my parents felt about a possible posting to France (by now they were aware of what I was up to and were pretty unhappy about it) and, of course, my own feelings after the conversations I had been having with, among others, a middle-aged sergeant. As far as I was aware, I was the only airman being interviewed on that day.

I have to admit that, by the time I was sent for a meal with instructions to report back early in the afternoon, I was having second thoughts and I think my interviewers had realized this. There was time to kill after eating and so, with nowhere specific to go, I decided to disregard my self-imposed rule not to venture anywhere I didn't have to and to look around this station which, even in my only just nineteen-years-old innocence, I knew to be of some repute. I was confident that, for the first time since enlistment, I would see some aircraft on the ground and might even be able to have a close look. The sun-drenched airfield and runways were, however, deserted and not one aeroplane was visible through the heat-haze. Now I realized why I had thought the place unnaturally quiet upon arrival; subconsciously I think I had expected, knowing something of the station's history, to find aircraft buzzing around with all the associated activity on the ground. What a let-down!

I turned a corner between some buildings and almost literally bumped into the sergeant I had recently left. I soon realized that this was no chance encounter: he had come looking for me and, to my amazement and not a little consternation, proceeded to bombard me with what some readers may be disturbed to hear described as religious twaddle. I get very fed up with anybody trying to ram anything down my throat, especially religion. I came from a churchgoing family, two of my uncles were Church of England priests and I was quite happy to continue in my role as a confirmed member of that Church. I thought it grossly unfair, and probably wrong, for a senior NCO member of the permanent staff to inflict himself in this way upon a humble visiting erk who he already knew to be in a state of some inner turmoil; I couldn't tell him to "push off" in view of his rank and it was difficult even to attempt to argue. I had to put up with him until it was time to return for the afternoon's further, somewhat shorter, interview, following which I took my leave of Kenley to return either to Sheffield or to Chelmsford, I only wish I could remember which!

Either way I was back at Norton on the evening of Wednesday 12 August following my leave and, if confirmation of my posting hadn't already arrived, it very soon did as RAF Form 64 (Airman's Service and Pay Book) was issued to me on Monday 17 August. Only airmen posted overseas received a pay book; it contained among other things provision for a "Record of Woollen 'Comforts' Supplied", "Particulars of Artificial Dentures" and a specimen Will providing for my silver wrist watch to be given to my friend John Jones. As I had neither a silver wrist watch nor a friend John Jones I decided not to make a Will at that time.

Having disposed of my electric iron and 'cleared' from the station by trailing around getting the necessary signatures on the form which I had originally used to 'arrive', I think I probably left Norton on Friday 21 August. My posting to AAFCE took effect on Monday 24 August. However, an entry in my civilian Post Office Savings Bank book (Wood Street, Chelmsford No.312) reveals that I was at home on that day and must somehow have wangled more leave. My departure from Norton was somewhat propitious: I had learned at a CO's conference that, on the Saturday of the following week, i.e. 29 August, the station was to suffer a mock attack by a local Army unit. It was not known what form the attack would take: however, although no live ammunition would be used, realism was to be achieved. "It is likely that people could get hurt" said our cheerful CO. One of the directions from which it was considered most likely that the attack would be launched lay to the rear of SHQ and who was to defend that sector of the perimeter? SHQ staff, including me! And where was I at the time? Hundreds of miles away, in France!

As a postscript to my seven months or so at RAF Norton, some indication as to its importance might be gained from the fact that it was to be no less than 34 years before I was to meet anyone who had heard of it. At Lytham St Annes, Lancashire on 10 July 1987 I was introduced by a friend to Mr David S. Bain who, as an officer in the RAF's Education Branch, had not only heard of Norton but, many years previously, had actually visited the station.

HQ AAFCE was located at Fontainebleau, the best part of forty miles south-east of the French capital, and I viewed the journey there by public transport with some trepidation. [In later years, as a result of the French withdrawal, militarily but not politically, from NATO, the HQ moved to Mons, in Belgium.] Thursday 27 August found me at RAF Stanmore, Middlesex where I was to spend the night and travel to France on the following day. At Stanmore I was hugely relieved to encounter another AAFCE-bound airman, also due to travel on posting the next day. A native of Grimsby, he had 'signed on' to do three years and said he was an engine mechanic. I took this to mean MT (motor transport) engines. "Oh no" he said, "aircraft engines". Aircraft? Surely there wouldn't be aircraft at an international headquarters such as that for which we were bound?

At a loose end after tea, I persuaded my new-found friend to accompany me to Wembley speedway where, after watching the Lions defeat the Wimbledon Dons 58–26, we were treated to a firework display. The not-too-full stadium seemed an eerie venue for a noisy speedway meeting. I have only visited the place once since: many years later, the coach upon which I was a passenger became traffic-bound and arrived at the stadium in time for me to attend only the second half of an England v Czechoslovakia football international. From my position standing at the very top of the end banking, the match seemed to be taking place about half a mile away and proved a huge disappointment. I was told it ended goalless.

Friday dawned sunny and promised to be a bit on the hot side for lugging full kit and civvies abroad. Our first stop had to be at the War Office in Whitehall where an Army NCO presiding over a small desk at the far end of the enormous pillared hallway issued us with the movement orders which we required in lieu of passports for our journey. Continental holidays hadn't got going in 1953 and few people held passports. Then to Victoria for the boat train to Dover upon which we had the good fortune to encounter two airmen, one a corporal (Dave Evans) of whom initially we were somewhat in awe and the other an SAC (Terry Ward). Returning from leave in the Midlands, both were headed for AAFCE. Neither appeared too unhappy at the prospect — indeed a smile rarely deserted the little corporal's face — which seemed a good omen for my own future.

We were soon to learn that the acronym AAFCE was pronounced "affsea" and that, discipline in the unusual circumstances of an international camp being fairly relaxed, NCOs there were human beings the same as airmen and were usually addressed by Christian names rather than their ranks. The corporal and his chum (with whom I was later to become quite friendly) gave us a lot of useful advice and offered to accompany us on our journey.

At Dover Marine station the British Railways 'packet', or ferry-boat, for Calais appeared huge to my innocent eyes. By 1990s standards it was minuscule. It conveyed only train loads of foot passengers who jostled and struggled their way up the gangplank, burdened down by their respective shares of the mountain of luggage with which the vessel was soon to be crammed. By sailing time it was almost impossible to walk around. Mercifully for my first voyage the sea was almost the proverbial millpond, the sun shone out of a cloudless sky and, sitting on deck with my new-found comrades, I thoroughly enjoyed the experience of being the first member of my immediate family ever to venture abroad.

Advice from the corporal as the vessel approached the quay in Calais harbour and we observed with interest a small army of men, wearing blue overalls and black peaked caps and wreathed in smoke the pungent odour of which was already assailing our nostrils: "Whatever you do, hang onto your gear and don't let any of that lot get hold of it!" Each screaming *"Porteur"* and pointing to the number which I could now see emblazoned on his cap, the small army was swarming all over the vessel literally before she had docked. Using long leather straps to facilitate the carriage of seemingly impossible weights, the suitcases and other luggage of passengers who had neglected to take our corporal's advice was disappearing over the side with amazing rapidity. Those relieved of their accoutrements were then faced with the dual problems of, first, finding 'their' *porteur*, then rustling up sufficient French money to get him to withdraw his outstretched hand.

If you had no French money, he was grudgingly prepared to accept large denomination English coins.

The train for Paris was nearby and, French stations being devoid of platforms as we know them in the UK, we hurled our kit aboard and climbed up after it. The SNCF (*Société Nationale des Chemins de Fer Français*) steam locomotive was one of those huge black pipe-encrusted monstrosities which I had, of course, previously seen only in pictures. On the footplate lounged Biggles, Marks I and II, resplendent in goggles. Even the dull and featureless landscape of north-western France seemed like magic to me, resulting in the journey of 150 miles or more passing very quickly. *En route* we were exhorted in four languages -

> *Ne pas se pencher au dehors*
> *Nicht hinauslehnen*
> *E pericoloso sporgersi*
> Do not lean out of the window

so we didn't. We did however learn that LAC Grimsby wasn't on a wild goose chase as the RAF apparently had a small communications flight based at an airfield near Melun. I also learned that AAFCE was, for the RAF, a regulars-only posting and that I would be the sole National Serviceman there. Had someone blundered? Would I be sent back?

It was early evening when we drew into Paris, Gare du Nord. We were never more grateful to Corporal Dave Evans than now. "Hang on a minute, before you lug all your kit down to the Métro, let's have a look round at the back of the station." What did we find parked there? Nothing less than one RAF 15cwt truck, the driver of which soon appeared! Yes, he was from AAFCE and, yes, we could all have lifts. First call would be at a café — *"Les Aviateurs"* — situated on the road running past Orly Airport, where one of the waitresses was reputed to wear nothing under her apron. Known to the RAF as "The Aviators", this café was conveniently located on the road between Paris and Fontainebleau and was apparently much used by AAFCE personnel in transit. Between the Gare du Nord and the café those of us ensconced in the back of the truck witnessed no less than three minor road accidents, in one of which a lady was knocked from her moped. Driving standards in the madhouse they called Paris were appalling; quaint vehicles thronging the streets included innumerable drunken garden sheds on wheels ('corrugated iron' Citroëns to be slightly more accurate) and, what was more, they all seemed to be driving on the wrong side of the road. Our phlegmatic denizen of the MT negotiated the mayhem with suitable British aplomb.

The café proved to be a cross between a bar and a small restaurant and was typical of those to be found all over France. Embarrassed by a lack of French currency, I was rescued by Cpl Evans: would I like a sandwich? Ham, perhaps? Anticipating a round of bread in the usual English fashion I was astonished to be presented with the best part of a crusty loaf, slit lengthways, liberally plastered with butter and stuffed with fairly undistinguished ham. I suspect nerves were by now getting the better of me and I was able to dispose of only about half my loaf before we were back in the truck and off on the final leg of our journey. Still in suspense? The waitress *did* wear something underneath her apron!

It was well into the evening and quite dark when we reached Camp Guynemer, carved out of the forest and situated in the Avon district of the town of Fontainebleau in the Seine-et-Marne Département. On duty in the brightly illuminated police post at the entrance to the domestic side of the camp could be seen one SP, one USAF air policeman and one French *gendarme*. To celebrate the commencement of my international career I had in my **small** suitcase a half-eaten crusty French loaf which, rapidly becoming stale, was to haunt me for the next two or three days: I couldn't find any means of disposing of it!

CHAPTER 8

FONTAINEBLEAU IN FIFTY-THREE

Camp Guynemer, named after Capitaine Georges Guynemer (1894–1917), a distinguished French airman of World War I, was divided into two separate sections by the Rue du Rocher d'Avon, a busy public road giving access to the French main road network via the Route de Moret (nowadays — but not in 1953 — a dual-carriageway). The small town of Fontainebleau was situated to the north-west of the camp, its showpiece — Napoleon's magnificent palace — lying perhaps a little over a mile away.

To the west of the dividing road stood the AAFCE Headquarters building, a two-storey cement rendered edifice consisting on both floors of a wide central corridor giving access to five wings of offices on either side as well as a spacious cafeteria. An imposing entrance graced the western end of the building, to the front and rear of which were surprisingly little-used car parks. Happily, substantial remnants of the 42,500 acre *Forêt de Fontainebleau* lay within, and fringed, the boundaries of the site.

To the east of the road was situated the 'domestic' site, housing all the facilities necessary to support the HQ with the exceptions of married and officers' quarters and a hospital, all of which were located elsewhere in Fontainebleau. A large single-storey office building of similar layout to the HQ across the road housed separate support units for each of the air forces represented here, and there were of course barrack blocks (for airwomen as well as airmen), messes, equipment stores, MT sections, sporting and recreational facilities and all the other resources required at a large international centre.

Only a couple of years' old, the camp as a whole was a wonderful example of intelligent planning: well designed and laid out and I am sure all the better for the NATO (which in reality implies United States) resources which lay behind its construction. The general ambience was enhanced by occasional trees as well as remnants of forest which had been left to flourish between and around buildings. I don't think there had been a single tree at Norton: indeed this camp was an eye-opener to me!

The RAF barrack blocks were located at the very rear of the site, close to its eastern boundary. Between those blocks and the perimeter security fence was a substantial belt of trees; beyond that fence, in a cutting, ran the SNCF railway line, leading northwards via Fontainebleau-Avon station and Melun to Paris (Gare de Lyon) and southwards to Nemours, Montargis and Sens. Even in the quiet of the night the electrically powered trains were rarely audible from the barracks.

But I am jumping ahead of my story! I had only just arrived, it was dark and virtually nothing of the camp was yet clear to me. I very soon found myself allocated to a four-bedded room on the ground floor of the centre of the three RAF barracks (block 12M). No one was there to welcome me but Pete Chatten, a dark and very quiet long-serving LAC from Norfolk (whose trade I don't think I discovered), soon appeared to claim one bed. The remainder of the room was strewn with cooks' 'whites', and an unpleasant odour of stale food did nothing to lift the gloom which was rapidly descending upon me. I was very tired after my long journey and the excitement of the day had rapidly dissipated following arrival at my destination.

I cleared the debris from the bed and locker which Chatten indicated were 'spare', installed my gear and myself and took stock of my surroundings. In theory the accommodation really couldn't have been bettered: four beds ranged around the walls, four double-doored steel lockers, four chairs, one small square table, waste bin, full-length mirror on the inside of the door, green linoleum with under-floor central heating, as well as excellent 'ablutions', including showers, just along the corridor. Any complaints? Only the inward-opening windows which were a potential hazard in warm weather to the two airmen (including me) whose beds lay thereunder!

In practice, however, sharing a room with cooks proved unfortunate to say the least. Not only did our two seem to have twice as much kit as ordinary mortals, much of which found its way into my portion of the room when I wasn't looking, but both they and their gear had clearly become permeated by cooking smells. At every RAF establishment there appeared to be a contest to find the cook with (a) the filthiest 'whites' and (b) the most ridiculous hat; our two appeared to be in the running to win (a) at least! Cooks work shifts and it was usual for one or both of 'ours' to be thundering about at unearthly hours of the morning, disturbing the beauty sleep of others still abed. The younger of the pair, in civilian life a pastrycook in Bradford (would I never be rid of the Yorkshire accent?), was newly-arrived and quite friendly towards me. His colleague barely passed the time of day. All in all, I hardly felt happy in my new abode.

But I had come to AAFCE not to fret about my living conditions but rather to practice my skills as a shorthand typist. I felt sure that at least I would find my work at this important international headquarters sufficiently interesting and rewarding to offset other lesser worries. I was again to suffer disappointment. I was ordered to work, not in the headquarters, not even in the RAF Support Unit itself, but for the RAF Education Officer (Flight Lieutenant Stevenson) who had an office in the separate chaplains' block pleasantly located in trees close to the support units. My desk was actually in his office, one long wall of which housed a sizable English-language library. I did very little typing and, as far as I can recall, had no opportunity to practise my shorthand.

The Education Officer was rarely at his desk — I had no idea how he filled his day — and my instructions were simply to look after the day-to-day running of the library and to try to restore some order to the chaotic state in which I found it. A card-index purported to provide a record of book loans but, not having been maintained for some considerable time, was in fact quite useless. Not knowing who anybody was, much less who might have borrowed which volumes and what books existed anyway, and being left to my own devices, I decided the only course open to me was in effect to make a fresh start with the index and ensure that all returns and loans were henceforth properly recorded.

Most, if not all, my visitors were officers and their wives but not all were British: certainly US and Canadian officers appeared and there may well have been an occasional Dutchman. During my National Service I became somewhat paranoid about saluting and I was grateful that, at a desk and hatless, problems of identifying who was, and who was not, an officer did not arise. One could not easily forget the exhortation at square-bashing that "WHEN YEW MEET AN HOFFICER YEW WILL SALEWTE. LONGEST WAY HUP, SHORTEST WAY DAHN. HIF YEW DEW NOT SALEWTE YEW WILL BE HON A CHARGE. YEW ARE NOT SALEWTIN' THE HOFFICER, YEW ARE SALEWTIN' 'IS KERMISHUN". The problem was of course compounded at an international camp seemingly awash with officers whose badges of rank sometimes bore no relation to those of the RAF.

Six members of NATO were represented at AAFCE. The air forces of France, the UK and the USA provided the largest contingents and those of Belgium, Canada and the Netherlands were present in lesser numbers. A small detachment from the Royal Signals represented the British Army. One of the RAF barrack blocks was shared with the Dutch; the Belgians shared with the French and the Canadians with the Americans. One block, a little aside from the other twelve and surrounded by notices forbidding access by males, was occupied by airwomen from France and the US, to be joined during 1954 by half a dozen WRAF nursing staff. I wondered at the absence of notices forbidding female access to the airmen's accommodation! There were three messes located near to the barracks: one exclusively for the RAF, another for the French (who were joined by the Belgians) and the third the US 'chow hall' used also by the Canadians and the Dutch (who, having apparently been given the option of dining with either the RAF or the US, obviously realized upon which side their bread would be buttered).

But to return to the chaplains' block wherein I struggled with my card-index. Only one chaplain lingers in my memory: Squadron Leader Daly, the diminutive, bespectacled and ever-smiling Irishman who was the RAF Roman Catholic chaplain. To him everyone, irrespective of nationality or denomination, was "son" and, in return, he was "father" to all. He was eminently sociable and would do his best to help anyone with a problem. The next office to my library was filled with radio equipment and it appeared that, by appointment, US Servicemen could attend to speak to their relatives "Stateside" (as they termed the USA — returning home was referred to as "shipping Stateside"). It was of course not possible in 1953 simply to pick up a telephone as one can in the 1990s; the telecommunications explosion had not by then occurred and the USAF had obviously deemed it worthwhile to provide this radio facility for their men (and women).

Was there anything comparable for the RAF? Not exactly: the RAF

Support Unit did however boast a Post Office run by veteran cockney Cpl George Hammersley who was pleased to sell stamps to those moved to write home and then arrange for the despatch of their letters!

* * *

At this point in the writing of this narrative I suffered a heart attack whilst cycling, on my own, on a minor country road. So much for my enthusiasm for the bicycle — in Chapter 3 I said "... in my sixties, I still ride out for pleasure and exercise ...". A lot of good it appears to have done me!

Whilst in hospital I encountered my first National Service pilot. A fellow patient, originally from the Orkney Islands, undertook his Service during the late 1940s. Trained initially as a radar fitter he was one of fifty to respond to an appeal for volunteers to train as pilots and one of only three to receive 'wings'. Stationed at RAF Honington, Suffolk during the Berlin airlift he flew several sorties into Tempelhof as co-pilot of a Douglas DC-3 (Dakota). He flew over 700 hours in all.

* * *

But, to return to 1953. After an inauspicious start to my 'overseas' career, my circumstances had improved in several respects by the turn of the year.

Not an RAF station as such, it would have been inappropriate to have a SWOman at Camp Guynemer. Many of the duties of a SWO were in fact undertaken by the formidable Flt Sgt Allan and, a few weeks after my arrival, I plucked up the courage to have a beef at him about the circumstances in my billet. To my surprise he couldn't have been more reasonable, agreed that airmen working shifts should never share accommodation with others and, having consulted a large wall-chart in the corridor of the Support Unit, gave instructions that I was to remove myself immediately to a room in the other wing of block 12M.

I found myself sharing with two clerks, LAC (later SAC) David Mollart-Rogerson and LAC Brian Simpson, both of whom worked in the HQ (in the Central Registry and the Logistics Directorate, respectively). My recollection is that the fourth bed had recently been vacated; it was quite soon to be occupied by a new arrival, SAC Derrick Smith, a fellow shorthand typist. These three will all figure later in this story: suffice it to say at this juncture that I consider myself fortunate to have enjoyed their company and comradeship for the next year or so.

At the time of my arrival there was, so far as I knew, only one other RAF shorthand typist at AAFCE, SAC Ray Mills who worked in the HQ. Unbeknown to me, he had applied to transfer to the RCAF where pay and conditions were infinitely better than those in the RAF. What was more, he would have the opportunity to travel to Canada at no expense to himself. His application having been accepted he left Camp Guynemer quite swiftly and, at short notice, I was told that I would replace him in the HQ. I don't think the Education Officer was too happy with this: I had been in his office for only a few weeks and had just about got to grips with sorting out his library. I have to admit I was a little apprehensive at the prospect myself: I had been told I would be working in the office of the Commander.

It was necessary first for me to be security-cleared to the highest level ('Cosmic Top Secret') and for this purpose I was subjected to an exhaustive interrogation by an RAF squadron leader in the Security block. I had to supply detailed information about my parents, home background, schooling and civilian employment, as well as the name of the police force covering my home area. I don't think it would have mattered had I a criminal record; rather any untoward political leanings needed to be unearthed. Reds under the bed again! I was photographed, prison-style as at Padgate, this time peering over my name and the initials RAF, before being issued with a beautifully produced forerunner of the modern credit-card style identity pass with the photo heat-sealed in plastic. I noticed that my initials were incorrect and the whole process had to be repeated before the pass was deemed fit to enable me to enter the hallowed portals of the HQ building. All entrances were guarded by RAF or other police and HQ passes had usually to be shown. We shall shortly learn what awaited me when I was able to breach this security barrier.

Things were definitely looking up and, my domestic and working circumstances having changed, hopefully for the better, I wondered whether there was any other aspect of my Service life which could improve. There certainly was — pay! By the end of the year I had received no less than three increases: first, 2s.9d a day local overseas allowance from 3 September; second, 6d a day from 8 November having completed one year's service; and third, 1s.0d a day on promotion to SAC from 8 December. Gross daily pay had therefore increased in three months from 6s.6d to 10s.9d, totalling £3.15s.3d a week. Deductions of 10s.6d (1s.6d a day) for my POSB account and 3s.0d for National Insurance left £3.1s.9d (£3.09p) net, a not inconsiderable sum with accommodation and rations provided. My new-found wealth moved me to increase my daily savings to 4s.0d as from 1 January 1954, thereby reducing my net weekly pay to £2.4s.3d (£2.21p). We received our pay in multiples of 100 French francs, roughly equivalent in 1953 to 2s.0d (10p). My civilian POSB book reveals that various sums were deposited during September and October, presumably by my parents as the result of my sending Postal Orders home — I had never been so well off!

Promotion to SAC had been gained as the result of passing the appropriate trade test. As at Credenhill when I attained the standard for LAC, only modest speeds were required — an increase in typing speed from 32 to 40 words a minute and in shorthand from 50 to, I believe, 60. I wasn't completely confident about typing because there's a limit to how fast you can go using only about two and a half fingers while still achieving accuracy — but I passed. The shorthand was a doddle for one with a certificate at 120 words a minute, especially as I was by that time using it in my work and therefore well practised. Unable for obvious reasons to enlist my mother's services on this occasion I had perforce to make my own best fumbling attempt at sewing the three-bladed 'props' badges on to my greatcoat and two uniform jackets.

Soon after arriving at Camp Guynemer I was befriended by a room-mate of Terry Ward, the SAC from the Midlands encountered on the boat train at Victoria station. Hailing from Manchester, AC1 Richard (Bill) Rudman, assistant armourer, whose emporium was located in the equipment stores building, had the misfortune to support Manchester City FC. In spite of this he took it upon himself to introduce me to the delights of the camp, in particular the NAAFI, and generally to steer me in the right direction during those first few tentative and slightly nerve-wracking days familiar I am sure to all new arrivals on any camp. Especially in view of the unhelpful — almost unfriendly — disposition of my early room-mates and as, furthermore, I was working initially with just one officer, Bill's guidance and friendship were invaluable. With dark hair and pale complexion, his main claims to fame seemed to be his girlfriend in Manchester — Angela — and an over-indulgence in Coca Cola which had apparently landed him in hospital. He proposed to avoid a repetition by diluting the American import with rum and introduced me to the resulting rum and coke, a drink of which I became quite fond. He had kept goal for the RAF Support Unit football team — once — conceding a dozen goals; he was more successful acting as scorer for the cricket team.

Why was an erk named Richard known as Bill? His full Christian names were Richard William; he didn't wish to be called Richard or Dick so, although certain of his 'friends' annoyed him with an exaggerated "Ricky", most of us compromised with Bill. The practice of calling people by anything but their real names, or indeed those by which they preferred to be known, seemed to be endemic at AAFCE. My own Christian name is Edward and I prefer to be known as Ted; neither of these names was used at AAFCE: I was either Eddie (which I now dislike) or, more often, Kate — derived from my surname.

But, to work! The Commander's office occupied one first-floor wing of the HQ building. Fully carpeted (apart from one small office), double-glazed and provided with both net and velvet-type curtains, working conditions couldn't have been bettered. Furniture was metal and modern and everything was in co-ordinated shades of green. There was a surplus of accommodation and all the rooms on one side of the central (carpeted) corridor were locked: in fact I never saw the inside of these rooms which, I was told, had been used by the previous Commander to house French-speaking personnel.

There was only a small staff: the Commander himself was the legendary Air Chief Marshal Sir Basil Embry KCB, KBE, DSO (and three bars), DFC, AFC, RAF. Sir Basil had taken over command from USAF General Lauris Norstad only the preceding July, the latter having become Air Deputy at SHAPE. His personal staff, in the office and at his residence, as well as his chauffeurs, were all RAF personnel — he would have it no other way notwithstanding the international nature of his command and of his HQ. The office staff comprised Sqn Ldr George Lewis (Personal Staff Officer), Plt Off (later Fg Off) Robin Lees (Aide-de-Camp), W/O Fred Custance

99

(Secretary, who occupied the non-carpeted room), Sgt Stan Fenney (Clerk) and, now, myself (deputy secretary and general dogsbody). W/O Custance and the principal chauffeur — Cpl Clifford ('Nobby') Clark — had arrived at Fontainebleau with Sir Basil, having worked for him at Fighter Command HQ where he had been C-in-C. It was a privilege to work in this office and, needless to say, all those mentioned will appear later in this story.

The suite of offices included a shower-room cum dressing-room for Sir Basil's personal use as well as a fully equipped kitchen. With access only through his own office there was also a map room, the curtained off walls covered by maps and charts illustrating in surprising detail the dispositions of the armed forces and military hardware of NATO and the Eastern bloc. This information was up-dated once or twice a week by personnel (RAF only!) from the Intelligence Directorate. An internal footbridge led to the neighbouring first-floor wing wherein was housed the office of the Chief of Staff, Air Vice-Marshal John Plant CBE, AFC, RCAF, subordinate to whom were two Deputies. The two wings shared a private ground-floor VIP entrance guarded by a solitary policeman.

The Commander's office establishment provided for an additional clerk (a corporal) but the post had been left vacant because, frankly, there wasn't the work to justify filling it. The mail from the UK didn't arrive until late morning and, as it was the practice to deal with all of it on the day of arrival, mornings were often partially occupied by crosswords, in my case that in the *Daily Mail*. This raises the interesting question as to why the day's English newspapers were available in W. H. Smith's kiosk on the ground floor of the HQ building several hours before the arrival of the UK mail! However, afternoons when Sir Basil was in his office were often hectic and could result in late teas for Sgt Fenney and myself.

In normal circumstances Sir Basil dictated his correspondence to W/O Custance who, in order to share the load, re-dictated to me the less important items. Our very early version IBM electric typewriters then came into their own (remember this was 1953!). Much of my share of the dictation related to the work of the RAF Escaping Society. Sir Basil was Chairman at the time and the Secretary was in London. On occasions when Sir Basil dictated direct to me he would invariably ask when he had finished "Is that all right?" This from the man who, as AOC of 2 Group, had in his De Havilland Mosquito flown with his squadrons on tree-top level daylight attacks on pin-point targets in occupied Europe!

I soon settled down to my new responsibilities and, what with more congenial living arrangements, increased pay and the relaxed atmosphere of the camp when compared to that of a normal RAF station, I began to enjoy life. I improved my lot still further by investing in a bicycle. Notwithstanding that I fear mustachioed LAC Kingdom 'saw me coming' slightly in the number of francs he extracted therefor, I acquired his British-built racer and accessories, due allowance being made for the fact that the rear brake cable was broken. Possession of this machine not only allowed me to resume, to a limited extent anyway, the cycling which had always been my abiding passion, but it also provided a means of getting to and from my duties (it was a long walk between the billet and the office) and, most crucial, it eased my paranoia concerning saluting! In the British Services — although perhaps this didn't apply to some of the other nations — one was not required to salute whilst riding a bicycle, presumably to obviate the possibility of falling off at the feet of the salutee. The most that was required was a smart 'eyes left' or 'eyes right' as appropriate — much less of an embarrassment when accorded in error to a non-officer than the much more obvious salute. Before taking to the streets on the bike it was necessary to purchase at minimal cost from a sweet shop in Fontainebleau the requisite licence and to carry it in my saddlebag at all times.

Possession of my own bicycle ensured that I was not one of a party of erks which went into Fontainebleau one day to hire bikes. Finding a garage, closed but with a fleet of cycles outside, they helped themselves intending to pay after their ride. Upon their return they were given tickets bearing their time of arrival and it transpired that the owners of the bicycles had paid a fee to park them at the garage and our erks had in effect stolen them, albeit temporarily.

To revert briefly to my concerns regarding saluting, I happened one morning to be following near the NAAFI a Royal Signals private. Crashing along in his great Army boots he perceived coming towards him a scruffy little Belgian who I knew to be a private too but who was wearing a British Army officer type raincoat bearing no badges of rank. I sensed clearly that our Royal Signaller was in a quandary and, not to my surprise, he threw up a huge salute to the Belgian who responded with a bit of an arm-wave before passing by me doubled up with mirth. I used to have nightmares that I would do something similar and spent some time studying the dual-language booklet 'Know your Allies'/'*Connaissez vos Alliés*' published by SHAPE, a copy of which I found in my desk in the Commander's office. Badges of rank for all nations, all Services, all ranks were illustrated and, particularly when working in the HQ, the information was invaluable. Unfortunately, SAC's props were depicted upside-down and in a circular instead of a square badge.

Once established in the Commander's office I soon began to understand the overall NATO set-up and to appreciate where I fitted into the jigsaw. In addition to the six nations represented at AAFCE, eight others — Denmark, Greece, Iceland, Italy, Luxembourg, Norway, Portugal and Turkey — were members by 1953. West Germany was admitted to membership during 1954 — indeed, a couple of *Luftwaffe* officers were glimpsed in the AAFCE car park shortly before my own departure in October that year.

NATO's political headquarters were housed in a modern concrete building situated in front of, and therefore largely obscuring from view, the Palais de Chaillot in Paris. On the face of it, this seemed to me to be an unfortunate location in which to build. The military headquarters (SHAPE) were located just to the west of Paris, at Marly-le-Roi. For operational purposes there were three 'regional' military headquarters, Allied Forces Northern Europe (at Oslo, Norway), Central Europe (at Fontainebleau) and Southern Europe (at Naples, Italy) each with a Commander-in-Chief.

Subordinate to him in each 'region' were Naval, Land and Air Forces headquarters, each with a Commander. Thus, Sir Basil was in command of the air arm of NATO's forces in the Central European area but answerable to an overall 'regional' Commander-in-Chief, an Army officer: Le Maréchal de France Alphonse Juin had taken part in the invasion of Tunisia and the Italian campaign in World War II.

The Central European Army and Naval Commanders were also French — Général Carpentier and Vice-Amiral Jaujard respectively — and, at Sir Basil's suggestion, the three Commanders used to meet as a Commanders' Council about once a month, joined by Maréchal Juin's Chief of Staff, Général Bailly of the French Air Force. Thus Sir Basil was comprehensively outnumbered by his French colleagues, only one of whom was an airman, and, in the light of his strong views as to the importance of air power and what I am sure was his preference for working with fellow nationals in general and RAF personnel in particular, it would have been interesting to have been a fly on the wall at these meetings. The Council met in turn at each of the three headquarters and I cannot recall that even W/O Custance attended for the purpose of note-taking when the meetings were at Camp Guynemer — he didn't speak French anyway!

Internally the Air HQ was organised into a number of Directorates — two dealt respectively with Logistics and Operations for example — each headed by an Assistant Chief of Staff (ACOS) of Air Commodore or equivalent rank. The matter of public relations figured quite highly in NATO's priorities and it was therefore not surprising to find an Office of Public Information located in the HQ. I have already said that a large proportion of the staff were officers and this applied especially in the HQ. There were also a few civilians, principally Canadian and US women so far as I had occasion to discover.

In an international formation of this sort it was not surprising to find a large proportion of officers and it seems not inappropriate at this juncture to list below in order of seniority the highest of the commissioned ranks in the RAF:

> Marshal of the Royal Air Force
> Air Chief Marshal
> Air Marshal
> Air Vice-Marshal
> Air Commodore
> Group Captain

The more junior commissioned ranks, and the non-commissioned ranks, were listed in Chapter 6 (pages 73 and 86 respectively).

To revert to personal matters, the mildly euphoric condition induced by my changed circumstances and improved pay became somewhat tempered by news from home. My brother Geof, having attained the age of eighteen on 3 October, was now heading inexorably towards his call-up and had opted for the RAF. Like me he had been one of a group of twenty gathered at Southend-on-Sea. However, in his case they were all told on arrival that the RAF would take none of them and that all would go into the Army whether they liked it or not. The outcome of expressed preferences for the RAF was simply a matter of luck and timing; the RAF was heavily oversubscribed and Geof was one of the many unlucky young men. In the event he served in the Royal Army Service Corps and had quite a rough time in the Canal Zone of Egypt.

Before the close of the year I had occasion to be very grateful for certain advice tendered to me by Bill Rudman, namely, that it would be in my best interests to procure a passport for myself. The attentive reader may recall that I had travelled to Fontainebleau with the benefit of a movement order collected from the War Office in Whitehall. According to Bill, travel with such an order necessitated the wearing of uniform. Having struggled all the way to AAFCE on a boiling hot day weighed down with full kit, including greatcoat, as well as my small suitcase containing civilian garb, it would certainly not have been my wish to return home for such leave as I might be granted wearing other than those civvies. My recollection is that each year I, as the lone National Serviceman, was allowed one period of fourteen days UK leave, with travel paid, as well as seven days local leave (regulars were allowed more); however, I twice went home for a fortnight during 1954 but can't now remember how I managed to wangle this. Maybe I said I'd had no leave at Norton.

The solution to the uniform/civvies problem was a passport and we shall soon see that I had good reason to be thankful that I took action to obtain one without undue delay. The requisite form having been sought from the British Embassy in Paris and necessary miserable-looking photographs taken in a shed-like studio at the rear of the premises of JAN, 109 Rue Saint-Honoré, Fontainebleau, my application was approved and, for the princely sum of £1, passport No.C.486148 was issued to me by Her Britannic Majesty's Consul General at Paris on 9 November. In those days passports were quite imposing documents, strongly bound in substantial covers. According to my description on page 2 I had no special peculiarities: that was a relief anyway!

Discipline was fairly relaxed — it wouldn't have been a simple matter in the circumstances of an international camp to make it otherwise. Reveille for RAF personnel was at 0630 but, with no Tannoy system between the various buildings and no fire picket, enforcement would have been a problem. An attempt was made during the late autumn to tighten things up a bit but, apart from threats, not a lot happened and blokes tended to arise in time for breakfast as previously.

There was no question of going around painting things which didn't move because it was of course not the RAF's camp to play with. Officially there was a 'bull night' — Tuesday if I remember correctly — and SROs announced each week which of the three RAF barrack blocks would be the subject of a kit inspection the following morning and in which of the other two lockers would be inspected. In the third there would be a general room inspection. In practice I was not aware that anything was ever inspected —

which was perhaps just as well. Very nearly every week block 12M was allocated the locker inspection. Although basically I was happy with this, as it was a relatively simple matter to keep the inside of one's locker clean and tidy, nevertheless I wasn't particularly happy to have to leave both doors wide open for the whole of one morning. Obviously civilian clothing and other personal possessions, as well as uniform and other kit, were somewhat at risk. I used to store such items as my camera in my **small** suitcase and tuck that away on a top shelf but that would have been no defence against any potential thief. Happily the world was a more honest place in those days than it is in the crime-ridden 90s and I heard of no untoward incidents in my block.

Much of my free time, especially during the evenings, was spent in the NAAFI complex which provided, in addition to an all-ranks cafeteria, a cinema showing English-language films most evenings, a well-stocked sales kiosk, a snooker room and other amenities. There were weekly bingo sessions, sometimes with top prizes of sports cars, and occasional live entertainment on stage in the cinema. Most of the films featured were pretty up-to-date UK releases: I recall for example seeing the 1953 comedy classic *Genevieve*, starring Kenneth More, Dinah Sheridan, Kay Kendall and John Gregson, and *Conquest of Everest* had been shown by late November, i.e. within six months of the event. With the exceptions of the British manageress and her deputy all the NAAFI staff were French. The sales kiosk was 'manned' by gum-chewing Jeannette, a young lady with long blonde hair, who had the, to me, irritating habit whilst meeting my needs for toothpaste etc of gazing past my right ear at something or somebody presumably of much greater interest than me. It was rumoured that one could live with her for 28 'mill' (a thousand francs was always referred to as a 'mill') a month: only Canadians could afford such luxuries. At the time the pound was equivalent to about 980 francs; a 'mill' was therefore roughly £1.

The cinema projectionist was a wild-haired chain-smoking Frog (sorry — we always referred to the French as Frogs) who also drove the camp bus, itself a source of amazement to me as it was the first vehicle I ever encountered equipped with flashing indicators. A vast improvement on semaphore signals, which might or might not work and were not especially visible anyway, it took me a while to get used to the sight of lights seemingly flashing all over this vehicle. A free bus service operated regularly all day from the camp calling at a number of locations in and around Fontainebleau, including the officers' quarters and the railway station, and was a valuable amenity. Access to the cinema projection room was gained via an outside ladder and rumour had it that, having started the first reel, our wild-haired friend sprinted down the ladder, did a circuit of the town in his bus and was back up the ladder in time to change to the second reel. As with the story of the drum major hurling the mace over the railway bridge in Chapter 2, one has to draw one's own conclusion!

Tea in the mess having been taken at the early hour of 1600, it was not surprising that many of us were ready to eat again later. Most evenings I partook in the NAAFI of *un œuf* or, if I was feeling flush, *deux œufs, pommes frites et* beans. Some evenings the cafeteria staff had difficulty keeping up with the gastronomic demands of the RAF, who were the dominant patrons of the NAAFI. There was no problem relieving us of our francs; a large and elderly French lady who seemed to be a permanent fixture presided very efficiently over her cash register.

American canned beers — Schlitz, Blatz and Budweiser — were cheap and pleasant but not very strong, while bottled Worthington and other English beers were very expensive. It seemed strange that Americans sometimes started behaving in quite childish fashion after just one or two cans of their own beer, whereas most of our erks seemed to be able to down copious quantities with little or no effect. One of my chums, who shall remain nameless, is alleged to have disposed of 36 cans in one session! On the other hand another anonymous airman, from the Midlands, who was to be seen staggering around the camp at weekends permanently blotto was sent home with alcohol poisoning.

There was a sudden decrease in the demand for evening meals in the NAAFI when it came to light that, officially, the RAF provided four, not three, meals a day. It may be recalled that, during my time at Norton, I had been required to type the details of (admittedly fictitious) meals on to weekly menu forms providing for breakfast, dinner, tea and supper each day. Some barrackroom lawyer type at AAFCE discovered that a meal had to be provided for any erks presenting themselves in the mess for supper at, I believe, 2000 hours. Obviously it was possible to save oneself cash in this way and, to the horror and consternation of the duty cooks, increasing numbers of erks began turning up and asking to be fed. Although the fare provided was not too special we persisted and the cooks became obliged to make reasonable preparations even to the extent that, by the time we arrived, inverted chairs had been removed from some tables and cutlery produced — if this doesn't ring true with former erks, please await Chapter 9! In fact, I think I am correct in asserting that, on any station, any erk genuinely hungry could present himself in the mess at any time, when the duty cook was obliged to provide sustenance.

When my duties made it possible for me to be there, morning sessions in the NAAFI cafeteria were an especial pleasure and provided one of my abiding memories of AAFCE. Aglow with the sun's rays streaming through the picture windows, the large airy room would be awash with cheerful chatter, clattering crockery and tinkling cutlery while the instrumental number *Swedish Rhapsody* (*Alfoen*) would belt out incessantly on the juke box; well, almost incessantly: if you were lucky you might get to hear Doris Day render *Secret Love* or even catch the jazz classic *Way Down Yonder in New Orleans*!

A memorable Saturday evening in the crowded cafeteria saw a slightly inebriated US airman making his unsteady way across the room, in the general direction of his friends' table, bearing above his head and balanced upon one upturned hand a large trayful of opened cans of beer and glasses. Rather in the way that fighting at Arnhem reputedly ceased while the combatants watched Flt Lt Lord VC fly his blazing Dakota to and fro over what had been the dropping zone (while his RASC despatchers pushed much needed supplies out of the aircraft and into the hands of the German Army) before crashing in flames, conversation in the NAAFI dwindled while, spellbound, we all observed the Yank's progress. Sure enough, he made it — almost! Those with the keenest eyesight were able to discern just the slightest sideways slide by the contents of the tilting tray before the whole lot crashed to the floor via the persons of the nearest unfortunate drinkers — happily not RAF who, needless to say, raised a tremendous cheer. *Swedish Rhapsody* ground on unperturbed.

But, to return to less pleasurable matters. It has to be said that certain advantages accrued from working in the Commander's Office. It was usually possible, for example, to avoid some of the less agreeable tasks attendant upon Service life, so much so that 'Moll', one of my room-mates, re-Christened me 'SAC Slimey' and affixed to the wall over my bed a giant-sized bedcard to this effect. Notwithstanding this we are on speaking terms over forty years later! One duty I could not escape: on sunny but chilly Saturday 19 December 1953 I found myself in a USAF staff car, in the company of the amiable RCAF flight sergeant from the office of the Chief of Staff, travelling in convoy on an exercise designed to test the ability of the HQ to transfer to what would be its wartime location and send a message to 2 TAF in Germany to mobilize them to intercept a Russian attack.

Our USAF driver was much frustrated by the convoy's designated speed — 25 mph — and rarely managed to get the powerful staff car out of third gear. After an hour or two of this agony he pulled off the road and stuck his head under the bonnet, telling the escorting APs (air police) that he "could fix it, bud". The tail of the overtaking convoy having disappeared around a bend in the road, he and the flight sergeant enjoyed a smoke while I lounged on the rear seat. After a suitable interval we set off like a bat out of hell to resume our place in the convoy, our driver having given vent to some of his frustrations in the meantime.

Lunch was an embarrassment. The convoy halted to enable all personnel to enjoy the packed meals provided by their respective messes. My companions, both fed by the US 'chow hall' of course, produced from the boot (or should I say 'trunk'?) of the car capacious boxes containing cold chicken portions with salad and other goodies — not forgetting bottles of wine. My brown paper bag yielded, to the best of my recollection, a sandwich and an apple. To their credit my international colleagues, both of whom out-ranked me, offered to share their feast with me but I didn't feel it would have been proper to do so. We shall see in Chapter 9 that Sir Basil displayed a more than keen interest in the food provided in the RAF mess. His comments upon the respective fare provided on this occasion would have been enlightening I am sure.

I travelled as the representative of the Commander's office and in the boot was an empty wooden crate simulating my typewriter and stationery. As I assume I signed RAF Form 4216, the Official Secrets Acts presumably prevent me from identifying the whereabouts of the complex for which we were bound. However, it was in the Paris area and proved to be the secret underground HQ constructed during World War II for Adolf Hitler's use when directing Operation Sealion, the invasion of the British Isles. Instead, Generalfeldmarschall Walther Model used the complex in 1944 to supervise the Germans' retreat from France! Hitler's own vast wood panelled office was home only to a desk at one end: Sir Basil would have been located here.

My office, a small concrete cell, was located at the far end of the corridor leading to Hitler's and contained only a small table upon which I placed my empty crate. Not a lot happened after that although I was given to understand later that we lasted only two minutes before being annihilated. We weren't permitted to return home until we had endured a night in cockroach-infested billets with straw palliasses and canvas sheets, shaving outside in cold water and, the ultimate indignity, a British Army field kitchen. This was the only occasion on which I used my mess-tin and, yes, the rumour was true, everything went in the tin gloriously mixed together.

Christmas was upon us and, four days after our return to Camp Guynemer, I received more than adequate compensation for the trials of the weekend. First though I had to endure a rude awakening by Moll (mentioned earlier and the inevitable abbreviation for SAC Mollart-Rogerson) departing the billet at 0500 on Tuesday 22 December in order to catch the 0815 boat train from the Gare du Nord *en route* to Calais and Christmas leave in the UK. Good for him; but it appeared that, for the first time ever, my own family would not be able to spend Christmas together. However, in the office on the following day: "How would you like to go home for Christmas?" asked Sqn Ldr Lewis. Taken aback I probably spluttered something incomprehensible in reply. "Air Commodore Wykeham-Barnes is flying to the UK on Christmas Eve. I'll see if I can get you a lift with him."

I was somewhat in awe of Sqn Ldr Lewis but frequently had good reason to be grateful to him as, during the next year or so, he increasingly became something of a surrogate father to me. Dark and middle-aged, his family came from the Eastern Mediterranean and had strong UK links. He spoke eleven different languages fluently and had joined the RAF soon after the start of the Second World War, during which he served with distinction in the Mediterranean theatre, and was awarded the Greek AFC following the allied withdrawal from Greece in 1942.

As for Air Commodore Peter Wykeham-Barnes DSO, OBE, DFC, AFC, RAF, he was now ACOS Operations at HQ AAFCE, having been a colleague of Sir Basil's on the low-level wartime attacks mentioned earlier when in command of 140 Wing. An imposing, ruddy-complexioned man, he strode the HQ corridors wearing brown brothel-creepers; only someone of Air rank would have dared to do this. I was obviously to be in good hands for my first flight, especially as the third occupant of the aircraft would be LAC Grimsby, with whom I had arrived at AAFCE on 28 August and who was an engine mechanic with the small RAF communications flight. "Them's good engines" he was to assure me.

Christmas Eve dawned foggy as had many of the preceding autumn days. The groundcrew truck hurtled northwards through the murk for about 15 miles to Melun/Villaroche airfield, my presence therein resented, understandably perhaps, except by LAC Grimsby. We had been due for an early take off but conditions were such that even I realized this to be impossible. Sent on one abortive expedition to the met office high in the control tower (the French weather men refused to speak any English to me although I was sure they were well able to do so), I spent the rest of the morning gazing at the fog and being studiously avoided by the groundcrew. Early in the afternoon conditions showed signs of improvement and the air commodore arrived driving a minute car. He parked in the hangar outside which had reposed all morning an aircraft of vaguely sinister appearance which I learned was the Avro Anson in which I was to fly. This aircraft formed part of the RAF communications flight which, as well as one or two other Ansons, also included Sir Basil's personal aircraft — initially a De Havilland Devon and later a Hunting Percival Pembroke. A Douglas DC-3 Dakota was at Melun, at least temporarily: the POR clerk, SAC Les Goddard enjoyed a return flight to RAF Tangmere, Sussex on board such an aircraft in the company of a couple of WRAF personnel. On a subsequent occasion I was to observe landing at Melun the Belgian Air Force's entire communications flight — a Mark 1 Anson which somewhat resembled a flying greenhouse.

The Avro Anson was the RAF's first operational monoplane with a retractable undercarriage and served from 1936 until 1968. Over 300 were in service at the start of World War II and Ansons were the first RAF aircraft to become operational in the war: one carried out the first attack on a U-boat on 5 September 1939. I was almost certainly to fly in a post-war C19/Series 2 version. The slightly truculent groundcrew fitted a seat in the passenger cabin to give me somewhere to sit and, with contrasting alacrity, insisted I sign the 'blood chit' absolving everybody from HM The Queen downwards from any liability in the event of injury to my person. LAC Grimsby, unlike me familiar with aircraft, was deputed to join the air commodore in the cockpit and 'work the maps', navigation being no more complicated than visual observation of the ground.

Assailed by a mixture of indescribable smells and conflicting emotions I climbed into the aircraft and was shown how to strap myself into my lonely cabin seat. "Them good engines" (Armstrong Siddeley Cheetah 16 radials of 420 hp each) chomped away reassuringly as we taxied to the end of the runway before opening up for the take-off run. I don't think anyone is able to forget their first ever take-off, the edge of the runway seemingly slipping away from the aircraft as the ground appears to bend away. I think I began to enjoy myself once we had climbed to our cruising height and set course for RAF Bovingdon, about 250 miles away near Berkhampstead, on the Hertfordshire/Buckinghamshire border. My seat was situated over the starboard (right-hand) wing and, from his position on the port side of the cockpit, Air Commodore Wykeham-Barnes several times turned to give me reassuring smiles; one of my 'mixed emotions' was undoubtedly apprehension and I am sure he recognized this. I worried a little when I noticed small amounts of what I took to be oil appearing from an aperture on the top of the starboard engine casing.

Conditions were pretty good: the fog had disappeared and there was only broken white cloud. The English Channel came and went, to be replaced by the green fields of England, and, within two hours of taking off, we were letting down for Bovingdon. There was some consternation in the cockpit which I didn't understand until after landing — which was just as well. Apparently the requisite green light would not come on to show that the undercarriage was properly lowered. RAF Bovingdon had been constructed as a bomber base in 1941/42 and was used alternately by the RAF and the USAAF during the war. At the time of my visit it was home to RAF Fighter Command's HQ communications squadron and to the 7531st Air Base Squadron, USAF. It closed in 1972 and became the site of a prison.

There were no formalities after our landing: no Customs examination; no reporting at a guardroom. The air commodore was met by his wife, who was accompanied by a large car and a large dog. Could he give either of us a lift? Without using my loaf I replied "No thank you, Sir, I have to go into London" while LAC Grimsby said he would be hitch-hiking to the north. Too late I remembered that Wykeham-Barnes had been CO at RAF North Weald, in West Essex, until not many months previously and that almost certainly he would have been heading in that direction and could have taken me well on my way home. I consoled myself with the thought that, as a non-dog lover since being bitten on the ankle at the age of about five, I wouldn't have enjoyed sharing the back seat with the enormous hound prancing around on the tarmac.

I have dwelt at length on the events of this day because I think everybody's first flight is a momentous occasion which registers deeply in the mind and, in my case, the circumstances of its occurring were of such importance to me at the time. I vividly recall waiting outside the camp for a bus into Watford, gazing up into the late afternoon blue sky dotted with fluffy white clouds and thinking "I've just been up there!" The wording on the poster "Fly with the RAF!" came to mind and I think it was at this point that I felt the first glimmerings of pride in my Service and in the uniform which, in the circumstances of my flight, I had of course been obliged to wear. It has to be appreciated also that, by 1953, commercial flying had not taken off (no pun intended) in the way it has since; the foreign holiday explosion had not then occurred and, in any case, virtually all travel abroad was by sea.

From Watford I made my way by rail and Underground to Chelmsford, arriving home about mid-evening. I met my two brothers at the door, on their way to acquire Christmas cheer from the off-sales at the 'Fox and Hounds'; on the strength of my unexpected arrival they decided to buy an extra bottle of cheer. Investigating the cause of the kerfuffle at the door, my parents thought they'd seen a ghost — a ghost in RAF uniform admittedly.

My mother wouldn't let go of me and my father, an undemonstrative man, in an unexpected gesture laid his hand on the shoulder of my best blue. It was nice to feel wanted and to have 'made' my family's Christmas. We didn't realize it at the time but, due to the demands of National Service and girlfriends, this was to be the last occasion upon which my family were to spend the whole of Christmas together.

The next three days sped by, only one incident remaining in my memory: on Christmas morning I cycled into the town and withdrew £3 from my POSB account at the GPO in Chelmsford High Street. This was the maximum sum which could be withdrawn on demand and I must have had a premonition that I was about to require funds. Incidentally, what would today's trade unions have to say about a situation where, not only were main post offices open until noon on Christmas Day, but there was also one delivery of mail (or post as we called it in those days)?

Air Commodore Wykeham-Barnes was due to fly the Anson back to Melun on Monday 28 December. No firm arrangement had been made as to the time of take-off; it had simply been left that LAC Grimsby and I would present ourselves at Bovingdon as early in the morning as reasonably possible. Despite catching one of the first buses into Chelmsford, it was well into the day by the time I completed the protracted journey by public transport. There was no sign of the Anson. "Left about an hour ago with two on board" somebody told me. Would anything else be going to the Paris area? "Not today, try the Yanks, over there in the nissen hut" I was advised. "No, bud, nothing for France today" drawled an American, reclining on a bed in said hut.

Calamity indeed! It was by now late in the morning, I had already been travelling for several hours to no useful purpose and I had to be back at Camp Guynemer in time for work on the morrow. At least having taken Bill Rudman's advice I had a passport in my pocket (I had needed no movement order to travel in the Anson) and, as the result of my Christmas Day visit to the GPO, hopefully had the means to pay my way. I decided to fly. More hours elapsed while I made my frustrated way to London Airport (Heathrow), where the BEA desk advised me to try Air France. "Yes, Sir" (Sir? In an SAC's uniform?) "We can get you on a flight to Orly in about an hour" they said. Darkness was falling by the time I boarded the half-empty Douglas DC (7 I think). I felt a little conspicuous in my best blue and tried to adopt a nonchalant pose: the other passengers had to get the impression that I flew all the time! In reality I was praying I wouldn't be airsick — I didn't feel quite so confident in the different circumstances of a larger aircraft and, at night, nothing to be seen through the windows to which to relate oneself. But all was well and, from Orly, the airport bus conveyed me to Paris, depositing me at the Aéro-Gare des Invalides (known to the RAF as "the Invalids").

I now found myself in a wet and dark Paris, alone for the first time, and faced with the necessity to find my way across the city in order to locate and catch a train to Fontainebleau. Presumably I had sufficient commonsense and some French francs to offset my initial panic because, via the Métro with one change of trains and the Gare de Lyon, I eventually found myself on the wild-haired Frog's bus taking me on the final leg of a very long and tiring journey back to camp. What would I have done had I no passport? Sought help at an RTO (Railway Transportation Office) perhaps? How would I have managed without sufficient English and French cash? Busked on a street corner possibly? These questions were best not thought about. Instead, the good old NAAFI provided *deux œufs, pommes frites et* beans and a can of Schlitz!

My mentor, Sqn Ldr Lewis, had given me an official Allied Forces Central Europe Christmas card (his message being "With the Best of British Luck to you, The P.S.O.") which, interestingly, pictured the flags of seven nations. The seventh appears to be that of Luxembourg, a small state without a navy or an air force, but whose army presumably contributed to NATO's Central region.

From its commencement in the wilds of Cannock Chase to its conclusion in the grandeur of Fontainebleau Forest, 1953 had been quite an eventful year for me. I wondered what 1954 would bring — demob at the very least I trusted!

CHAPTER 9

WORK AND LEAVE, HOME AND AWAY

The year started well enough — with one and a half days off! New Year's Day fell on a Friday: not in 1954 a holiday in the UK, our international partners celebrated it as such and so it was an AAFCE holiday too. We were also given the Saturday morning off, which made sense as long as the Russians didn't decide to start anything before the Monday. We normally enjoyed one Saturday morning free per month, which accorded with the RAF arrangement in the UK of one '48' each month. In fact 48 and 36 hour passes were never required: we simply came and went as we pleased. The orderly room in the RAF Support Unit needed only a small supply of RAF Forms 295: as far as I was aware passes were only required by personnel going on leave to the UK.

W/O Custance had chosen this first weekend of the year to start a fortnight's leave and so, from Monday 4 January, I became directly responsible for the first time for Sir Basil's letters and other typed work. Mr Custance (W/Os were entitled to be referred to as "Mister" and in fact this was how Sir Basil referred to Fred Custance) did not spend this leave in the UK because, with his family, he rented a house on one of the various roads traversing Fontainebleau Forest. Long-serving, middle-aged (by my standards pretty elderly actually!) and chain-smoking, he had joined the RAF as a boy entrant, possibly as long ago as in the late 1920s — I'm not sure that he might not in fact have been one of 'Trenchard's Brats' at RAF Halton.

I have to admit that I did not enjoy the happiest of relationships with Mr Custance. I can recall no problems so far as our work in the office was concerned: such friction as existed between us arose from other matters. There was, for example, the saga of my 'abominable' groundsheet. I was more or less instructed to lend it to Mr Custance so that his son might have the use of it whilst camping during the summer. It wasn't easy to try to refuse what amounted to an order from a warrant officer but, nevertheless, I demurred: in the short term, I would be in trouble in the event of it not being available for a kit inspection; in the long term, it was one of the items of kit which I would be required either to hand in, or pay for, on demob and I knew full well that, once loaned, I would have the utmost difficulty getting it back. I asked many times for the return of this groundsheet even, one Saturday afternoon, cycling through the forest to the Custance residence to try to retrieve it myself; he wouldn't even allow me through the front gate but fobbed me off with some convoluted explanation or other as to why it wasn't available. Eventually, a matter of days before I returned to the UK, he produced a groundsheet: it wasn't my groundsheet; it wasn't even an RAF groundsheet; it was the wrong colour and, from the Service number it bore, I deduced that it was probably an Army groundsheet. I was left to worry what the reaction would be when I tried to hand it in on demob.

There was also the affair of the 'putt-putt'. Mr Custance travelled between home and the office on a quaint but commonplace French moped. He was one of the many senior NCOs and others who appeared most unhappy with the new-fangled berets. Unlike the younger 'sprogs', our elder brethren had never had the benefit of tuition by DIs in the arts of beret shrinking and wearing and that of Mr Custance, after a trip on the 'putt-putt', was really quite indescribable. Very much oversize it would balloon in the air, somehow defying the elements' attempts to snatch it away. Anyway, one summer morning I was told to ride the 'putt-putt' to a garage in Avon where repairs of some sort were to be carried out. Again I demurred. I had never driven or ridden anything with an engine and certainly lacked the confidence to do so for the first time in a foreign country and with no proper instruction: Mr Custance didn't even propose to venture outside the HQ to give me a demonstration. As with the groundsheet, as an SAC I found it impossible to refuse the demands of a W/O. Luckily I couldn't start the thing and so pedalled it — hard work with a too low saddle and in the broiling sun — to the garage where they didn't appear to be expecting it and there was also a language problem. I decided to leave it there anyway and walk back to the office.

To revert to Sir Basil's work, I think I must have made a satisfactory start because, two days later, on Wednesday 6 January he signed my copy of Anthony Richardson's book *Wingless Victory*. Telling the story of Sir Basil's escape from occupied France in the summer of 1940, this excellent volume was issued by The Companion Book Club in 1953. I think W. H. Smith's kiosk in the HQ needed to maintain a standing order for bulk supplies of the book and I obtained mine after placing my own order with the nice young French lady in charge of the kiosk. It was interesting in the outer office to observe the differing nature of the approaches made to us by various personnel desirous of having their copies of the book signed by Sir Basil. Those not used to calling at the office tended to enter with extreme diffidence, some non-Britons not quite sure whether Sgt Fenney or myself might in fact be Sir Basil. Some of the Americans in particular wished to leave personal details on the mistaken assumption, presumably, that their copy would be endorsed on the lines of "To Elmer. Congrats on the swell job you're doing. Yours, Baz". They all got the same as I did — "B. E. Embry" and the date! It was not unknown for 'Basil' to be pronounced by Americans to rhyme with 'hazel'.

Thursday 21 January was a sad day for my parents: my brother Geof reported to Aldershot to begin his National Service in the RASC where, initially at least, he had a far harder time than I had in the RAF. We were to see very little of each other during the next two years as, long before my return from France, he had been posted to HQ Middle East Land Forces, initially in Egypt but later in Cyprus. I am left with the feeling that parents, naturally protective and having themselves survived at least one world war, sometimes suffered more than did their more adaptable offspring over National Service. In the case of my own parents, with three sons close in age, we weren't together as a family, with its attendant 1950 values and spirit, between my own enlistment when we were respectively aged 15, 17 and 18 and my youngest brother Den's demob. By then marriages were looming to break the family up for good.

I barely saw Geof during my own fortnight's leave due to commence on Friday 5 February: his fleeting Sunday visits were occupied mainly by expeditions on his bicycle to the home of a girlfriend on the other side of Chelmsford. We were in the midst of a spell of wintry weather, including snow which did not, however, lay deeply on Camp Guynemer. Collective advice was that one travelled on UK leave by the 'night ferry' from Dunkerque to Dover, thereby gaining the best part of one day at home. Having received 12,000 francs (£12.4s.11d or £12.24½p — a fortune) in leave pay on Thursday 4 February, I proposed to accompany Bill Rudman and two others I will refer to as LACs Bell and Platt on the night ferry that evening.

As we had tickets for Friday's 0900 train we had to call at an office above the platforms at the Gare du Nord to seek permission to travel instead by the evening train. There we were told that conditions in the Channel were too rough for the ferry sailing and that consequently the connecting train would not run. *"Ce n'est pas possible"* they said. Normally this train included some *wagons-lit* (sleeper coaches) which were conveyed by the ferry and on to London (Victoria) without disturbing the snoozing occupants. It was by now late in the evening and, expecting that we would be able to travel next day, we had either to spend the night in Paris or return to camp and start again. We all decided to remain in Paris. LAC Bell said he wasn't going to spend a night in this glamorous city without enjoying himself and disappeared into the darkness. Perhaps because of the cancelled sailing, hotel accommodation in the vicinity of *la gare* seemed to be at a premium but we managed to secure a room for three at a handily situated but slightly crummy hotel. Unfortunately the room possessed one small double and one single bed. We tossed for the single: Platt won and so Bill and I 'enjoyed' an inconvenient night.

Next morning we met a philosophical but penniless Bell at *la gare*. All his leave pay had been squandered on the two Parisian 'ladies' with whom he had spent the night. The cross-channel services between Dover and Folkestone on the one hand and Calais and Boulogne on the other were operated jointly by British Railways and SNCF. At Calais we embarked on what turned out to be a French vessel and, while still in harbour, had a lonely meal in the restaurant. I wonder who paid for Bell's! We commented on large ice floes drifting past the windows (portholes? — I'm not sure at what point a window becomes a porthole) by our table. I didn't know this at the time but Essex had been suffering severe weather during this week, with blizzards sweeping the County and similar ice floes around the coast. Of the meal I can recall only a huge helping of spinach. As the vessel left the protection of the harbour it started to roll in what we hadn't appreciated were still rough seas. Without a word I hurriedly deserted the table *en route* to the nearby gents, wherein I spent the most miserable journey of my life cursing the RAF, the ship, the sea, the weather, the meal and, above all, the spinach; it is a fact that in these circumstances you say you want to die. I emerged years later, when I sensed the motion changing as we entered Dover harbour, to discover that, at the request of my worried friends, messages had been broadcast over the ship's Tannoy seeking to discover my whereabouts. Obviously the Tannoy wasn't audible to those closeted!

I spent a quiet leave and very little money — evidenced by the fact that on the day before returning to camp I deposited £10 in my civilian POSB account. I had intended to go to London on my first Thursday at home to see the musical *The King and I* at the Theatre Royal, Drury Lane. Possibly as a consequence of the inclement weather or, more likely, due to lack of a ticket, I stayed at home. I did spend 3s.6d (17½p) on the purchase of a copy of *Pitman's Pocket Shorthand Dictionary* for SAC Smith, a sum which I trust he reimbursed and no longer owes me. Derrick Smith was another to whom the AAFCE blight on names applied: for some reason best known to himself he wished to be known as Del or Dingle. His RAF friends simply couldn't go along with either of these so he was known as Smithy or, more likely, Smiffy. A shorthand typist, he succeeded me as the RAF Education Officer's sidekick. Short with very fair thinning hair and a pale cheery complexion, he hailed from Hoyland, Barnsley. In spite of his South Yorkshire accent I became very friendly with him and, apart from my chance encounter in Innsbruck with a square-bashing colleague (mentioned in Chapter 5), he is the only one of my ex-RAF comrades upon whom I have set eyes since my demob — he came to stay with me in Chelmsford during one of his leaves from AAFCE in early 1955.

I had a long and lonely journey back to camp on Saturday 20 February. This was the first occasion upon which I had undertaken a journey of this magnitude alone. Having bid my brother Den farewell at the local bus stop, it wasn't until one Eastern National bus, two British Railways trains, one London Underground train, one ship of unknown nationality, two SNCF trains, two Paris Métro trains, the wild-haired Frog's bus and twelve hours later that I greeted my RAF friends and, no doubt, adjourned to the NAAFI for the usual repast.

I hadn't long to wait before the next break from routine. "How would you like a trip to Nice?" asked Sqn Ldr Lewis on Thursday 4 March. "The Devon is going down tomorrow and you would stay the night and return on Saturday morning". Needless to say I was excited at the prospect but could foresee difficulties. My companions would be Sqn Ldr Paston-Williams, Sir Basil's personal pilot and CO of the communications flight, and Flt Lt 'Johnnie' Walker, his deputy who, when not himself piloting the aircraft, acted as navigator. Quite apart from the fact that I wouldn't be able to afford the standard of hotel chosen by officers — whose expenses could well have been paid by the RAF anyway — it wouldn't have been seemly for an erk to presume to join them and, thus, I would be on my own once we had landed. I was also a little concerned as to how my trip would be justified in the event of awkward questions at either end of the journey. As he usually did, Sqn Ldr Lewis understood my worries. If I supplied the name of an airman who I would like to accompany me and who could get clearance from his own superiors, he (Sqn Ldr Lewis) would 'fix it'. To resolve my concern about justification for the trip (a) if necessary I was to say that I and my potential fellow erk were there to refuel the aircraft (two office wallahs refuelling the Devon would have been a laugh had this been necessary!) and (b) I was to place two sheets of blank A4 paper inside a sealed envelope addressed to Sir Basil and endorsed "TOP SECRET — BY HAND". This envelope (unopened) was still in my possession a few years ago. Sir Basil was with friends near Nice and I believe the purpose of the flight was actually to convey Lady Embry home.

I must not convey the impression that I owed my good fortune on this and similar occasions solely to Sqn Ldr Lewis; Fg Off Lees was very much involved also and I am indebted considerably to them both.

I asked LAC Simpson if he would care to accompany me on the flight. Brian Simpson was one whose name became little corrupted: to nothing worse than Simps and indeed his correct Christian name was often used! Of slightly chunky build, he was by nature quiet, serious-minded and slow to smile but nevertheless a good companion on several weekend visits to Paris (described in Chapter 10). A native of Liverpool, I believe both he and his father worked for the Dunlop Rubber Co., Ltd., and he spent many hours studying in pursuit of some business qualification, poring over the books and papers which he had brought from the UK. For light relief at AAFCE he played hockey although for whom I'm not certain.

Brian hesitated about accepting my invitation. I don't believe he had flown previously and he was doubtful about approaching RAF Air Commodore T. C. Dickens, ACOS Logistics and head of the Directorate in which he worked. The eventual outcome was that he was given permission to fly but not until so late on the Friday morning that he had no time to return to the billet for his civvies; needless to say we both had to travel in uniform but my trusty **small** suitcase conveyed my civvies. I can't remember by what means we reached Melun/Villaroche but reach it we did, swiftly to board Sir Basil's personal Devon C1. This low-wing aircraft was the military version of the De Havilland Dove, the UK's first post-war airliner, and was powered by two 380 hp Gipsy Queen 70 engines. With a crew of two, it seated at least six passengers in reasonable comfort.

During my somewhat sheltered existence I had never set eyes on a mountain — from any angle: we don't have too many in Essex although certain hills seem like mountains when being ascended on a bicycle. The flight of over 400 miles and approaching three hours took us some 500 feet above the snow-covered peaks of *les Alps Maritimes* — for me a fantastic sight and an unforgettable experience. Sir Basil met the aircraft on the airstrip alongside the sea at Nice. "Hello Clayton" (he never did get my name right — surely he couldn't have confused me with Group Captain 'Tubby' Clayton DFC, with whom he had flown during the war!) was all he said as I left the plane, trying hard not to look as if I had just been airsick for the first and only time. The Devon had been flown by Flt Lt

Walker who, having crossed the mountains north of Nice, had descended to the airstrip rather in the fashion that he would have brought down one of the fighters he was reputed to have flown in World War II. Simps was looking a bit green but had managed to contain himself. Happily for both of us a bowser from one of the civilian fuel companies (there was no military presence at the airstrip) had reached the aircraft by the time we disembarked and had set about refuelling.

The officers gave Simps and me a lift into Nice in their taxi, showed us the rather grand-looking seafront hotel in which they would spend the night and told us to be on the pavement outside at a certain hour in the morning. We were then left to our own devices. Nice was then, and still is, an expensive resort; Simps and I were both strapped for cash and our first priority was therefore to find a reasonably priced hotel. Obviously we had to get well away from the seafront Promenade des Anglais and, four streets back, at 20 Avenue Georges-Clemenceau we found the Hotel Scribe on the corner of the Rue Paganini: *"Le meilleur confort dans un quartier central et tranquille. L'installation sanitaire la plus moderne, réalisée en 1953"* said the blurb. Although an imposing building, we decided we could afford *"le meilleur confort"* and checked in. I still have the bill which I assume relates to both of us. The room cost 1,190 francs and breakfast 200 which, together, represented £1.8s.5d or £1.42p, somewhat more than we would have paid in Paris. Nice appeared not to have crummy hotels to match those in the capital!

The sea was rough and, although I in my sports jacket and grey flannels and Simps in his best blue with beret tucked into his belt didn't find it cold, our fellow strollers on La Promenade des Anglais were expensively wrapped up in fur coats and the like. We patronised Nice Souvenirs at 23 Avenue de la Victoire, my few mementoes costing 540 francs (10s.9d or 54p) in all. I am including these price details to illustrate the incredible degree of inflation which has occurred during forty years and to reveal what apparently paltry sums were of such importance to us at that time. I don't have a note of the cost of the back-street meal we enjoyed at L'Auberge, 7 Rue Paul Déroulède but it had to be cheap or we would have gone elsewhere!

The officers' stay had evidently been slightly more expensive and eventful and they may well have invested at the casino. Next morning they appeared a little the worse for wear, one in particular, when we returned with them by taxi to the airstrip. Sqn Ldr Paston-Williams flew us back to Melun and his flying bore out the description of him given by Sir Basil in a letter to a potential passenger, namely, "a first-class airline type pilot". I would guess he spent the war in Transport Command: he certainly wouldn't have been suited to single seat fighters. I cannot now recall whether or not Lady Embry joined the flight.

After the adventures of the last few weeks, work and social life settled back into routine. Bill Rudman had decided I needed a pen-friend and I was by now corresponding with Valerie, who lived in Wythenshawe on the outskirts of Manchester, and was a friend of Angela, the girl of whom he rarely ceased to speak. Valerie wrote very long letters to which I found it difficult to do justice when replying; she proved to be a very pleasant person when eventually I met her but I have to say that I didn't find it easy writing to a complete stranger. I think Bill was trying to act as a matchmaker; whenever a letter arrived for me from Valerie he would have snatched it from the wallrack in the other wing of block 12M and hurried it to my billet before I had even realized that the mail had arrived.

My only other correspondent at this time was my mother to whom I tried to write regularly. When clearing her house after her death in 1984 (my father had died eight years' earlier) I came across every letter I had written to her from Hednesford, Norton and AAFCE, neatly bundled in date order in their original envelopes. For some inexplicable reason I couldn't bring myself to read them through but consigned the bundle to the skip. Had I retained those letters my self-imposed task in writing this story would undoubtedly have been made much simpler: they contained a fairly detailed résumé of my activities which would have helped me now to establish dates and so on.

By 1954 letters to and from the UK were being sent via BFPO 6, bearing ordinary British postage stamps purchased from Cpl Hammersley in the RAF Support Unit, who also transacted other Post Office business such as the sale of postal orders. He may well have acted as *bureau de change* as well. Previously mail had been sent through the French postal service. I have the covers from books of 15 franc stamps, implying that postage on a letter to the UK would have been less than 4d or about 1½p. On the other hand two or more 15 franc stamps might have been required; if only I had kept those letters ...

Entertainment continued to revolve largely around the NAAFI. I went there to the cinema on at least one evening each week, my 50 franc (1s.0d or 5p) ticket being torn in half by the wild-haired Frog in between bouts of bus driving and film showing. The elderly lady from whom I had just purchased the ticket, seated in the kiosk about one yard to his left, was reputed to be his mother. The RAF, along with any Pongos who might be present pursuant to reciprocal arrangements made with the British Army cinema at Quartier Chataux in the town, sat in the cheap seats at the front while Americans, Canadians and anyone else who might understand English paid a little extra to avoid us. The Dutch, whose command of English was usually pretty good, invariably arrived as a mob escorting in their midst a lone US airman who had learned their fearsome language and from whom they appeared to have become inseparable. A series of films about Scotland Yard was shown; each time the words "Scotland Yard" appeared in the captions the entire Dutch contingent yelled "S C O T L A N D Y A R D". It kept them happy.

"Do I look like a typical American?" asked a scruffy, bespectacled and gawky looking character in a US film one evening. "Y E E S S ! !" roared the front seats. This character happened to bear a striking resemblance to a US airman on the camp who, fortunately, was not in the cinema at the time. The US Army allowed us to attend the cinema on their camp in the town on the strict understanding, however, that we weren't admitted until it had become clear that no US personnel would thereby be displaced. As this involved a long walk with no guarantee of admission I attended only once, watching the film from a vast armchair-like seat in the back row whilst stuffing myself from a bag of popcorn.

I often went to the British Army cinema. During the performance on one occasion the film was stopped to allow the orderly sergeant to enquire from the stage whether any AAFCE personnel were present — we were of course all in our civvies and therefore indistinguishable from the Pongos apart from being much better looking. We were informed that 'trouble' was expected in the town and that we should return to Camp Guynemer, preferably immediately or if we preferred at the end of the film, but in any event all together as a group and without dallying on the way. There was a strong Communist element in Fontainebleau and there were certain bars and cafés in which the British were not, shall I say, as welcome as in others. One, Les Cascades, was actually out of bounds to the RAF. On the other hand in the bar run by pro-British 'Pop' were pictures of King George VI, our present Queen and Sir Winston Churchill. I didn't often visit the bars in the town: when I chanced into one it was usually for a game of table football (which, played the RAF way, frequently resulted in the table leaving the floor) and a rum and coke or, occasionally, a glass of very light and refreshing French beer (pronounced "bee-air"; if you said "burr" you got a small glass of colourless firewater called Byrhh).

But to return to the cinema, we all decided that as we had paid our money we would stay until the end, by which time it was dark. There were about ten of us and, making our way through the unnaturally quiet streets, we became aware of headlights bearing down upon us from our rear on the wrong side of a road with no footway. First inclination was to run but we stood our ground and waited with some trepidation to see what was behind the headlights. "You lot going to AAFCE?" We had never been so pleased to see a Pongo! He had been despatched with his 3-tonner to see that we were OK and dropped us off at the entrance to our camp.

English and French were the official NATO languages. It was apparently therefore felt appropriate to place in charge of the AAFCE library, of all places, an elderly Flemish-speaking Belgian Air Force W/O whose command of English was somewhat fractured. We held some excruciating conversations during the course of his visits to the Commander's office. A likeable man with a smile for everyone, he was splendidly attired in a somewhat Ruritanian uniform festooned with orange aiguillettes (rope with knobs on!) etc. Sgt Fenney asked him to obtain for Sir Basil volume 3 of the *History of the Swiss Navy* and didn't put him out of his misery until several days and many anxious visits later.

On my first ever visit to the RAF Support Unit I had observed through the open door of a small office the forbidding figure of a flt sgt SP who gave me the once over as I passed. "Strewth" I thought "I'll have to watch my step here!" Identified by the nameplate on his door as Flt Sgt Charles Collyer BEM, he always left the door open and never removed his hat. It transpired that he was at all times anxious and waiting for the opportunity to salute an officer and sat at his desk, door open and hat on head, ready to leap to his feet and salute any officer who either chanced to pass or, incredibly, happened on the other end of his telephone. Yes, he saluted the telephone receiver! A large, quietly spoken and gentle man, he was a most unlikely occupant of his rank and trade. He was married to a French woman who, allegedly, had hit him over the head with her frying pan during the course of a domestic dispute the details of which are best left unsaid.

In his capacity as Deputy Supreme Commander, Field Marshal Viscount Montgomery had visited AAFCE in an earlier year. Rumour had it that, each time his official car stopped, Collyer was there to whip open the great man's door and throw up a huge salute. He was said to have pursued the car on his bicycle. "By Jove", Monty may have thought to himself, "the Air Force seem to have plenty of these flight sergeant chappies — and they all look the same, what?" Reference to the field marshal always reminds me of the wartime newspaper headline "MONTY FLIES BACK TO FRONT"; no wonder we won the war with such versatile leaders!

I don't think Collyer can have done very much police work: living in the Fontainebleau area with a 'native', so to speak, he had become something of an expert on local taxes and so on and his knowledge and experience were of great help to other married personnel similarly living outside the camp. Sir Basil recognized the value of this expertise, frequently summoned Collyer to his office to seek his advice and vetoed repeated attempts to post him elsewhere. He didn't take kindly to being addressed as "Chief", "Chiefy" or "Flight" — he said that he was neither a Red Indian nor a bird — but wished to be called "Flight Sergeant". It is therefore difficult to believe now that I, a humble SAC, had the temerity to goad such an outwardly imposing and frightening figure while he awaited Sir Basil's call in our outer office: "Come on, Chiefy, have a seat and take the weight off your feet. Why not take your hat off while you wait?" He did, just once, and proved to be nearly bald.

He wanted to know where I had been stationed before coming to AAFCE. "Norton, ah yes, Norton, and where is Norton?" he asked "and who was in charge of the police at Norton?" I explained and a faraway look came into his eyes. "Cpl Simmons, ah yes, Cpl Simmons, yes I remember Cpl Simmons well. And how is Cpl Simmons?" "Don't know, Flight, I haven't seem him since last August". Before I had time to explain that, in any event, it wasn't the practice of erks to make friends of, or socialize with, SPs, he had vanished, saluting, through the communicating door to the officers' room adjoining mine. To be fair to the SPs at AAFCE they weren't a bad lot as SPs go. Their main task was, after all, in company with their international colleagues to maintain the security of the camp as a whole and the HQ in particular rather than to go around harassing the likes of me.

As was the case with Cpl Simmons at Norton, I was in quite a fortunate position so far as SPs were concerned. They were billeted in rooms on the floor above mine in block 12M and I was the only man in the block to possess an electric iron — and I had several. I can't explain why, but I did.

SPs were, of course, avid pressers of uniforms, a power point for this purpose being available in the common room between the two wings of the block. My irons were available to all for hire at 10 francs a time (about 2½d or 1p). One iron had a temporary fault in that it appeared to blow up after a few minutes' use but was all right again when it had cooled down; it was hired to any SP who might have incurred our displeasure and it was good to see his embarrassment when he returned it, apparently broken. It wasn't all profit: one of the irons ceased to work and I decided it needed a new element. A stroke of genius led me to ask in the electrician's emporium in Fontainebleau for *un élément*; I fitted it using my cycle toolkit and it worked.

To turn to one who didn't hire my irons, unhappily mustachioed AC1 Leon ('Firmy') La Porte was a frightened little Frenchman, admin orderly by trade, who had exercised the little-known right available to citizens of NATO countries to undertake their National Service in the armed forces of a fellow member-country. The horrors he must have endured during square-bashing don't bear thinking about. A Parisian, 'Firmy' had done well to wangle himself what was effectively a home posting. We were each rationed to 300 English cigarettes a week, obtainable from the gum-chewing young lady in the NAAFI kiosk at 50 francs (1s.0d or 5p) for twenty. After more than forty years it is probably doing 'Firmy' no disservice to say that, each Friday evening, he drove to Paris with his car (yes, he owned a CAR!) stuffed with non-smokers' cigs sold to him at a small profit and destined for the black market. As far as I know he never got caught although I believe an SP involved in the same trade was apprehended. The same SP was later to become involved with a married woman and absent himself without leave. Caught in Switzerland he was brought to book, the story reaching the London national newspapers. As for 'Firmy', he eventually transferred to the RCAF and increased pay!

In Paris I was once offered black market English cigs in the street; it was interesting to speculate as to where they had started their illegal journey: in the back of my locker perhaps? The frequency of locker inspections in block 12M precluded the stockpiling of cigs for 'Firmy' although, using our blue perforated ration cards, we were able to buy last week's, this week's and next weeks's rations, i.e. 900, in one transaction.

On or about Maundy Thursday 15 April Sgt Fenney and I were both given the opportunity to fly to the UK in the Devon, a snag being that there would be no return flight after Easter. The Devon was by now long overdue for a major service and, to my surprise, Welshman Stan Fenney hesitated and eventually decided he wouldn't go. My surprise arose from the fact that, during the war, he had been aircrew, a flight sergeant navigator in fact. However, he had been the sole survivor of a Lancaster bomber shot down over Beauvais: sheltered by the French resistance, he evaded capture until the arrival of the British Army. This experience didn't prevent him flying home with me later in the year. Having left the RAF after the war he very soon applied to re-join. He was not permitted to re-gain his previously held Commission in the Equipment Branch and now found himself, as a sergeant, little more than a filing clerk — a sad little tale really. Another long-server patently unhappy under an oversize beret, he still had his officers' raincoat which, without any indication of rank, he donned during inclement weather, leading to confusion among our allies as to whether or not he merited a salute.

Although I believe Stan's personal circumstances were such as to give him cause for unhappiness and he was to a certain extent a very private character, outwardly he was robust, amiable and sociable. It was noticeable on days when I didn't use my bike but walked to and from the office with Stan that nearly everyone — and not just RAF personnel — was greeted with the inclination of the head and the clucking of the tongue which were his trademarks. Not so the young French office cleaning lady if she was still around when we arrived in the morning. Instead: *"Voilà"*, waving a bunch of keys, *"les clés de mon cœur!"* followed by an aside to me in English which had better not be repeated in a family story. Her blushes were exceeded only by those inflicted by Stan upon poor Betty, the redheaded Deputy NAAFI Manageress who was eventually to become his wife.

Possessed of a somewhat rolling gait, better suited perhaps to a sailor than an airman, Stan was to remain at AAFCE until December 1958; walking alongside him tended almost to induce in one a state of seasickness! To Stan I was "my boy Kate" and, in the office, he would occasionally try to get away with referring to Fg Off Lees as Robin or "the boy Robin". The considerable difference between their ages and the fact that he had previously been an officer of more senior rank presumably gave him the confidence or cheek to attempt this. The response was invariably stony!

Stan had played semi-professional soccer for Hereford United and Newport County and was still on the books of Swansea Town for whose Reserves he turned out when on leave. His main claim to fame was playing for Newport County when they were defeated 13–0 by Newcastle United in 1948. He remembered being a member of a Hereford side at Chelmsford, a match at which, as I said in Chapter 3, I may well have been a spectator. Although no longer a youngster 'Twinkle', so termed for his twinkling feet, was still a fine footballer and he captained and ran both the RAF AAFCE team and the international HQ team. The latter side didn't take life too seriously and featured at left back a Canadian officer who didn't really know too much about what was going on, as well as myself making up the number at right half. It was good experience to play alongside Stan, solid as a rock, in the centre and, very occasionally if I did something right, to hear his "Well done, Kate!" "Tough as old boots" my mother would have said of him; "ouch!" was more likely from opposing forwards as they bounced off him.

I suppose I must have taken my dreadful old football boots out to France although I can't remember doing so. Every time I used them I ended up crippled by nails from the worn down studs sticking through the 'wooden' soles, not to mention the rock-hard toecaps. I also had a few Wednesday afternoon outings with an RAF team, playing on one occasion in a proper stadium before a crowd comprising three beret-clad Froggies, a small boy and an elderly dog. I didn't play in any of the weekend matches against teams from small towns and hamlets where there was a wartime connection with the RAF and about which my goalkeeping friend Moll has commented as follows:

"Oftentimes they laid on food, wine, beer, a dance and even the young ladies in their pretty frocks. I did not miss one game whilst at AAFCE unless on leave and during my tour we never lost a game. I concluded that the French teams let us win as a thank you to the Brits for liberating their country from German occupation. Great days — great games, once we won 18-0 and I scored a penalty."

But enough of football! Because of Stan's hesitation I dithered for a while about the Easter trip in the Devon. However, I learned that the purpose of the flight was to return a visiting Army general — Lieutenant General Sir Frederick Brownjohn — to the UK and eventually I decided that, if his important life was to be entrusted to the Devon, then who was I to worry about mine? I accepted the offer and, by now feeling quite experienced at this flying game, decided to return by air under my own steam on Easter Monday. Sqn Ldr Paston-Williams duly flew us from Melun to, I believe, Bovingdon and I surprised my family by turning up unexpectedly for three full days at home.

Undoubtedly Geof was at home some of the weekend: my last sight of him until January 1956. On Good Friday I cycled to the speedway at Rayleigh and enjoyed seeing the Rockets defeat the Swindon Robins 50-32; I gave the following evening's match against the Exeter Falcons a miss. On Saturday I withdrew £2 from my civilian POSB account, no doubt with an eye to the expensive travelling day to come on the Monday; the sums involved appear quite ridiculous now. On Easter Monday 19 April I returned via Heathrow and BEA to Paris Le Bourget (now Charles de Gaulle) Airport. I had very much hoped to fly in one of the modern and much-vaunted four-engined turboprop Vickers Viscounts. 444 of these fine aircraft were built and many are still in use. No such luck: the aircraft was an Elizabethan, in earlier days known as the Airspeed Ambassador. I was to wait thirty-six years before flying in a Viscount. In May 1990 I flew on holiday from Southend Airport to Guernsey via Jersey in a fairly clapped out specimen proclaiming itself, on the outward journey, to be the Gambia Air Shuttle. On return to Southend, a mechanic was working on the starboard outer engine even before I had disembarked.

Simps and I both had cameras on camp, mine being the modest Hawkeye I had used while at Norton. I had taken a few photos around the billet area and at Nice but, on Saturday 1 May, we decided upon a photographic expedition around the town and the grounds of the palace to give our families at home some idea of what Fontainebleau looked like. Unfortunately the palace itself wasn't open to the public. Wandering around its grounds we wondered whether there was any truth in the tale that Napoleon used to row Josephine out to the pavilion on the tiny island in the lake at the rear of the palace; we didn't know but what we did know was that the lake contained giant carp which, unlike other visitors, as impoverished airmen we didn't feed. My photos show sparsely populated streets and deserted palace grounds — on a Saturday afternoon! The town was pleasant enough with adequate shopping facilities — the *Prisunic*, France's answer to Woolworths, being the source of many of our modest requirements such as notepaper and envelopes. There were some very poor areas within the town, where the overriding odour was one of drains rather than the usual garlic and Gauloises. It was said that handfuls of one franc coins strewn around (worth about one farthing or one tenth of a new penny each) would produce hordes of scrabbling locals.

Upon completion of eighteen months' service my pay increased again on Monday 3 May to the level enjoyed by regulars. The attentive reader may recall from Chapter 1 that such an increase was introduced as a sop to pressure groups when the period of compulsory service became two years in 1950. The increase of 3s.0d a day, less income tax for the first time in the RAF at 2d a day, took my net weekly pay to £3.4s.1d (£3.20½p) at which rate it remained until my demob. Most weeks my actual pay was 3,100 francs, equating to £3.3s.3d, and the method of payment was very civilised. Fg Off Lees or someone deputizing for him withdrew from a bank in Fontainebleau the cash required to pay all Sir Basil's personal staff and my share was handed to me at my desk: no more tiresome pay parades for me!

One other aspect of daily life became unusually civilized during my time at AAFCE. The normal RAF practice whereby mugs and 'irons' were taken to and from the mess ended when someone in authority realized how undignified this appeared to the other nations' airmen especially as, there being no separate corporals' club, the junior NCOs shared the mess with the erks. To make matters worse the usual tanks of alternately scalding and freezing water had not been provided for mug and iron rinsing and it was therefore necessary to wash our crocks back at the billets. Presumably the camp's architects had thought better of us in this respect and, in the cases of the other nations, they had been right to do so. We were surprised one day to discover that tables for four were laid ready with cups, saucers and cutlery and that a corporal Mess Orderly — a bespectacled and vertically challenged older man known as 'the Mekon' — had been appointed to oversee what went on in front of the serving counter.

All very luxurious but unfortunately a gradual deterioration in the standard and variety of meals in the mess occurred during 1954. It by some means came to Sir Basil's notice that the food was not all that it might have been and he paid a surprise visit one tea time, trailed by ADC Fg Off Lees sporting golden aiguillettes. Only I, sworn to secrecy, knew what was afoot. The consternation among the cooks, resplendent in their filthiest 'whites' and wearing their most ridiculous hats, was a joy to behold. I don't suppose any of them had ever set eyes on so much 'scrambled egg' and 'fruit salad' — apposite terms in the circumstances — adorning the uniform of one individual. The catering officer, a former pilot who had been obliged to cease flying due to eyesight problems, was not present and the can had to be carried by, I believe, a sergeant.

"Any complaints?" Sir Basil and his entourage approached every table except that at which I was sitting. Nobody said a word. Next morning Sir Basil called me into his office, sought my opinion of the meal (toad in the hole — he asked whether there was actually any toad in my hole!) and, in the light of my critical comments, asked why I thought he had received no response in the mess. I could only suggest that the airmen were possibly intimidated by the presence of the catering sergeant and perhaps also nervous about complaining to an officer of his high rank. Half a dozen airmen were next collared at random and wheeled in to give Sir Basil their views in private. The catering officer was then on the wrong end of a hefty rocket, threatened with the loss of his job, instructed to sort out the failings in the cookhouse and told to get up to the Paris food markets and use a bit of imagination. The food improved dramatically. One eminently sensible change: the Bradford pastrycook with whom I had shared a room initially was given responsibility for all sweet preparation. As it happens I have a sweet tooth and I was sometimes the grateful recipient of a double helping when he was serving up his own, often quite excellent, creations. It wasn't what you knew that mattered but who you knew!

It was in the mess another tea time that we first became aware that the much heralded and, in Bill Rudman's case, long awaited influx of WRAF nurses had arrived — all six of them, apparently in the charge of one WRAF officer upon whom I never set eyes and who was a replacement Adj. Bill couldn't wait for the opportunity to start issuing items of ladies' underwear over the stores counter. As we queued for our tea, Bill pointed in the general direction of the half dozen civvies-clad and reticent young ladies and exclaimed "That one is — MINE!" We didn't know to whom he was referring but he seemed happy enough, Angela in Manchester or no Angela in Manchester — and he continued to be happy enough with 'his' WRAF (LACW Diane Lawson) until posted in August 1954 to RAF Horsham St Faith, the site of Norwich Airport! We understood it had been considered necessary to supplement the hitherto all-male nursing staff at the hospital with some females in view of the rapidly increasing birth-rate among the wives of RAF personnel.

There was some freak weather in England during May; snow fell heavily in some areas, including parts of Essex, on 17 May. In contrast, although we had as yet no inkling of this we were about to experience quite a long, hot summer in Fontainebleau. My brother Geof's summer was to be a lot longer and a lot hotter: on Wednesday 2 June he left a foggy Liverpool by troopship for the Canal Zone. My parents were very upset at having a second son posted abroad; to them, France was probably just as far away as Egypt even if a little less hazardous. As it happened I was about to surprise and cheer them up a little by spending the first weekend in June at home. Sir Basil was himself to fly the Devon to RAF Northolt, in West London, to collect an air chief marshal — Sir William Dickson, Chief of the Air Staff, I believe — and fly him back.

I should perhaps explain that officers of Sir Basil's rank were not expected to pilot themselves. However, Sir Basil had always 'led from the front' and invariably relegated Sqn Ldr Paston-Williams to the right-hand seat while Flt Lt Walker found himself in the unenviable position of navigating from the passenger cabin. All my flights were in the nature of 'gash flips', covered by my signature on the 'blood chit' mentioned previously. Never once did Sir Basil question my presence on an aircraft: not many erks can boast of being flown by an air chief marshal.

On this occasion Cpl 'Nobby' Clark took me to Melun/Villaroche in the front of the left-hand drive Humber staff car, calling at the Hôtel de Bellune to collect Sir Basil on the way. This fine house, built in the late eighteenth century, had been provided by the French Government as a residence for the AAFCE Commander. Staff there comprised one sergeant and one corporal, both RAF, to whom I spoke on the telephone but never met. 'Nobby' told me to wait in the car while he went into the house which, secluded behind trees, I was unfortunately therefore unable to see. As anticipated Sir Basil indeed took the controls of the Devon. We were met at Northolt by Sir William and, with his chauffeur, I stood saluting on the tarmac as Sir Basil, in his element, taxied out for the return trip. The chauffeur, a corporal, kindly conveyed me in the front seat of an identical, but right-hand drive, Humber to Sloane Square Underground Station, close to which his chief had a flat, and promised to meet me there for the return journey (which he duly did). I remember going into the flat but cannot think why!

I have no recollection of the weekend, save that I cycled to speedway on Saturday 5 June to see the Rockets win a close encounter with the Ipswich Witches 43–41. On the morning of my return trip, Sqn Ldr Paston-Williams had brought Sir William back to Northolt and I believe the afternoon flight was the occasion when, with Lady Embry aboard, we encountered over Paris the most vicious storm clouds imaginable. We flew straight into them, our world turned black when not illuminated by blinding flashes of lightning, the poor old Devon did everything but invert itself and water poured from around the escape hatch on to my best blue. Needless to say I was strapped into my seat and couldn't move elsewhere to escape the deluge. In her seat on the other side of the aircraft Lady Embry continued with her knitting, for all the world as if she was sitting in the drawing room of the Hôtel de Bellune. "You seem to be sitting in the wrong seat" she said.

Stan Fenney was aboard one flight with me, *en route* to Wales for UK leave. I believe the aircraft was the Devon and I think we landed at RAF Northolt (today still an RAF station). This was the only time I was required to clear Customs before or after an RAF flight — no problem as far as I was concerned but Stan's case contained many hundreds of cigarettes covered by a thin layer of clothing. We arranged that I would present myself first in the small Customs shed and try to engage the lone officer in conversation while he checked my **small** suitcase and found nothing untoward in the hope that, in the process, he would more or less overlook Stan. This worked and his guilty case wasn't opened.

Another flight to the UK occurred quite soon after the delivery of Sir Basil's replacement aircraft — a Hunting Percival Pembroke C1. He spent the day it arrived at the airfield and flying it around and we didn't set eyes on him in the office. The Pembroke was a new high-wing communications aircraft powered by a pair of 550 hp Alvis Leonides 127 radial engines. With a crew of two it conveyed eight passengers and I found it a pleasant and comfortable aircraft. The high wings afforded passengers a much better view of the ground than obtainable in low-wing aircraft, a bonus for those on 'gash flips'. A few were still in service with the RAF in Germany in the late 1980s.

I flew in the Pembroke to Northolt, the reason for the flights in both directions being to convey Lady Embry to and from the UK. When I presented myself at Northolt for the return flight, due in the morning, I learned that Lady Embry wished after all to fly to Melun from RAF Hendon in the afternoon and it was therefore necessary to reposition the aircraft. This flight of only seven or eight miles over North-West London was obviously made at low level and was a novel and interesting experience. Hendon airfield — best remembered as the site for the pre-war annual RAF air displays and spectaculars — is now the site of the RAF Museum.

It appeared that Hendon hadn't previously seen a Pembroke because as soon as we disembarked we (Sqn Ldr Paston-Williams, Flt Lt Walker and I) were surrounded and questioned about the aircraft by interested officers and airmen. Leaving me to face the inquisitors the two officers disappeared, presumably in the direction of the officers' mess for drinkiepoos and lunch. "I've got to get out of this" I told myself, hardly the best bloke to deal with technical queries, "and quickly". Aware at what hour Lady Embry was expected I decided to get off the station without delay and kill time elsewhere. I don't remember reporting to the guardroom before leaving but I suppose I must have done so.

From the nearest Underground station (Colindale) it was a direct trip on the Northern Line to Embankment. The weather was fine but not too warm, leading me to wonder whether this trip perhaps occurred as late as in September, and I simply strolled around for an hour or so, leaning on the parapet of Westminster bridge for a while watching the river traffic. Returning to RAF Hendon my saluting nightmare came to life. Walking along the road outside the station I espied coming towards me an individual who simply didn't look like an officer. He seemed too short and untidy and was wearing a raincoat like Stan Fenney's, with no indication of rank. I decided not to salute. "COME HERE AIRMAN, WHY DID YOU NOT SALUTE ME?" followed by the inevitable harangue, all the more embarrassing for taking place on a public road. I explained that his raincoat bore no indication of rank — which I am sure it should have done — and he mellowed somewhat. "I'll give you a tip airman" pointing at his hat "look at the cap badge in future". He wanted to know who I was and what I was doing. As soon as I uttered the words "Air Chief Marshal Sir Basil Embry" his whole manner changed and it seemed almost as if I had been ticking him off rather than the other way round! Telling me to hurry along and join my flight, we exchanged salutes and he scuttled off down the footway.

It must appear that I spent an awful lot of time gallivanting around on 'gash flips'; well, perhaps I did, but I think I would have been foolish to turn down the never-to-be-repeated opportunities presented to me by Sqn Ldr Lewis and Fg Off Lees. Very few National Servicemen I am sure were given the chance to fly as often as I did and, as I intimated earlier, even fewer had the honour — yes, it was an honour — to be flown by a man of Sir Basil's rank and fame.

Time needs to be spent on the more serious side of life at AAFCE but, before tackling such more weighty matters, I would like to say a little about Paris and my several off-duty visits to the magic city!

CHAPTER 10

PARISIAN INTERLUDES

The date: Saturday 19 June 1954. The time: probably before noon. The place: a traffic island in the centre of the Avenue des Champs Élysées. The scene, facing north-west towards the Place de l'Étoile and with the Place de la Concorde behind me: a serene and untroubled vista, closed by the distant Arc de Triomphe, revealing one pedestrian on the right-hand footway, half a dozen parked cars in the middle distance on the left, the nearest moving vehicle at least one hundred yards away, and acres of exposed tarmacadam. Although I have a photograph to prove it and in spite of the fact that I was obviously there to hold the camera, I still find it difficult to believe that I saw the heart of Paris so deserted at a weekend. A leisurely stroll along the tree-lined boulevard as far as l'Étoile revealed to LAC Simpson and me a pair of *glacés* salesladies, their two-wheeled handcarts unpatronized and not a pedestrian in sight. Incredible!

Simps and I were enjoying one of the several weekend expeditions to the capital which we had decided it would be foolish not to undertake while we had the opportunity. On a weekend when we were both free on the Saturday morning, we would travel to the Gare de Lyon either by train No.108 (at 0914) or train No.208 (at 1004, later 0953) from Fontainebleau-Avon station. The journey took around 40–50 minutes. First priority always was to locate a cheap (even if perhaps crummy!) hotel in which to spend the night and have breakfast on Sunday morning. My recollection is that we usually headed for the back streets on the smaller of the two islands in the Seine — the Ile St Louis — but, strangely, the two hotels which I am still able to name were miles from there! The Grand Hotel de l'Union at 65 Rue du Chateau-d'Eau was in the north-eastern quarter of the city, not far from the Gare de l'Est, while the Hotel de Saumur at 22 Rue de Bellechasse was much more centrally situated, in the vicinity of 'the Invalids'.

Our weekend breaks were very sedate: neither Simps nor I was the type to 'live it up'. Rather we preferred to see as much of the city as we could at minimum expense. Although he was a regular airman and therefore somewhat better off than I (until I had completed eighteen months' service anyway), neither of us had a lot of cash to spare. Usually we got around on foot, using the Métro only to travel longer distances. I found the Métro to be both cheaper and easier to understand than the London Underground system. For a start the fare — 45 francs 2nd class — was standard for all journeys. Although this equated to as little as about 11d (or 4½p), one could reduce it to 30 francs (about 7d or 3p) by buying for 300 francs a book of tickets *(un carnet de billets)*, not in fact a book as such but five separate tickets each of which could be used twice. One *carnet* between the pair of us probably lasted the weekend.

Inside the foyer of each Métro station was a map of the system.

Pressing the button alongside the name of one's destination station revealed the best route to take, illuminated in the different colours allocated to each of the various *lignes* and clearly indicating the *correspondances* or stations at which to change trains. At the *correspondance* one merely looked for the name of the terminus of the required *ligne*. A couple of things not in common with London's Underground of which one had to be wary: at some stations a metal barrier closed across the access to the platform as each train arrived, presumably to minimize the possibility of accidents especially at busy times. No problem on the face of it but these barriers closed without warning and with such rapidity that it wasn't beyond the bounds of possibility for an innocent RAF passenger to receive a nasty clout. Similarly, the sliding doors on the trains whipped across with a bang and one had to watch out for one's person! Presumably to confuse foreigners still further, train doors didn't open automatically; passengers had to do this by pulling sideways a lever on one of the pair which had the effect of opening both.

One Saturday, on my own for some reason on this occasion, I was standing just inside the doors of a train resplendent in my very English looking civvies 'uniform', rolled *Daily Mail* under one arm and neatly folded raincoat over the other, when fellow nationals in the form of a youngish couple, two small children and luggage collapsed into the carriage and spent the next few minutes trying to make sense of the diagram of the *ligne* on display. In a somewhat unseemly and un-British flap they decided they needed to disembark when next the train ground to a noisy halt and waited for the doors to open. When they didn't part panic ensued until, without saying anything, I reached forward and pulled the doors open. "*Merci beaucoup*" said the Englishman to the (I would have thought) obviously English man, the accent being on an excruciating par with many of those heard at Camp Guynemer.

It isn't really fair to be unkind to these poor people. There was very little tourism in the early 1950s and it was quite brave of them to venture abroad with two young children. There was probably no such thing as a package holiday; I doubt if the expression had been invented. On our expeditions around Paris we weren't plagued with the crowds — or the attendant crime — with which the city is now beset and we were really exceptionally fortunate to have the opportunity to see Paris at its best. We never used buses; they looked far too complicated, not to mention uncomfortable to the point of being dangerous. It was cheapest to travel on an open platform at the rear and accordingly that was where virtually everyone tried to stand. There seemed to be no limit to the numbers allowed on a bus and I marvelled sometimes that these decrepit old vehicles didn't stand on their tails and paw the air in desperation.

Two of our weekends in Paris were basically photographic expeditions. On 19/20 June, in addition to the Avenue des Champs Élysées and the Arc de Triomphe already mentioned, we covered such locations as La Tour Eiffel, Palais du Luxembourg, Palais de Chaillot (and NATO HQ), Hotel des Invalides, Sacré Cœur, Hotel de Ville and Notre Dame. We must have walked miles, lunching modestly *al fresco* near La Tour Eiffel. We might well have splashed out on *jambon* with our standard *deux œufs et pommes frites* but would have been unlikely to have got beans if we had asked for them. A basket of bread and a small bottle of red wine, about as far as Simps usually ventured on the alcoholic front I believe, completed the meal. We usually ate pretty frugally in view of our financial situation, although we once ventured into 'Le Marly', Café Tabac Brasserie, on the rather posh and expensive shopping street, Rue de Rivoli. Surprisingly, we also bought souvenirs at a couple of nearby shops, Levasseur & Cie and Holvoet, *Couture Frivolités Monchoirs*. We always ensured that we were back at Camp Guynemer in time for Sunday tea, thereby saving the expense of one meal. I would guess we usually travelled on train No.3251 which left the Gare du Nord at 1421 and arrived at Fontainebleau-Avon at 1513.

Our second photographic weekend wasn't until 2/3 October, one month before my demob, when we spent much of our time along the banks of the Seine. Photographs featured bridges, the Préfecture de Police and myself buying an original etching from one of *les bouquinistes* along the Quai de la Tournelle (on the left bank). The picture, *"dessiné, grave, impremé par l'artiste, Ch. Lebeau"*, features my favourite bridge, Le Pont Neuf, and hangs framed in my home. It might, but on the other hand might not, be worth a fortune! I became more adventurous with my Hawkeye this weekend, photographing one of the Seine bridges at night with an exposure of two minutes and capturing the magic of the Métro, underground on the platform at Gare de Lyon station.

In his quiet way Simps was a good companion in Paris. Unlike myself he had taken the trouble to discover something of the city in advance and was therefore able to point us both in the right direction most of the time. The weekends made a pleasant change from the increasing boredom of the camp where there was little in the way of worthwhile off-duty activity during the day. There was no television or radio. I had my bike, of course, for the occasional lone spin; Fontainebleau town and the palace were at hand; we sunbathed and kicked a football at the rear of the billet; and, despite the risk of getting lost, some of us ventured into the forest (where I was surprised to find a few rocky outcrops) for the occasional stroll. To this day I suspect Smiffy still believes we spotted therein a crocodile of the amphibious reptilian variety; we never let on that we were referring to an organized gaggle of small children disappearing into the trees. What with the heat of the 1954 summer and the sandy soil in the area, he could perhaps be forgiven for appearing to swallow our story.

A Parisian break from the monotonous and unimaginative fare of the airmen's mess and the NAAFI was welcome too. We couldn't afford to experiment very much but at least the style of cooking was different and the ambience of a typical French restaurant had something which neither the mess nor the NAAFI could ever hope to match! It shouldn't be assumed that meals revolved entirely around *œufs et pommes frites* — because they didn't — but I have to confess that my favourite dish consisted of a goodly helping of *jambon*, eaten straight from the circular metal pan in which it had been cooked, with at least *deux* lightly done and therefore somewhat runny *œufs* on top. A side dish piled high with real French *pommes frites*, thin and piquant, and a glass of light beer would complete a meal fit for a king — or an SAC at any rate!

Our strolls around the aromatic streets of Paris — nostrils were seemingly always assailed by at least one odour, be it coffee, cooking, garlic, Gauloises, drains, traffic or just hot air from a footway grating — were basically free from incidents or difficulties. We just enjoyed the ever-changing scene and the seemingly permanent good weather, grateful for the opportunity to do so. There occurred one minor irritation. I had arranged to meet Simps on a Saturday afternoon outside the source of a good cup of English tea — W. H. Smith's colonnaded bookshop situated just off the Place de la Concorde at the most expensive end of the Rue de Rivoli. I arrived first and was perusing the books on display in the window when I became aware of a small ball of grease on legs, wearing a shiny grey suit, loitering on my right. Eventually it approached. "You are Eengleesh?" it asked. I suppose I could have denied this, but didn't. Pity I couldn't have replied in Swahili or Icelandic or something. Anyway, it (the greaseball) tried to persuade me to go to its place, which I was assured had every luxury, for tea. I told it in effect to "shove off" but it wasn't inclined to do so. Accordingly I resorted to the same ploy as on a previous occasion when I had been approached in similar, but not identical, fashion (by a railwayman at Liverpool Street station, when travelling home from RAF Norton). Now, as then, I introduced into the 'conversation' the magic letters R, A and F and for the second time my tormentor backed off rapidly. Must be something worthwhile about our Service — at least its acronym — after all! The greaseball was still lurking in the distance when Simps emerged from the Métro entrance on the other side of the road, permitting himself just a little grin.

I paid two weekend visits to Paris other than in Simps' company. For some unexplained reason an erk hailing from Portsmouth (I think, although I can't be certain, that he was LAC Platt with whom I had travelled on UK leave in February) selected me for the doubtful honour of accompanying him to the capital one Saturday in high summer in order to meet and escort for the weekend two sisters, also from Portsmouth. Although Platt had the whole complement of Camp Guynemer from whom to chose, the invitation was put to me in such a way as to imply that if I didn't accept the poor girls would be let down and it would be my fault. As in the case of the Sheffield nurse with the wooden leg, how could I let a lady — worse, two ladies — down?

The weekend was an utter *débâcle* as far as I was concerned. One of the girls lived or worked in Paris and her sister was coming over to join her for a break. Platt and I were to meet them on the Saturday afternoon. We duly travelled to Paris after breakfast on what must have been just about the hottest day of a hot summer. Before mid-day I was suffering from a severe migraine headache, literally the first I can recall of the succession which have plagued my life ever since. Crossing one of the many Seine bridges I recall saying "I'm sorry, I just can't go on, I've got to do something about this headache". I was able to buy from a kiosk at the end of the bridge one of the pink and blue paper strips of Aspro tablets familiar to sufferers in the UK at the time and somehow convey myself to the hotel into which we had booked and the whereabouts of which I am glad to have forgotten. Meanwhile a disgruntled Platt went off to meet the girls. I believe he thought I had done it deliberately but I would assure him or any other doubter that nobody has a migraine pain for the fun of it.

I was in bed for the best part of twenty-four hours with virtually nothing to drink or eat, a scenario which I now know to be entirely wrong for a migraine — at least for a migraine of the sort to which I am subject. It is in fact very important to eat regularly, to drink plenty and, in my case, not to lie down. By Sunday lunch-time my fragility had eased just sufficiently to enable me to join the other three for a stroll around the lakes in the Bois de Boulogne, the magnificent area of parkland to the west of the city — all I had to show for the only weekend visit I would prefer to forget.

My second trip without Simps proved to be a very different kettle of fish! SAC David Mollart-Rogerson, a room-mate, was due to celebrate his twenty-first birthday on Tuesday 26 October, just four days prior to my return to the UK. (Incidentally, he was never known by his Christian name but usually as Moll or, occasionally, Danny — a perceptive erk, Sandy McLaughlan, had thought he resembled Danny Kaye, the entertainer.) With Smiffy, we decided to spend the previous weekend in Paris, I to return to camp Sunday evening and the other two Tuesday evening, i.e. on Moll's birthday. Tall, slim, ruddy complexion, too much hair to hide in a beret and of vaguely agricultural gait, Moll, from Southampton, was a fine goalkeeper. He worked in the HQ Central Registry.

Weatherwise, we had an appalling weekend. My hopes of a relaxing cruise along the Seine on one of the imposing Bateaux-Mouches were soon dashed by the rain which fell almost non-stop on the Saturday. Smiffy and I were reduced to wearing the raincoats which, as part of our 'uniforms', should of course have been carried over our arms while Moll, with only a short green jerkin, suffered most from the elements. It goes without saying that we didn't have any headgear. We established ourselves in the Hotel Solférino, close to the Métro station of the same name and in the vicinity of 'the Invalids', where we were each obliged to pay the princely sum of 500 francs (10s.0d or 50p) per night for bed and breakfast — in bed! And it wasn't crummy either — although the bed might have been crumby! We hadn't been in Paris long before we allowed ourselves to be conned into contributing to a street collection in aid of *La Journée Nationale des Paralysés et Infirmes Civils*.

Our main objective during the wet Saturday afternoon was to book ourselves seats for the evening's show at the Folies-Bergère. We made our way to the theatre at 32 Rue Richer, in Montmartre, and were peering at the model of the auditorium on display in the foyer when a scruffy herbert emerged from a dark corner and, in fractured English, explained to us the details of the model which, as intelligent young airmen, we found clear

133

anyway. Nevertheless we thought "What a nice man" and thanked him, whereupon out shot his hand in anticipation of a tip. Needless to say he wouldn't retire to his dark corner, like a spider awaiting its next prey, until we had coughed up. After this inauspicious beginning things could only get better. We ate in Montmartre (at 'Dupont Métropole') and were back at the music-hall, to use the correct term, in good time for the show — *Une Vraie Folie* — at 2030. Seats at the side of the second balcony had cost us 510 francs (10s.2d or 51p) each and, but for the fact that I had left my trusty John Lennon specs back at Camp Guynemer thereby preventing me from appreciating the finer points, I think we all enjoyed the show.

Sunday morning was heavily overcast with intermittent rain. Our principal activity, costing 50 francs, was to ascend by lift to the top of the Arc de Triomphe from which eminent position a magnificent view and some optimistic photography were spoiled by the inclement weather. By afternoon the rain appeared to have ceased, at least for a while, and we took ourselves off to the Stade Buffalo, on the southern outskirts of the city, to witness the France v England stock-cars international. It cost us 400 francs each (8s.0d or 40p) and we didn't really get value for money. Perched high on concrete terracing upon which one couldn't sit in comfort for very long, we were miles from the action, such as it was. The English team, which included one lady (Tanya Crouch), were driving what I had recently seen in use at Rayleigh speedway stadium, namely, 'old bangers' modified by the removal of such unnecessary luxuries as seats and windows and the addition of safety measures like roll-bars and mesh windscreens. The French team appeared to be driving cars little short of specially built for the purpose and, accordingly, I believe in every race all the French competitors finished in front of all the English. The only excitement I can recall arose when one of the French cars was seen to be on fire. The flames were extinguished when the vehicle passed through one of the huge puddles on the track, the driver seemingly unaware of what had transpired.

As arranged I returned to camp on the Sunday evening, leaving the other two to make the most of two more days. I am aware that, on the Tuesday (Moll's twenty-first), they saw the American film *Three Coins in the Fountain*, with Clifton Webb, Dorothy McGuire, Jeanne Peters, Louis Jordan, Maggie McNamara and Rossano Brazzi, presumably at the Ermitage cinema. *Fontaine des Amours*, the French language version of this 1954 film, which was not only in Technicolour but also in the new-fangled CinemaScope, was showing in three other Paris cinemas — the Max Linder, the Alhambra Ciné Music-Hall and the Cigale. I don't somehow think my friends would have preferred that version.

So much for Paris. I may not have appreciated fully at the time — although I certainly do now — just how fortunate I was to have the opportunity to get to know that fair city so well before the days of mass tourism and largely at the expense of Her Majesty's Government. Chapter 13 will show that I did return a few years' later; things had changed and certainly not for the better.

In passing, it might be worth mentioning that one day I most certainly did *not* visit the capital was Wednesday 14 July — Bastille Day and a French national holiday. An AAFCE holiday too, we in the RAF were expressly forbidden to go to Paris in view of the harm which might befall innocents abroad on such a day. Instead, some of my comrades saw fit to stagger home at about 0500 the next morning having attended a dance organized for the military in Fontainebleau.

CHAPTER 11

FINAL MONTHS IN FRANCE

"Ein zwei, ein zwei, ein zwei" cried Sqn Ldr Lewis, goosestepping through our outer office. It was to be years before I discovered that *"ein zwei"* didn't mean "left right". On the other hand he taught me correctly how to answer the office telephone in French: extensions 2051 and 2059 were, respectively, *"vingt, cinquante et un"* and *"vingt, cinquante-neuf"*. One morning he arrived for work suffering badly from the effects of a car accident the previous evening. Two black eyes and severe facial bruising were merely the obvious signs of injury. Sir Basil took one look and told him to return home and I believe he did so later in the day. I am afraid AAFCE personnel proved to be somewhat prone to traffic accidents with the result that the wreck of a crashed red saloon was positioned just inside the entrance to the domestic side of the camp for all to see when entering or leaving; a USAF master sergeant had in fact been killed late in 1953.

During one of Sir Basil's frequent absences from the office (often he was away for several days at a time visiting NATO formations in West Germany and elsewhere), I allowed myself to be goaded into strutting around his office wearing one of the spare uniform jackets stored in his dressing-room. I must confess I thought I looked pretty good with pilot's wings and five rows of medal ribbons! And I wouldn't reach my twentieth birthday until 7 July! But I was to surpass even that, presumably, chargeable offence on a celebrated occasion in June or July to which I will admit shortly.

I have already alluded to the long, hot summer from which we were all benefiting or suffering according to one's individual point of view. Sir Basil had been concerned for some time about the fact that most, if not all, our international colleagues had the benefit of lightweight summer uniforms whilst the RAF could do no better than revert to shirtsleeve order, i.e. jettisoning uniform jackets, rolling up shirtsleeves (neatly of course) but continuing to perspire under the usual heavy trousers. Admittedly those who had served in the Middle or Far East and had retained their KDs (tropical kit) had permission to wear them but I think Sir Basil felt, as did the rest of us, that we would become a laughing stock mooching around in khaki Eric Morcambe-style long shorts (or were they short longs?). As it was the RAF — and, for that matter, our Army colleagues — felt themselves second-class citizens. Sir Basil felt sufficiently strongly to have represented the position to the Air Ministry on a number of occasions and, although I can't substantiate this, I did understand at the time that Monty, over at SHAPE, had been in touch with the War Office at the same time. There just might have been some collusion but, whether or not, no progress was made.

Of far greater moment, Sir Basil was not too happy about certain aspects of the NATO situation — upon which I am not competent to comment but upon which he elaborated in his autobiography *Mission Completed* (Methuen, 1957) — as well as being concerned about a number of the conditions to which RAF personnel were subject, especially when compared to those of their colleagues in the other five Air Forces, e.g. pay, allowances and, of course, uniforms. He made himself somewhat unpopular by making noises in high places about all these matters with the eventual result that, subsequent to my own departure for demob, he was invited to retire early from the Service.

Included in those 'high places' was Royalty in the person of HRH The Duke of Edinburgh who accepted an invitation to visit AAFCE during the summer of 1954. Escorted at high speed by police motor-cyclists, the Duke's convoy forced an unfortunate French civilian's vehicle into a ditch during the journey to Camp Guynemer. The Duke arrived in the uniform of Admiral of the Fleet. Fg Off Lees accepted the proffered gold-encrusted cap which, after the Duke had disappeared into the private office, was plonked upon my head by one of the officers. I've often speculated as to the possible offences with which I could have been charged on this occasion. Impersonating an officer (or a Duke)? Lèse-majesté? Could it be relevant that HRH now has about as much hair as I have?

Bill Rudman was a member of the guard of honour this day and some of my fellow erks became part-time waiters at the inevitable cocktail party. During the course of his visit the Duke planted three rhododendrons in the grounds of Fontainebleau Palace, crouching in the midst of which Smiffy — ecstatic — and I — grinning — were later photographed by Simps. One of the three shrubs died. I don't suppose anyone told HRH.

The Central Band of the RAF were in attendance for the Duke's visit. Queuing with some of the bandsmen in the NAAFI cafeteria I was astonished at the scruffy appearance of their uniforms when viewed from close quarters. The present-day band's uniforms are a far cry from those of 1954 when they were little better than standard best blues.

An earlier Royal visitor, prior to the arrival of either Sir Basil or myself, had been Prince Bernhardt of the Netherlands.

The Americans never do anything by halves. It came to the notice of the USAF that, as I mentioned in Chapter 8, Sir Basil's accommodation included a fully-equipped kitchen which had been put to no use — not even to make a pot of tea — since he took over from General Norstad in July 1953. Could the USAF use the facilities to cook a meal next time Sir Basil entertained official visitors? The great day dawned. When Stan Fenney and I arrived for work, the kitchen was already a hive of activity. Half a dozen USAF chefs were in evidence, spilling from the doorway of the quite small but well equipped room. I didn't get to see the main course but, for a luncheon party of no more than four or five, the Yanks had baked an apple pie at least two feet by eighteen inches and filled a vast insulated — I think 'barrel' is the only word to describe it — with ice-cream. I have a great fondness for apple pie and, even more so, for ice-cream and I am happy to say that I benefited from the surplus of both! Sir Basil had a great admiration for the industry and enthusiasm of Americans and I doubt if he was displeased either!

Undoubtedly on the occasion of the lunch in question I would have been required to undertake my most detested task — the ritual of *eau-glacé*. The Thermos-type insulated water jug from Sir Basil's office had to be taken to the HQ cafeteria for iced water whenever he had visitors who presumably liked it with their whisky. Unfortunately my ill-fitting serge clad arrival in the midst of the ultra-smart American women (civilian and military) who thronged the place invariably caused a log-jam in the queue, leading to my embarrassed unpopularity with staff and customers alike. The fact that I wasn't required to pay anything for this service didn't seem to help. Stan Fenney offered to undertake the duty once or twice; this could well have had something to do with the anticipated presence behind the counter of a certain redheaded Deputy NAAFI Manageress. My dislike of the task was well-known in the office. A few days before my departure from AAFCE Fg Off Lees presented me with page 786 from the issue of *Punch* magazine dated 30 June 1954. The full-page cartoon featured a civil servant, his shadow a huge figure armed with a whip, and the caption reading "According to *The Economist*, the Civil Service has become 'a despotism that is practised by the most conscientious and industrious tyrants that the world has ever seen'." Underneath he had added "For our Mr Caton — A first-class Eau-Glacé carrier — Robin Lees". The fact that I had been a local government officer and not a civil servant was beside the point: it was the thought that counted.

The use of the Christian name surprised me: in spite of our closeness in age, Fg Off Lees had always been a somewhat distant figure, like me (and quite properly) conscious of the gulf between our respective status as officer and erk. Fair haired, tall and slim, athletic in build, he represented the RAF at tennis, squash and hockey. With a Fg Off Nicholls he was to win the RAF tennis doubles three times. The son of Air Marshal Sir Alan Lees KCB, CBE, DSO, AFC, eyesight problems had prevented him from emulating his father as a pilot; however, he was destined in the 1980s to head the RAF's Administration Branch in the rank of Air Vice-Marshal. He specialised in being photographed partly hidden by, and several paces to the rear of, Sir Basil, adorned with the golden aiguillettes of his ADC-ship, clutching the official briefcase and appearing anxious.

Aware that Fg Off Lees was to meet in the final of the AAFCE tennis singles championship a USAF officer who had once played in the US clay-courts championships, I and several chums went along to the courts — located more or less between our billets and the NAAFI — one Saturday morning to discover Lees one set down and a trifle despondent. The gulf between 'them' and 'us' — officers and erks — was swiftly bridged by overriding considerations of national pride and, possibly to Lees' surprise, we gave him our support; after all he was British and the American's attitude appeared to be that he had some God-given right to win. The upshot (I like to think with the advantage of the 'crowd' on his side) was that Lees gritted his teeth and gradually clawed his way back into the match. The more he did so, the greater the number of mistakes made by the Yank who, inevitably it seemed, began to lose his temper. Lees eventually got his nose in front and won.

'SAC Slimey' or no, I wasn't always able to skive off the unwelcome tasks visited upon unwilling erks and found myself undertaking incinerator duty (on one occasion only) and weekend airfield guard duty (again, only once). Incinerator duty wasn't so bad and merely entailed being a member of an international three-man team (one officer, one non-commissioned officer and one airman) detailed to dispose of classified waste from the HQ in the brick-built incinerator hidden in a small area of forest near to the main entrance. I have to confess that I am unable to remember even the nationality of my team-mates, if they can be described as such; I, as the airman, burned the waste supervised by the non-commissioned officer, in turn supervised by the officer who, I seem to recall, wasn't very much in evidence when I undertook this duty.

Airfield guard duty was a bind. Two erks spent the weekend in the building housing the control tower and the RAF's office accommodation at Melun/Villaroche and, in effect, acted as fire picket in support of French firemen. On my weekend there I don't think we ever left the office building. From the cookhouse on Saturday morning I collected the weekend's rations, consisting solely of a tray of eggs, prior to being hurtled out to the airfield in the front seat of a small truck. MT drivers only knew one speed when no-one in authority was aboard — flat out. My endeavours to safeguard the 'rations' nearly came unstuck at the last moment when the truck was driven up the several steps leading to the building's main entrance and left at an angle of roughly 45 degrees to the horizontal. This was apparently the normal practice and resulted in descent from the cab with a tray of eggs being not the simplest of operations.

Fortunately my guard colleague had done this duty before and was something of a culinary expert, at least to the extent that he could produce amazing omelettes a foot across and about two inches thick. The secret appeared to be to beat up separately the whites and the yolks before folding one (I can't recall which!) into the other. We survived on omelettes and tea and might have played the odd game of cards; otherwise we didn't do very much at all. During the course of the weekend I was offered "feelthee peectures" by a Frenchman who was probably one of the firemen; as an upright citizen of the UK I declined politely.

I understood the French used the airfield for experimental purposes; some extraordinarily loud engine noises emanated from the far side of the field but nothing was ever visible. Melun/Villaroche had a long history: in use during the First World War, it housed the HQ of the Royal Flying Corps briefly in September 1914; the *Luftwaffe* were in residence during the Second World War, Junkers 88 long-range bombers carrying out attacks on the UK during the Battle of Britain; Douglas A-20 Havoc light bombers of the USAAF Ninth Air Force arrived from the UK in August 1944; and now, in a small way, the RAF were there!

I took part in only one parade during my fourteen months at AAFCE — at a weekend, when I wasn't able to avoid it. Best blue'd and big 'atted a large RAF contingent marched through the domestic side of the camp, out of the main gate, left wheeled on to the Rue du Rocher d'Avon, right into the Route de Moret and thence I know not where. I would guess we probably wheeled right again and then right into the main entrance to the HQ where the car park was often used for ceremonial parades. At least we of the RAF made a satisfactory noise when we marched, which was more than could be said of the Yanks. I recall an occasion when, idling along the road in front of the RAF billets, I sensed rather than heard behind me the approach of a considerable body of marching American airmen. I narrowly escaped being mown down by taking hurriedly to the grass, the silence induced by their soft-soled boots lending an almost ghostly quality to the Yanks' progress.

On the occasion of the RAF parade mentioned, I remember feeling impressed that such a disparate body of men, not involved regularly in martial activity, were able to put up a pretty good show for the few Frogs around at the time. We marched with the almost imperceptible swagger peculiar to the RAF; the Army march bolt upright while the Navy, as befits their seagoing potential, roll all over the place. We weren't burdened with rifles because foreign troops weren't normally permitted to bear arms in France. This restriction may have something to do with the fact that, arriving for work one morning, I was surprised to observe the USAF air policeman on duty at the rear entrance to the HQ unbutton his pistol holster and produce therefrom a packet of cigarettes and a lighter.

It must not be assumed from the fact that we didn't usually carry arms that Bill Rudman had nothing to look after in the armoury. On the contrary, not only had about three hundred .303 rifles to be maintained in good order but there were also a number of .38 revolvers, some Sten guns and Sir Basil's sword. I never found myself included in one of the parties of airmen taken out to a range somewhere in the forest to practise with the rifles and Stens.

The lone policemen of various nationalities detailed to guard the VIP entrance to HQ used to get pretty nervous at times; after all, their's was I suppose an awesome responsibility. During periods of inactivity the anxious SP, AP or *gendarme* on duty sat at a small table just inside the entrance. I have to confess that it was not unknown for members of the Commander's personal staff to creep out on to the carpeted landing and either speak or make some sudden noise, whereupon it was possible to observe our protector leap to his feet and stand smartly at ease having generally straightened and smartened himself up anticipating the descent from on high of Sir Basil, his Chief of Staff or someone else of importance.

To revert to lesser matters, Smiffy had been on a period of UK leave. Entering the billet on the evening of his planned return I was surprised to find not Smiffy — presumably keeping a low profile — but, instead, plonked on our small table an autochange record player of the type which, in the 1950s, was about as up-to-date as one could buy. Fifteen inches or so in width and depth, as well as in height, it had obviously been a pretty weighty burden, along with its attendant twelve inch 78 rpm records (long-

140

playing discs had only just about been invented at that time), for a small airman travelling all the way from Yorkshire. I can't recall the thing being put to any use; perhaps Smiffy hadn't appreciated there was a different voltage in France or had no suitable transformer. I've often wondered what happened to it when he returned to the UK for demob; he couldn't possibly have carried it along with all his kit and civvies. What I do know is that henceforth Moll, Simps and I had no table upon which to conduct our correspondence!

The rest of us were happy to seek our musical entertainment in the NAAFI. I have referred to the juke box and occasional live entertainment on stage in the cinema. A top singer of the day, the American Al Martino, performed on one occasion. Undoubtedly he rendered *Here in my Heart*, the number with which he was top of the first ever UK Hit Parade, published in the *New Musical Express* on 14 November 1952, the week after my enlistment at RAF Padgate. I was ashamed to be among the AAFCE audience when an English lady singer struggled to perform despite having lost her voice but, for her pains, was hooted off the stage.

An October 1954 highlight, the mid-week appearance of Ted Heath and his Band sent British morale sky-high! Having spent the day travelling by coach from Birmingham, the band arrived to find no special arrangements had been made even to feed them and they had perforce to join the rest of us, queuing for our usual *deux œufs, pommes frites et* beans, before starting their performance somewhat late. As a Ted Heath fan Moll was ecstatic. With Mrs Moira Heath sitting in the front row and all the stars present (apart from Lita Roza who was replaced by Kathy Lloyd) the band went through their celebrated routines — Johnny Hawksworth playing his double-bass horizontal on the floor for example. Don Lusher was there with his trombone, Denis Lotis sang; we returned to our billets well satisfied that night.

Entertainment of a French variety was provided some Saturday evenings. I wasn't present on the occasion when, a pair of unmentionables having been hurled from the audience to a lady performer, she changed into them on stage and threw her originals into the seething throng. (In my Preface I said this story was suitable for readers of a nervous disposition and I hope I haven't now betrayed that trust!) I took part in the much more respectable pastime of bingo on one or two occasions but won nothing, not even the monthly prize of a car! It was quite expensive to play (400 francs, about 8s.0d or 40p, an evening) and we tended to leave it to the Yanks and our own NCOs and officers who could afford it. Stout cards with square windows over which one slid a shutter when a number was called were employed and were re-usable indefinitely. A winner of the Coverall 'Giant Jackpot' on Friday 22 January 1954 — all numbers covered within the first 54 called — could choose from the following prizes:

> Crosley refrigerator
> Maytag washing machine
> Philco gas range

Dining table and four chairs
Demi-tasse set (15 pcs) or
140,000 francs (about £143) in cash

A far cry from tombola in the NAAFI at RAF Norton with prizes of a shilling or two!

By the date of my twentieth birthday, on 7 July, I was looking forward to another period of UK leave. I proposed to travel by the night ferry on Thursday 29/Friday 30 July, having received 12,800 francs leave pay from Fg Off Lees on the Wednesday. Representing just over £13, this largest-ever payment had enabled me to splash out on 600 cigarettes for my father, and Simps photographed me setting off from the billet, neatly folded raincoat over left arm and small suitcase containing fags in right hand, early on Thursday evening. I knew there would be difficulties with the Customs at Dover — the permitted maximum being 200 cigarettes per person — but I had my story ready. Despite the memories of my last (disastrous) crossing, I now had no qualms about travelling by sea. Having consulted George Will MPS, his friendly local pharmacist, my father had procured for me a small tin, clearly labelled POISON in red, containing a dozen tablets guaranteed to put an end to all forms of travel-sickness. And, in my case, they did: despite having ceased taking them even as a precaution many years ago, I've had no further problems to this day (touch wood). I am sure my self-imposed embargo on going anywhere below deck has helped. Accordingly, apart from the necessary visit to the purser's office to exchange my boarding card for a landing ticket, I spent the night of 29/30 July alone on deck.

During the period of which I write, it was the usual practice for virtually all pieces of luggage to be opened and searched by HM Customs. A chalked mark was then applied to all cleared items to enable their owners to leave the Customs hall. Whereas today they are looking for drugs and such things as explosives and weapons — not to mention illegal immigrants! — in the 1950s excessive quantities of tobacco products and alcohol, as well as cameras, watches, jewellery and similar items, were sought. I admitted to my 600 cigarettes even before my case was opened, explaining that I was a Serviceman travelling home for two weeks' leave, my ration on camp was 300 per week and I therefore had with me my two weeks' ration. "I've heard that one before" was the inevitable response; however, I think because I hadn't tried to hide anything and had taken care not to carry anything else dodgy, I got away with it. "Don't do it again" I was told; not that I would have the opportunity, demob being only three months away.

Inevitably, Bank Holiday Monday 2 August saw me cycling to Rayleigh speedway where I witnessed a rare Rockets' defeat, by 41–43 against Swindon Robins. The fifteen mile ride home seemed longer than usual. Next day I travelled to Manchester, booked myself into the Victory Club in Piccadilly (Manchester's equivalent of London's Union Jack Servicemen's Club) and made my way by bus to Wythenshawe to see my pen-friend, Valerie. I was a bundle of nerves and had the utmost difficulty in getting myself around the ham sandwich provided by her mother (echoes of 'The Aviators' café near Orly Airport). Valerie proved to be a very nice person but I think we both realized straight away that I shouldn't have made the trip. We spent a slightly strained evening walking around until, having missed the last bus going all the way into Manchester, I had some difficulty getting back to the Victory Club. I spent much of the next day in news theatres (cinemas showing newsreels), meeting Valerie during her lunch-break for something to eat and again in the evening when we went to — guess where? — another cinema! Next (Thursday) morning I left for home and our correspondence gradually fizzled out.

The only event of note during the remainder of my leave was the first ever stock-car race meeting at Rayleigh stadium, held on Saturday 14 August. I wasn't too impressed; the cars wrecked sections of the safety fencing and tore up the carefully prepared speedway track. Apart from the international meeting in Paris described in Chapter 10, I haven't watched stock-car racing since. Cycling home after dark with my brother Den disaster struck. I failed to see a very large pothole in the unlit A130 Southend road near the village of Howe Green and very nearly parted company with my trusty steed. As it was, both wheels were badly damaged and I had difficulty riding the final four or five miles home. As I was due to leave for AAFCE about nine hours later there wasn't much I could do about the incident at the time. However, Den and his school ruler cycled out to the scene next morning to photograph the (by then filled in) offending pothole, which turned out to have been about a yard in length and about a foot wide, and later arranged to spend a large proportion of my leave pay by having the wheels rebuilt with new rims, tyres and tubes. Try laying a ruler on the A130 these days in order to photograph it and you wouldn't last long!

Meanwhile my father wrote to the highway authority, my civilian employer Essex County Council, to complain about the incident and the expense I had incurred. An officer who was in later years to be a colleague of mine, Geof Leather (a wartime RAF sergeant pilot who became a POW after baling out of his shot-down bomber) drafted what I later learned to be the only possible reply. Because the pothole was not present as the result of misfeasance on the part of the highway authority (i.e. because they had done something positive to cause it) but rather as the result of nonfeasance (i.e. they hadn't actually done anything), then they accepted no liability and I had no claim on them. The law has since been changed and rightly so; it seemed quite invidious that, through no fault of my own, I had incurred expense and very nearly injury because the highway authority were able to argue a legal nicety. Nowadays they would simply refer the claim to their insurers who would settle on their behalf. All quite irrelevant to my story but important to me at the time!

All in all I had spent an unsuccessful fortnight's leave and wasn't sorry to be back at Camp Guynemer to see out the final two and a half months of my Service. Perhaps I had reaped a just reward for taking what was almost certainly an illegal second period of UK leave. I was a trifle luckier in

September: I occasionally 'invested' modestly in Moll's fixed odds football coupon and forecast the Fair 4 to result in four home wins, i.e. 1-1-1-1, on Saturday 25 September. Fair 4 matches were specially selected as being the most difficult to forecast and the least likely to result in home wins. Moll said I was mad but it so happened that I was also correct and so, with odds of 40–1 and a stake of 1s.0d (5p), I won £2. Not to be sneezed at in those days.

I have said very little about the RAF Support Unit, apart from the Education Office where I worked for a time, largely because I had very little contact with the personnel in it and therefore didn't learn too much about it. I have mentioned Cpl Hammersley, the aged postal clerk, as well as Flt Sgts Collyer (SP) and Allan (quasi-SWOman). The CO was Wing Commander R. G. M. Walker DFC; the Adj was Flt Lt E. A. Strange AFC, conspicuous by his height and grey hair and succeeded during 1954 by a lone and therefore equally conspicuous WRAF officer (Flight Officer Temple); Flt Lt Pacey was the Equipment Officer; Flt Lt Simnett was the Accounts Officer. The sergeant (accounts) was John Higgs and the orderly room corporal was Dick Rogers. Those most important of all erks, the pay clerks, were SACs "Jerry" Jerome from Swindon and Terry Ward (who I had encountered on the train at Victoria station) from Nuneaton; the POR clerk was a typist, SAC Les Goddard.

One or two commercial enterprises existed on the camp. Close to the Security block was a small colonnaded parade boasting a hairdresser, a laundry and an American Express office. The hairdresser — I can't possibly call him a 'barber' — was a lovely little old Frenchman who had previously had a shop in Fontainebleau and claimed he had cut the hair of King Edward VIII (or was it Edward VII?!). He paused in his labours, seemingly after every snip, to hold up his mirror and check that everything was to his client's satisfaction. Accordingly, haircuts seemed to take hours and, in spite of the fact that he spoke very little English, they were occasions which I very much looked forward to and enjoyed. The laundry looked after our civilian needs, including dry cleaning. The rather overpowering French lady in charge spoke very good American and therefore underpants became 'shorts' and trousers became 'pants'. (As elsewhere in the RAF we were of course able each week to send a small bundle of uniform items — shirt, socks, towel, etc — to the 'official' laundry).

I never had occasion to call at the American Express office and suspect that it may have been open to US personnel only. Certainly available exclusively to American citizens was the vast PX — Post Exchange — located nearby but not on Camp Guynemer itself. Here we understood that Yanks and their families could buy literally almost anything, from a pin to a motorcar, at extremely advantageous prices. I wouldn't be in the least surprised to learn that enterprising erks had befriended Yanks willing to obtain from the PX whatever items constituted the latest craze so that they might sell them on to RAF colleagues, perhaps at a small profit, or even hang on to them!

The Americans more or less succeeded in securing exclusive use of the sports field located close to the barrack blocks. In the early days the RAF (those "Goddamned Limeys"!) and possibly others had been able to use the field for soccer training but the Americans commandeered it for their own version of football — that strange series of short periods of activity interspersed between long lulls during which groups of players get together for a chat. I attended one or two 'games' on Saturday afternoons but never managed to stay the whole course. The Yanks didn't consider the occasion worthwhile unless at least one broken bone had resulted from it. The pitch was surrounded by a grass running track used for training purposes but only once, as far as I recall (on Wednesday 30 June 1954), for organized athletics. I felt that, on a camp the size of ours, this was a gross misuse of limited facilities. With the exception of tennis there was no provision for other sports which, if played at all, had perforce to take place elsewhere. I understand the situation did in fact improve following my departure when, after the personal intervention of Marshal Juin, an adjoining area of the forest was made available for a comprehensive sporting facility — to be known as the Embry Stadium.

Generally speaking the airmen of the six nations tended to keep themselves very largely to themselves. I have already spoken of the Americans' quite childish behaviour at times, especially after a can or two; perhaps I was over-sensitive about the fact that a group of them used to repeatedly circle the main camp roads on motorcycles during evenings but this certainly irritated me. I was never sure quite what the French got up to in off-duty hours: certainly they didn't make as much use of the NAAFI as, for example, the Americans and British. Although it's difficult to believe that the French spent most of their time in their billets, an awful lot of noise frequently emanated therefrom. I think it's possible that our hosts spent more of their off-duty hours in the town's cafés than I might have appreciated at the time; after all, in their civvies they would have been indistinguishable from the locals.

The Dutch tended to be somewhat isolated from others by their seemingly incomprehensible language! Many of them large and loud, but eminently good-natured, they gave the impression that they were present in greater numbers than was actually the case. They usually seemed to have in tow a number of female Dutch civilians who, as far as I knew, didn't work at AAFCE. What they were doing on the camp, I hesitate to suggest. Several of the airmen had with them their vast Dutch bikes which I have no doubt they had pedalled from the Netherlands, across Belgium and down through France to reach Fontainebleau. They would have thought nothing of a ride such as this. In my dotage I have acquired an extremely high regard for the Netherlands and its people. With a group of colleagues from the former Anglian Water Authority, where I was working at the time, I took my own bicycle across to the Netherlands for short cycling holidays in each of the eleven years from 1981 to 1991. In ideal cycling country (flat with excellent provision for bikes) populated by the most hospitable of people supplying adequate cheap accommodation and great food, these were very enjoyable expeditions — except, of course, when it rained. Largely,

I think, because of events during the Second World War, the British are very popular with the Dutch in any case and they couldn't have done more to help us. I've even learned a few words of their language!

The Belgians and Canadians were present in numbers roughly comparable to the Dutch but seemed much less conspicuous — to me at any rate. I was very impressed by the few Canadians I had the good fortune to meet at one time or another. In spite of their similarity in speech, they were totally different in nature from the Americans; there seemed to be a greater maturity and somehow more responsibility about their general attitude and behaviour. Of the Belgians I can say very little. I felt they seemed to be slightly in awe of their 'big brothers' and hosts, the French, with whom they were obliged to share billets and mess.

By the end of August I had been at AAFCE for one, basically enjoyable, year. My demob was now only a couple of months distant but, before recounting the events — sad as well as happy — of that short period, I feel I should say something about the man who had dominated the previous ten months or so of my life — Air Chief Marshal Sir Basil Embry.

It would be quite wrong for me to attempt to tell the story of Sir Basil's career or of his escape from occupied France; I am not in any event competent to do so. Interested readers should try to beg, borrow or steal copies of *Mission Completed* and *Wingless Victory*, publishing details of which I have already given. Born in Ireland in 1902 and therefore in his early fifties by the time I was inflicted upon his office in 1953, Sir Basil was indeed a formidable figure. Greying and not especially tall, he naturally appeared to me quite elderly but his erect posture, steely eyes and usually unsmiling face surely struck terror in those who crossed him. I always felt that his Service cap detracted from the overall impression of severity and smartness — to me it appeared a trifle too large for him and he seemed somehow to peer out from under the scrambled egg on the peak. I am sure that, like so many others, he had been happier in earlier years surmounted by his forage cap. I never saw him wearing one of the dreaded berets.

Sir Basil didn't suffer fools gladly and, although I wasn't aware that this occurred at AAFCE, anyone who didn't measure up to his high standards very soon vanished elsewhere! During World War II, he rose to ranks in which he should not have been flying on operations but insisted on continuing to accompany his men over Europe. Always one to 'lead from the front', it was his belief that crews knowing that their commander was in the air with them, taking the same risks, would have greater confidence in the outcome of their missions.

Considered as a possible leader of the target-finding force about to be created by Bomber Command in the summer of 1942 — the 'Pathfinders' of 8 Group as they became known — I don't think a job such as this would have suited Sir Basil's aggressive nature one little bit. I doubt if he could have reconciled himself to dropping flares rather than bombs, even for the purpose of ensuring that following formations bombed the correct targets, and in spite of the fact that his own squadrons' missions were therefore crucial to the success of the whole operation. I once heard him described in the office as a man who needed a war: he was lost without an outlet for his energetic, one might say belligerent, approach to life; he wasn't very good at 'fighting a peace'.

He not surprisingly expected high standards from his personal staff at AAFCE. I recall a wintry occasion when he had been away visiting NATO units in West Germany. Fog was widespread and conditions at Melun necessitated the diversion of the returning Devon to Belgium, to Brussels Airport I believe. Not much of a problem on the face of it unless you happened to be Cpl 'Nobby' Clark, faced with the prospect of driving the Humber from Fontainebleau to Brussels and back (a round trip in excess of 400 miles), mainly after dark, in thick fog and on continental roads with which he was not familiar. A nightmare for 'Nobby' who, I seem to recall, told me the next morning that, on being returned safely to the Hôtel de Bellune, Sir Basil vanished inside with little recognition of his efforts. I suppose the Commander took the view that his chauffeur had a job to do, a job obviously considerably less onerous than much of what had transpired in wartime, and had got on and done it satisfactorily: and that was the end of that.

Needless to say I did my best with my work in his office not to upset Sir Basil and I think I succeeded. I was always on tenterhooks at times when Mr Custance was absent for any reason but can recall no disasters. It has to be said that the working relationship between those of such disparate ranks as air chief marshal on the one hand and senior aircraftman on the other is somewhat less daunting for the latter when he is sitting with his shorthand notebook on the corner of the former's desk than it might be when standing rigidly to attention before the great one. This lesson had been learned in 1951 when I was required unexpectedly and at short notice to take dictation from Mr John E. Lightburn, then Clerk of Essex County Council.

It goes without saying that much of our work was classified and, apart from the drawers of our desks in which we kept such inconsequential items as stationery, our only storage consisted of two safes, one a four-drawer filing cabinet and the other a double-doored cupboard similar in size to the steel lockers in the billets. The cupboard must have weighed a ton — literally — and how on earth it was lifted into the office I can't imagine: perhaps they built the HQ round it! On occasion the security people would change the combinations of both safes overnight, leading to difficulties the following morning until we had wrung the revised details out of them.

Sgt Fenney was responsible for the filing of official papers as well as Sir Basil's personal correspondence. Of the latter we always produced an extra copy which Stan filed away in alphabetical order of addressees, enabling us to overcome problems arising when Sir Basil announced that he wanted to write to Mr So-and-so and we hadn't a clue who Mr So-and-so was. Sir Basil was frequently called upon to deliver speeches to gatherings of one sort or another. Usually Mr Custance, but occasionally I, typed these in double spacing on pocket-sized pieces of card loosely fastened with a 'bootlace' (a treasury tag) to facilitate ease of use. All speeches were carefully stored away; when a new one needed to be written Sir Basil would invariably want to base it on one already delivered and woe betide us in the office if we couldn't lay hands on the old one.

I was surprised to find that Sir Basil received a number of what may only be described as begging letters, usually from charitable and other organizations rather than individuals. Most of these received short shrift but I remember on one occasion typing a letter to send a halfcrown (2s.6d or 12½p) book of postage stamps in response to an appeal and visiting Cpl Hammersley in his postal emporium to buy the necessary book. I was considerably more surprised one afternoon when Sir Basil emerged from his private office at an unexpectedly early hour to ask for his car to be summoned. He explained that there was nothing for him to do and that he therefore proposed to go home. In my lowly innocence I found it difficult to comprehend that a commander could find himself in such a situation.

On the coffee table in Sir Basil's office reposed a scale model of a Folland Gnat, a new single engined jet in which he believed there to be considerable potential. In fact this two-seater aircraft was to become the RAF's main advanced flying trainer and was the original mount of the Red Arrows aerobatic display team, replaced in 1980 by the Hawk.

Sir Basil was very keen to have a scientific adviser at AAFCE and was several times visited by Mr Archie Potts, who had been scientific adviser to Fighter Command when he was C-in-C. Mr Potts had been an expert in air defence issues and was one of the few scientists in 1953/54 to understand the implications of nuclear weapons. He was to join the staff subsequent to my departure.

Invited to retire prematurely from the RAF at the end of 1955, perhaps because of his views on the situation in NATO and the forceful manner in which he had expressed them, Sir Basil was replaced as Commander by another RAF air chief marshal, Sir George Mills. Within a few months he took up sheep farming in Western Australia, for which purpose he had been presented with a shepherd's crook prior to his departure from AAFCE. He died late in 1977 at the age of 75.

CHAPTER 12

DEMOBBED AT LAST

By the time I had returned from my slightly dodgy UK leave we were into the second half of August and demob had ceased to be a distant prospect — a sort of permanent mirage which appeared never to come any closer. Unlike some of my colleagues, I hadn't made myself a chart from which to cross the passing days and weeks; my AAFCE diary did, however, contain the one word entry for *Novembre, Mardi 2* — "OUT".

It was probably at about this stage that Fg Off Lees and others tried to tempt me into signing on as a regular airman, assuring me that promotion to corporal ('getting my tapes') would be just around the corner. Relevant to this, I believe, was the fact that my possession of the University of London School Certificate exempted me from the RAF Education Test, Parts 1 and 2, an appropriate item having appeared in PORs more than a year previously. I have often speculated as to what would have been my future had I decided to remain in the Service. Needless to say I took the assurance about promotion with a giant pinch of salt; what I did know, however, was that male shorthand typists were a pretty rare breed in the RAF and that I could have found myself working in practically any country in the world: I understood, for example, that it was usual for air attachés at our embassies to have male secretaries. However, no way was I going to be tempted; in common with just about every fellow National Serviceman in all three Services I had looked forward to the great day for nearly two years and I wasn't going to be denied the pleasure of its arrival — or should I say the joy of my departure?

On a personal level, a certain amount of tidying up needed to be done prior to my looming departure. On one of my UK trips I had acquired a replacement rear brake cable for my bike and, now in good and safe running order, I managed to sell it at only a small loss. I had an idea that I might have sold it to my friend Moll but he tells me this was not the case, so the identity of the lucky buyer remains forever a mystery. As for my collection of electric irons: it wouldn't have been right for me to sell them to anybody as I hadn't paid for them myself. I presented them to some budding *entrepreneur* (not, I hasten to add, an SP) whose identity, again, is forgotten.

It may be recalled that Simps and I had been on a number of photographic expeditions together. Not surprisingly we exchanged copies of some of our photos and the cost of doing so is illuminating. For fifteen 3¼" x 2¼" monochrome *épreuves* (contact prints) and four *agrandissements* (enlargements about 4¼" x 3¼") JAN of Fontainebleau charged me 225 and 136 francs respectively which, with the addition of some sort of tax at 11 francs, totalled 372 francs for nineteen deckle-edged pictures. Equivalent to 7s.6d or 37½p, you'd be lucky to get one standard sized (6" x 4") colour reprint made for this sum these days.

I had a few souvenirs to take home with me. I've already mentioned my Parisian etching and to this I added a china ashtray embellished with the coat-of-arms of Fontainebleau and a modest photograph album bearing on its cover a reproduction of Fontainebleau Palace — not as tacky as it sounds but I have to confess that the pages are now secured in the well-filled album by what appears to be an RAF shoelace. Among other odds and ends, such as book matches and a lady's pink handkerchief inscribed *"oh la...la!"*, were cloth badges with the coats-of-arms of SHAPE, Fontainebleau, Paris, Nice, Ile de France — and half that of Dunkerque! I have the left-hand bit, for 'Dunk', and cannot now explain this curiosity. Perhaps some other 'erque' has the other half!! Shopping and other expeditions into Fontainebleau weren't necessarily undertaken by the wild-haired Frog's bus. There was a route on foot incorporating a shortcut through, presumably, a remnant of the forest and, if I remember correctly, taking one into the town somewhere in the vicinity of the square in front of the palace. Unlit, the section through the trees was at worst a trifle spooky; in the modern crime-ridden age it would be foolhardy to attempt it, especially after dark and on one's own. 'Mugged' is the awful word used nowadays to describe what might have happened to you; I thought the word was 'robbed'.

Nearing the end of my time at AAFCE I had just about overcome my self-imposed restriction on venturing to areas of a camp where I was not actually required to be. The feeling of intimidation, apprehension, fear almost, endemic on RAF stations as such, was not present on Camp Guynemer. The dreaded "OI YEW, AIRMAN" preceding some contrived admonition or other simply wasn't heard; my inhibitions diminished.

I had also by this time become used to seeing around the camp and billets an erk who reminded me very strongly of my youngest brother, Den. I was sitting quietly on my bed, minding my own business, when he came into the room one evening, in uniform, to see my friend Moll and I had to restrain myself from asking "Hello Den, what on earth are you doing here?" I knew it couldn't be Den as he was not yet eighteen years' of age and therefore wasn't in the RAF but the resemblance was so uncanny that it gave me quite a turn! I think the cause of the trouble might have been LAC Skinner, from London, who was teaching Moll how to bet on the horses. When it became obvious that this was a waste of time (and money) Moll switched to the fixed odds football coupon, a move from which I was to benefit, as recorded in Chapter 11.

An erk of considerable repute, although as far as I knew I never set eyes on him, was an MT driver who in fact undertook very little MT driving. Most of his service was apparently spent at the RAF hospital at Halton, Buckinghamshire being cured of the unsavoury disease which, upon his return to AAFCE quickly followed by a visit to Paris, he promptly re-caught. An MT driver of very different ilk was Cpl 'Nobby' Clark, Sir Basil's chauffeur. A West Countryman, he was a little excitable when not behind the wheel. He lived locally with his wife and children and it was a particular source of amusement to Stan Fenney that he didn't appear to understand why his family continued to grow. His deputy, another corporal, was a very different character: older and quieter, he took life perhaps a little more seriously. Both men were first-class drivers; they had to be!

Although it hadn't actually been necessary to speak French very often during the course of my duties, the knowledge of the language gained at school had nevertheless frequently been very useful, not only in the office but also during off-duty moments in Paris and elsewhere. My first French teacher was in fact a minute French lady of advanced age, Mademoiselle Graemo, who I had difficulty in understanding and with whom I didn't make a lot of progress — with the language, I hasten to add! After one year of me she returned to France and the remainder of my tuition came from Mr 'Lefty' Wright (who, it may be recalled from Chapter 2, ran the school photographic society from which I derived so much) and Mr Tom Bone ('Boney', needless to say). Having obtained a Credit at the School Certificate examinations in 1950 I suppose I am indebted to all three teachers. What they (especially Mlle Graemo) would have made of the strange way in which many of us conversed at AAFCE I hesitate to think. Most erks had at least a smattering of French and got into the habit of introducing into their everyday conversations occasional French words, terribly pronounced. For example, an erk going on leave would say he was going on his vacancies — from the French *vacances*; or, if he was setting off to Fontainebleau to do some shopping, he might say he was making for the magazines (*magasins*) in the veal (*ville*). I confess I am still apt to speak in this way today! The British spoke of Fontenblow; the Americans of Fonnenblau (to rhyme with cow) — terrible really.

I had grown to feel very much at home in France and, as a result of my several weekend visits to Paris, came to know the capital better than I knew London. Despite living all my life only about thirty miles distant and having Londoners as parents, I have never felt at ease in our capital city. On the occasions when I have ventured there, from necessity rather than choice, once out of the Underground I've really had little idea of my whereabouts or orientation. On the other hand, I developed a 'feel' for Paris; I always seemed to understand the overall pattern of the city and, in effect, to 'know where I was going' at any time.

Shortly before my own departure, USAF Col Paul Tibbets was assigned to AAFCE to fly a desk in the directorate occupying the first-floor wing adjoining that in which I worked. Col Tibbets was the pilot of 'Enola Gay', the Boeing B-29 Superfortress which dropped the first atomic bomb. Called 'Little Boy' and equivalent to 20,000 tons of TNT, the bomb devastated Hiroshima, Japan, on 6 August 1945 and, with the second and larger weapon dropped at Nagasaki on 9 August, hastened the end of World War II. I recall Sir Basil asking to see Col Tibbets soon after his arrival at AAFCE.

In a moment of madness I confounded my incredulous room-mates by announcing that I thought I would be so pleased to be back home after my impending demob that I might continue my public service by joining the Civil Defence organization. I already had some idea of what would be involved, not only as the result of my father's wartime ARP activities but also because it so happened that I had worked at County Hall in close proximity to colleagues helping to administer the Service in Essex. Once home I thought no more of this idea!

At the instigation of Sqn Ldr Lewis it was decided somewhat against my wishes that my imminent demob should be marked by the issue of an appropriate publicity 'blurb'. Accordingly on Friday 8 October I presented myself at the Office of the Chief of Public Information where I was interviewed at length by a Canadian civilian, Miss E. Barber. On the same day, resplendent in my best blue and feigning work, I was photographed at my desk by an RCAF photographer. One airman each from the FAF and the USAF were then roped in and required to stand behind me while, still seated, I held up for their examination an almost blank sheet of paper. My supposed colleagues were both very nervous about being in the Commander's office and, not an English speaker, the Frenchman hadn't a clue what was going on. The intention was that press releases and photos should be sent to the relevant local newspapers in the UK, the USA and France. I was at a later date given a couple of spare 10" x 8" copies of the photo featuring just myself, in which I am surprised to note that I was pictured pretending to use a ballpoint pen; I didn't realize they had been invented by 1954. Although I saw a copy of the international photo, unfortunately there wasn't a spare for me.

Unbeknown to me at the time, on the day of the interview and photograph the wheels of my demob were well and truly set in motion in the RAF Support Unit when the CO signed RAF Form 1394, my Brief Statement of Service and Certificate on Discharge. When I was handed this form on the day of my demob I was a little baffled to note that my personal qualities of leadership had been assessed as "very good" as I didn't realize I'd had occasion to lead anyone. I was still 70¼ inches in height. I was notified that I had been deemed to be enlisted in Class H of the RAF Reserve to undergo part-time service with effect from 28 November, having been allocated to No.61 RAF Reserve Centre, Kenley, Surrey — Remobilization Station 'S'.

On Tuesday 26 October Sir Basil signed for me a copy of the official AAFCE photograph of himself standing, hands resting on desk and looking suitably stern, in front of his huge wallmap of Europe. This pose contrasted sharply with that in the official portrait of his predecessor, drawerfuls of which were apparently found in the outer office after his departure; General Norstad had been pictured filmstar style, with hat, and smiling quietly. On the same day Fg Off Lees handed me the page from *Punch* magazine mentioned in Chapter 11 and Sqn Ldr Lewis enquired whether I thought it might be helpful to me in the future if I were to be given some sort of testimonial as to my work in Sir Basil's office. Needless to say I felt this would be of advantage and he kindly put his signature to a document in the following terms, typed by myself on Commander's Office notepaper:

TO WHOM IT MAY CONCERN

This is to certify that SAC Caton has been employed in the office of the Commander, Headquarters Allied Air Forces Central Europe, Air Chief Marshal Sir Basil E. Embry, KCB, KBE, DSO, DFC, AFC, RAF, during the period September 1953 to October 1954, as a shorthand-typist and general clerk.

SAC Caton is a young man of outstanding ability, extremely pleasant, courteous, and obliging, who can always be relied upon to carry out his duties in a most satisfactory manner.

(sgd) G. E. Lewis

G. E. LEWIS

Squadron Leader RAF

Personal Staff Officer

26 October 1954

No, honestly, I didn't make it up myself! On the same day and although I wasn't of course aware of it at the time, the now long-defunct *Essex Newsman-Herald* published under the headline "He is Clerk to Sir Basil Embry at NATO" a much-reduced copy of my photo and the following report:

> Back to his old job soon
>
> Senior Aircraftman Edward Caton, RAF, 20-year old son of Mr and Mrs L. F. Caton, of Bruce Grove, Chelmsford, will return to his job as Junior committee clerk with the Essex County Council, when he finishes his National Service on November 2.
>
> He has been serving as office clerk to Air Chief Marshal Sir Basil Embry, RAF, commander of all NATO's air power for Central Europe, at the Headquarters of Allied Air Forces, Central Europe.
>
> SAC Caton says: "I've had the chance to see some of the top men who are organizing the growth of NATO. It comes to mean more than a name when you realize how many of the outstanding military men in Europe are working together to make it a success."

Three days later I was in the news again. The *Newsman-Herald*'s sister paper, the *Essex Chronicle* (still going strong today after more than 230 years), re-published the same photo and news item. It seems strange now that its rival, the *Essex Weekly News*, was almost devoid of photographs in the 1950s: so, no photo of me but, under the headline "From County Hall to NATO and back", *Sentinel*'s Essex Commentary led with the following item:

> Military service can bring some mighty interesting assignments, according to SAC Edward Caton, RAF, 20-year-old son of Mr and Mrs L. F. Caton, of Bruce Grove, Chelmsford.
>
> For the past year Caton has been clerk to Air Chief Marshal Sir Basil Embry, commander of all NATO's air power for Central Europe, at Fontainebleau.

By trade Caton is a shorthand-typist, and by implication he must be good, for Marshal Embry has no reputation for tolerating mediocrity.

COUNTY HALL JOB

"Shortly after joining the RAF," says Caton, "I read about Air Chief Marshal Embry's escapes from the Germans. And I heard of the raids he planned after he got back to England. The last thing I expected was to be taking his dictation."

Caton's military service finishes on Nov 2. After that he will return to the civilian job he left as junior committee clerk with the Essex County Council.

Fame at last — but had I really said what was attributed to me? Certainly I took some stick from so-called friends and former colleagues when I resumed my local government career in November!

Wednesday 27 October 1954 — probably the saddest of my 731 days as an airman. When describing Sir Basil's private office accommodation in Chapter 8 I mentioned that the information in his map room was up-dated regularly by RAF personnel from the Intelligence Directorate. W/O Bert Moylan, a single man in his mid-40s hailing from Portsmouth, and his smiling SAC sidekick from the West Country were the personnel in question. Bert, billeted in the small room at the end of my corridor in Block 12M and yet another old-timer unhappy under a beret, was never one to 'pull rank' but was a kind and gentle friend to all. He was an especially close friend to Stan Fenney. On my last Wednesday at AAFCE I expect I had more pressing things to do than play football and luckily I was not in the team for the afternoon's match, during the course of which our good chum Bert unhappily passed away. As usual, Moll was keeping goal and describes what happened thus:

"Bert Moylan was my right back. I have a very vivid recollection of events just prior to his tragic death when he took a goal kick on the right after which he spun round and fell. I ran to the right of the 6 yard box to render what assistance I could until I realized the full seriousness of the situation. We sent for the MO but he passed away before he arrived."

In my turn I have a vivid recollection of Moll, in a state of shock, sitting on his bed that evening trying to come to terms with what had happened — Simps, Smiffy and I not really knowing what to say. Leaving the mess after tea the next day I was told by 'the Mekon' that, during the following week, I would be a member of the funeral party as I was the right height. As it happened I would by then be in the UK and, possibly, a civilian to boot and it was nice to be able to disillusion an NCO somewhat full of his own importance even if the occasion was a sad one. A Court of Enquiry sat during the week of the funeral and Moll's attendance was naturally required.

I would guess that almost certainly I did not participate in the fateful soccer match because I was engaged in 'clearing' from Camp Guynemer at the time; alternatively, of course, I might not have been picked for the team! Although the camp was not an RAF Station as such, it was necessary to 'arrive' and 'clear' in the usual manner. During the course of 'clearing' I recall visiting the MO who informed me that I had gained the five pounds in weight by which I had been considered deficient at my Southend-on-Sea medical. Did this mean that I had improved from Grade II to Grade I, I asked? He said it did but, as far as I was aware, nothing to this effect was recorded.

In his autobiography Sir Basil Embry emphasized that he had always considered it important to know the names of those serving under him. As he pointed out, a man's name is his most personal possession. Nevertheless, when I took my leave of him he was still calling me "Clayton"! Before shaking hands, he thanked me for what I had done in his office, enquired what I proposed to do upon my return to civvy street and described me as "... a typical example of a young National Serviceman who came into the Service, did his bit to the best of his ability and returned from whence he had come as soon as he was able". Could have been worse!

Although I didn't fully appreciate it at the time I was just completing two of the best years of my life. The second year in particular contained some unrepeatable experiences, especially meeting and working with a man who was a legend in his own lifetime. Sir Basil's wartime exploits were legion; his escape from occupied France was sufficient by itself to distinguish him as someone special; and this was the man with whom I had just shaken hands.

So, this was it. All personnel other than those serving in the UK and West Germany had to travel to RAF Innsworth, Gloucester to undergo the actual process of demob. It remained only to pack up my kit and civvies and get myself back to the UK. Although I planned to travel to Gloucester via my home I proposed to wear uniform. Colder weather now upon us, this would enable me to don my greatcoat — the easiest way to carry it — and facilitate the carriage of all my clutter. Last time I was home I had left behind the bulk of my civvies and was just about able to cram everything into my kit bag and **small** suitcase. Certainly I did not propose to emulate veteran Cpl Hammersley, recently returned to the UK to retire, who swore that his kit bag would go home packed solid with cigarettes and that his ancient uniform would disappear out of the train window somewhere in France. He was replaced as postal clerk in the RAF Support Unit by SAC Roy Howard. Roy hailed from Lowestoft, a resort which held for me so many memories of boyhood holidays with relatives.

I had been issued with a set of decrepit 'irons' to replace the pristine set handed in when the mess changed over to civilized behaviour. I still have these; the fork is stamped with the Service number 1450891 and it would be great to hear from the old-timer to whom it was originally issued.

SAC Les Goddard, the POR clerk and a friend of Moll, proposed to take over my bed after my departure, planned for Saturday 30 October. Having bid farewell to my room-mates — Moll, Simps and Smiffy — and to other friends, especially Sgt Stan Fenney, I left AAFCE during the evening for the last time on the wild-haired Frog's bus. Inevitably, I suppose, I had mixed feelings; after all, a special chapter in my life was ending. I was to travel by the night ferry and have a clear recollection of the train's arrival in Dunkerque harbour and my departure from French soil via garishly lit passageways leading me to the ship. On a chilly but dry night, the sea happily not too boisterous, I found myself a corner on deck sheltered from the breeze and the funnel's acrid fumes and passed a lonely voyage wrapped up in my greatcoat, big 'at pulled down at the front. A patrolling Jolly Jack Tar gazed curiously at me on his regular perambulations of the ship but didn't utter a word. Probably thought I was daft.

Without incident I struggled home with all my gear quite early on Sunday morning and spent the next couple of days in a kind of limbo. I was still an airman but couldn't help but feel that it was all over. Then I did something which proved perhaps that I *was* a bit daft. My two years' service would end on Tuesday 2 November. Throughout those two years it had always been my practice to spend as much time as possible at home. Considering the circumstances of my imminent return to civvy street, I suppose I took this to a ridiculous extreme by not departing for Gloucester until the great day itself, admittedly at a very early hour. If I'd had any sense I'd have travelled on the Monday because the duration of the journey proved to be such that, by the time I'd reported to No.5 PDU (Personnel Despatch Unit) at RAF Innsworth, it was late morning and well past the time by which I should have been there to catch the start of that day's demob process. I would have to cool my heels until the Wednesday with the result that I would serve two years and one day. I would also miss the opportunity to meet up with any of my colleagues from square-bashing days who had been posted abroad — other than to Germany — as they would of course have been demobbed on the Tuesday, the correct day!

I was not alone in my predicament: I encountered half a dozen blokes from the Middle and Far East who had also arrived too late, all of whom were finding the bright but very cold weather on the day an uncomfortable contrast to the heat to which they had become used. As a group we were treated rather as lepers; nobody wanted to know about us and we were left to our own devices. Having blooded my 'new' set of irons in the mess, I went with the others in search of accommodation for the night. We found an unoccupied barrack hut and purloined from elsewhere the beds and bedding we would require. I cannot now remember why we were unable to get a stove going; I've a feeling the flue was blocked and maybe that's why the hut was out of use. It was a bitterly cold end to the day and I believe we kept warm in the NAAFI until we had to return to the hut where I spent by far the coldest and most utterly miserable night of my two years (and one day!) There was a sharp frost and our warm breath froze on the hut windows. I lay shivering under all the available bedding and clothing and don't think I slept a wink — and I was the one who hadn't arrived from a hot part of the world. The fact that this was the last night of my service was the only consolation; I think it was rivalled for sheer discomfort only by the one spent with Hitler's cockroaches the best part of a year earlier.

Wednesday was a beautiful day with continuous sunshine, but very cold again. The demob process consisted of a sort of mini 'arrival' and 'clearance' all in one go. At the equipment stores certain items of kit had to be handed in (but paid for if you couldn't produce them — I wondered what had happened to Cpl Hammersley if he really did chuck the lot out of the train window in France!) — and happily there was no problem over my Army groundsheet; the clerk hurled it into the oblivion behind him without a second glance. I had been aware for a long time that you were given the choice of handing in either your boots or your shoes. In my case each pair was of such good quality and so comfortable that I really would have liked to have retained both. However, I had many months earlier decided that the shoes would be likely to be of more use to me as a civilian and had thereafter worn my boots whenever possible. Thus I handed in the boots and was still wearing the shoes several years later. Most of the kit was of good quality and I have already mentioned that, over forty years later, I am still using the larger of the two shoe brushes with which I had been issued at Padgate.

I have, in my own schoolboy-like handwriting, a list which I made at the time of my demob of the items of kit which I was required to maintain in reasonable condition for use if and when called for part-time Reserve service, as follows:

1	Kitbag	
1	Greatcoat	
1	No.1 Home Dress	[best blue]
1	No.2 Dress	[working blue]
1	Cap S D (with badge)	[big 'at]
1	Beret (without badge)	
1 pr	Shoes	
1 pr	Slippers	[plimsolls]
1 pr	Gloves	
2	Towels	
4 prs	Socks	
2	Ties	
1	Pullover	
3	Shirts	
6	Collars	
2 prs	Pants	
2	Vests	
2 prs	Sleeping jackets and trousers	
1	Housewife	
1	Mug	
1	Knife	
1	Fork	
1	Spoon	
1	Button-stick	
1 pr	Braces	

In addition to the shoe brush (which, it would appear, I was not actually required to look after) I still have in 1997 the kit bag, big 'at with badge, mug and irons, as well as the buttons and badges removed from the greatcoat to enable it to be worn for cycling to and from work during cold weather. Most of the remainder of the kit 'got the moth'.

Other demobees had materialized from I knew not where (perhaps the nice heated billet to which all arrivers should have been directed yesterday!) and No.5 PDU set about processing the whole group with what was obviously well-practised efficiency. RAF Form 1394 (the discharge certificate which had been completed at AAFCE) was handed to me. Ration books didn't need to be returned as rationing had finally come to an end earlier in the year. We were all relieved of our 1250s. I was to be paid for my extra day's service (3 November), which would be followed by twenty-four days paid leave, my whole-time service ending on Saturday 27 November 1954. Service in Class H Reserve would commence the following day. I attended a final pay parade at which I received the sum of £10 on account, the balance owing to me to be forwarded later when final accounting had been completed. In fact it wasn't until almost Christmas and after one letter of reminder from me that a money order in the sum of £12 8s.1d (£12.40½p) was finally received.

Unlike the regular airmen, who were sent to Woking in Surrey for this purpose, those National Servicemen among us were not to be issued with the infamous demob suit. Neither would we receive any further payment by way of a gratuity or pay during service in the Reserve.

The RAF had one final trick to play upon me. No.5 PDU were, as I said, processing us efficiently and I was given to understand that the procedure was designed to ensure that we would all be cleared in time for transport to Gloucester station to catch the train for London (Paddington) departing at about noon. A clerk in 'A' Sqn was nearing that most magical moment — the issue of RAF Form 143, a warrant for a ONE-WAY railway ticket from Gloucester to Chelmsford — when the fire alarm sounded, he picked up his typewriter and ran from the hangar in which he was working. I wasn't letting him out of my sight and followed him outside, where I passed a frustrating half-hour or more sitting on the grass and twiddling my thumbs. Time was short when the fire drill ended, but a hair-raising ride in the back of a 3-tonner saw a group of us at the station just before twelve. Anticipating, correctly, that there would be a queue of erks in a similar state of panic at the booking office, I was first off the lorry and displayed a surprising turn of speed with my flailing kitbag in order to ensure that the ONE-WAY ticket for Chelmsford would be issued in time for the London train even if others weren't. Every man for himself, I'm afraid!

I caught the train (as did a few others) and arrived home in the late afternoon. My brother Den marched me down the garden to a patch of remaining sunshine where, still in uniform, I was photographed for posterity. It really was all over now.

I was to don the uniform on only one further occasion. Some years later, when my two brothers and I had all completed our National Service, my poor old mother thought it might be a nice idea to have a colour photo of the three of us in uniform. We all got dressed up — my best blue by now a trifle tight about my person — and we were beautifully posed indoors with Den and me (both RAF SACs) on either side of RASC Sgt Geof, all looking suitably severe. Using my father's Kodak Instamatic, my mother took her time before the flash fired and the great moment had passed. When the print arrived, we saw that our heads had all been cut off.

CHAPTER 13

AFTERMATH AND REFLECTIONS

Just about the first thing I did was to go out and spend my £10 demob payment (and some more!) on a Regentone record player. Not a sophisticated autochange model of the sort with which Smiffy cluttered up the room at AAFCE, my portable acquisition was nevertheless a modern three-speed (78, 45 and 33⅓ rpm) machine. To go with it I also bought my first extended play (45 rpm) disc. I couldn't very well bore my family with it indefinitely and so it wasn't long before I acquired the first of my collection of the new-fangled long playing (33⅓ rpm) records. I still have the record player and, almost certainly, the records.

It didn't appear to have been possible during my National Service to have access to the RAF Post Office Savings Bank account into which daily sums stopped from my, at first, meagre pay had been deposited on my behalf over the two years. However, shortly after my return home the account book arrived from the RAF POSB at Harrogate, disclosing that there was a sum in excess of £72 in the account. Suddenly I was rich and could afford to buy more records! I also invested in a zoot suit, a capacious single-button grey affair with vast lapels and huge bottoms, which must have looked slightly ridiculous.

I had decided to exercise my right to resume my former employment as a local government officer and restarted work at County Hall, Chelmsford on Monday 22 November at an annual salary of £245. Although this gross sum was virtually the same as my concluding RAF gross pay, I was in fact now worse off. Whereas I had been enjoying 'all found' luxury in the Service, obviously it was now necessary for me to pay my mother for my keep.

In spite of the fact that the winter of 1954/55 proved hard with abundant snow, at least in Essex, for some inexplicable reason I declined to wear any sort of coat or hat except during periods of actual snowfall, when I condescended to don cycling cape and my father's old ARP beret. I seemed to assume that my blue and gold Rayleigh Rockets scarf and a pair of gloves were sufficient protection from the somewhat severe elements. Coincidence or not, I became quite ill and spent one month off work with what my doctor called 'flu' but what the forerunner of the DSS thought must be something more severe. Having only recently resumed work there, I wasn't too popular at County Hall either.

Prior to my illness I received up-to-date news of AAFCE when Smiffy was good enough to spend two days of his UK leave with me in Chelmsford. He may well have been a little surprised to journey south from the frozen wastes of Yorkshire only to find the same conditions in Essex. Neither of us keen on the bright lights, we passed a quiet couple of days walking in the snow and visiting the cinema. Meanwhile Moll's great day arrived on about 10 February when, like me, he was demobbed at RAF Innsworth. However, as a regular he then went to Woking for his demob suit prior to starting one month's (paid) demob leave. Prior to leaving AAFCE he had been presented with a certificate as to his NATO service, signed personally by Sir Basil Embry. Informed subsequently that I had no knowledge of such certificates being issued, in spite of working in Sir Basil's office, Moll commented "You will see that Sir Basil signed my Cert, if you worked for him why did you not receive one, were they given only to best performers!"

I kept in touch with all three of my AAFCE room-mates and with Bill Rudman for a while but, inevitably I suppose, correspondence gradually petered out until, in 1995, I was able with the help of telephone directories to regain contact with Moll and Bill. Unfortunately the names Simpson and, more especially, Smith don't lend themselves to successful amateur detective work although I have tried to trace them.

The period of enforced idleness brought about by my illness gave me an opportunity to reflect on the events of my two years away from home and perhaps to begin to consider the effects of the experience on myself and my future. I was of course still not long removed from the situation common, without exception, to all National Servicemen, namely, possessed of an inability to see any further than the date of his own demob and no real enthusiasm for anything else. If I was being honest with myself, I was by now beginning to realize that it hadn't all been bad and that, again in common with other National Servicemen (at least those in the RAF), I had in fact been presented with an irreplaceable opportunity to 'grow up' in a disciplined and worthwhile environment. Without a doubt we had gone in as boys and come out as men.

I am convinced now that the discipline to which we were all subjected in the early stages, whilst admittedly unpleasant and seemingly taken to ridiculous lengths on occasion, certainly didn't do me any harm and, with very few exceptions, didn't harm anyone else either. I am aware that there were isolated instances of recruits committing suicide during RAF square-bashing — two in one eight-week period at Padgate in 1956 — but I do feel that a youngster with any sort of 'gumption' about himself could not only survive but acquit himself well into the bargain and end up a better person than when he started. One lesson we all learned: to know when we were well off and to stop complaining about nothing!

I am bound to admit that I was favourably surprised with respect to one aspect of my RAF life: on the whole I encountered considerably less bad language than I had anticipated would be the case. Naturally there was some pretty lurid profanity, notably on the part of the DIs at Hednesford, but generally speaking the incidence of swearing never reached the levels I had assumed would be the case. I served in three quite distinct environments: at Padgate and Hednesford we were all National Servicemen (apart, of course, from many of the permanent staff); at Norton there was probably about a half and half mix of National Servicemen and regulars; while at AAFCE all, apart from myself and one other NS airman rumoured to have arrived just

161

prior to my departure, were regulars. With only the very rare exception, I couldn't have asked for better crowds of blokes with whom to serve during the whole of the two years.

I wasn't aware of this at the time but it so happened that I had been serving in the RAF during the year (1953) when its strength reached its highest point since World War II, namely, 277,125 men and women and more than 6,300 aircraft. Pride in the Service, the first glimmerings of which (as I have already mentioned) began to emerge during my second year, wasn't something of which I recall being aware during the first few months after my return to civvy street. In fact, it wasn't really until many years later that my interest in, and feelings for, the RAF began to develop and forty years were to elapse before I felt moved to embark on the writing of this story. I will, if I may, return to the subject of pride later.

I became, temporarily at any rate, an 'only child' when my youngest brother Den entered the RAF at Cardington (by now home to the only remaining Reception Unit) during May 1955. He square-bashed at RAF Wilmslow and trade-trained at RAF Locking. My parents' anxiety at this time was compounded by the fact that my other brother Geof, still in Egypt and by now a sergeant in the RASC (at the tender age of nineteen), was contemplating signing on to become a regular soldier. Perhaps promotion had gone to his head. However the situation in the Canal Zone was deteriorating and my parents were delighted when, in a note accompanying a short recording which Geof had made in Ismailia on Saturday 18 June to send greetings on the occasion of my approaching twenty-first birthday, he penned the momentous words:

By the way, in case the flap is still on, please reassure all concerned that I am not, repeat NOT, signing on the dotted line. Two years is my limit now.

His decision was no doubt influenced by the demanding situation in which he was now finding himself, as described in a letter written earlier but also received with the recording:

Personally, I'm somewhat choked at the moment: perhaps I'd better explain why. Each morning this week I've been up at 4.30 for rehearsals for a church parade which is coming off shortly. I am on guard tonight [Thursday]; that is followed by Orderly Sergeant tomorrow [Friday]; that in turn is followed by another guard on Saturday night. That guard dismounts at 5.30 a.m. on Sunday, and church parade follows at 6.15. In my opinion, a procession of duties like this is absolutely no good to man nor beast; and it's certainly not doing me any good at all: not one little bit.

I was glad to have completed my own Service and, just as important, to have avoided the Army! However, as an 'H' Reservist I wasn't out of the wood yet, being liable until 2 May 1958 to be called-up if required for, at the least, a fortnight's training each year. I'm sure some former National Service airmen were summoned for annual training but neither I nor any of my contemporaries proved to be required. My guess is that those of a technical bent were more likely to be of use to the Service than pen-pushers and the like.

My final contact with the RAF came in a letter of 6 May 1958 from the RAF Record Office at Gloucester confirming that my Class 'H' Reserve liability had been completed on 2 May and that I had been transferred to Class 'G' (General) Reserve on the following day. I no longer had any liability for annual training but only for recall in the event of an emergency, for which purpose my uniform and other kit had to be maintained in a reasonable condition. What might be termed an emergency of a personal nature occurred the following month when, on 21 June, I was married at St John's Church, Great Clacton, Essex.

In the hope that it might add momentum to my burgeoning local government career, in the following year I succeeded after three years study in obtaining the Diploma in Municipal Administration awarded by the then Local Government Examinations Board. I have to confess that I transgressed by not notifying the Record Office on RAF Form 4304 of this success; neither did I inform them of my change of address upon marriage. I don't think I wished to remind them on either occasion of my existence in case this might give them ideas not of my liking!

I don't know what I was worrying about really: good fortune had certainly smiled upon me during my whole-time Service and why should my luck have changed? Most importantly, I had been accepted for the RAF at the outset. Then, having struggled through my training (where, it may be recalled, I missed the ordeal of the assault course), whilst I might not have been deliriously happy with my first permanent posting to Norton, to which salubrious parts of the world could I have been sent instead? I'd probably have been spared Korea as an airman (only Transport Command were involved, conveying troops) but possibly not as a soldier or sailor, the war there continuing until July 1953. But I could have found myself in the Middle East where, as I was only too well aware from my brother's letters, life was becoming very unpleasant. The emergency in Malaya, lasting until 1960, involved the RAF, as did operations against terrorists in Kenya.

And where was I? Having done the unforgivable and volunteered for something, I was living and working on a camp which, if not luxurious, was certainly far removed from the normal run-of-the-mill RAF establishment and situated, moreover, adjacent to a pleasant little French town graced by a magnificent palace. I had even timed my arrival so as to avoid being billeted in Caserne Damesme, the dreadful old rodent-infested barracks used by the RAF prior to the completion of Camp Guynemer (when the Headquarters were located in Cour Henri IV at the palace). Throw in for good measure a legend of World War II and high-calibre and friendly colleagues, and for what more could I have asked? A posting to an RAF station near my home perhaps? But, who knows, working and living conditions there might have been awful!

So far as the general quality of personnel was concerned, it has to be borne in mind that the demand for service in the RAF far outstripped availability of posts most of the time and the Service could therefore afford to be selective. With the greatest of respect to all concerned, it has therefore to be admitted that the Army ended up with the 'dregs', several hundreds of whom had each year to be taught to read and write before military training could commence. I understand that the object of the courses which these recruits were detailed to attend was for the students to be able to understand the Army's equivalent of RAF SROs by the end of a course lasting, I believe, about eight or ten weeks. Needless to say it must not be assumed from these remarks that all recruits to the Army were illiterate! Far from it; I merely make the point that the RAF were able to select from those opting for the air arm.

And what of France, my home for fourteen months or so? Did my experiences there lead me to become a Francophile? Have I spent much time there since my enforced residence all those years ago? Not really! Following my return home from AAFCE in 1954 I next stepped on French soil during the summer of 1957 when I travelled by train from Boulogne to Ötztal for a holiday in the Austrian Tyrol. I had noticed from the itinerary that the train would stop for about three-quarters of an hour to change engines at Laon, a town in northern France. I therefore had in my pocket the remaining francs with which I had returned to the UK for demob and, much to the chagrin of other passengers turned away with their pounds, shillings and pence, I was able to purchase refreshments in the station buffet. Unashamedly smug might be an apt description of me as I sipped my drink.

The following year found me organizing on behalf of the office social club an Easter weekend coach excursion to Paris for 39 persons. In a couple of respects reference to the trip in this story is perhaps justified. At an incredibly early hour on Good Friday 27 March our coach deposited us outside the run-down Hotel de Belfort situated in the very dodgy Rue du Faubourg Saint-Denis. The commotion awakened a short, plump and excitable crone who appeared wearing a pink dressing-gown, as well as an ancient, unkempt gent with a bullet-hole through the left lens of his spectacles. There was chaos on the narrow stairway leading to the crone's 'office' where, before I could fight my way through the milling throng to try to get things sorted out, she began handing out room keys for double and triple rooms simply by reference to the list of passport numbers I had been required to supply prior to the trip. My own list showing agreed room occupations remained in my pocket until, eventually, I was in a position to try, in my halting French, to regularize the situation. The crone didn't speak English and very soon several 'wrong' pairs and trios were installed in rooms and, in some cases, sleeping soundly after their night in the coach. After prolonged argument without getting anywhere, I remembered where I had worked at AAFCE and stormed *"Moi — je suis le Général; je suis le Commandant-en-Chef: voilà, la liste officielle!"* at which she hurled down the remaining keys on to what passed for her desk and stormed into the inner recesses of wherever it is crones like her disappear to.

Included in the same weekend trip was a half-day excursion on our English coach to Versailles and Fontainebleau. Naturally, I hoped there might be an opportunity to glimpse Camp Guynemer either from the coach or perhaps on foot if time permitted. Unfortunately things didn't work out like that: we spent so much time at Versailles that, by the time our driver had found somewhere to park in the square in front of the palace at Fontainebleau, he was already agitating to be back on the road to Paris. Not surprisingly he was concerned about the prospect of being caught in the evening rush-hour traffic.

We had only about thirty minutes in the town, during which short period it was at least possible to enjoy a brief reunion with Mme Tamara Jakowleff and her mother (*Mamotchka*), two lovely French ladies who had befriended us in Austria the preceding summer and who had driven from their home at Bourg-la-Reine in the southern suburbs of Paris to meet our coach. There was further consolation as, during the return coach journey, a collection was taken for me as organizer of the weekend, with the proceeds from which I was able to buy two books on Paris.

Camp Guynemer no longer houses AAFCE or, for that matter, any other NATO formation. France withdrew militarily (but not politically) from NATO many years ago and the HQ of AAFCE are at present at Mons, just across the border in Belgium. NATO's military HQ (SHAPE) are also now in Belgium, at Chievres which I believe to be near Brussels. The presence of the Embry Stadium led to Camp Guynemer becoming the national sports centre — the base for all French athletes and sportsmen doing their National Service — although, in 1988, a holidaying ex-SAC Les Goddard thought it looked like a naval base.

As well as further rail journeys to Austria and a second Easter weekend in Paris (by air and rail and an absolute disaster happily organized by someone else!), I have since visited France only three or four times on day excursions via Dover to Calais (of which I am not very fond) and Boulogne (which I do like). It will be apparent that I have not so far had an opportunity to visit Fontainebleau again.

Gradually during the next thirty years or so I developed a growing interest in the RAF and became a voracious reader of whatever books I could lay my hands on, especially those dealing with World War II. What I term my own RAF library now extends to some ninety volumes and my reading has helped to further my growing pride in the Service. "Don't they make you feel proud?" asked my wife as, with my family, I watched a display by the RAF's aerobatic team, the Red Arrows, over Oulton Broad near Lowestoft during the 1970s. I had to admit they did; after all, I had in my admittedly humble RAF existence worn the same uniform as those blokes hurling those Gnats — as they were in those days — around the Suffolk sky.

I can't raise very much enthusiasm for the modern fast jets. Just as my interest in the RAF extends mainly to World War II, so it is also the aircraft of that era in which I can get excited! This being the case I am very fortunate to live only one hour's drive from the Imperial War Museum's site at the former RAF station at Duxford in Cambridgeshire. Many a happy hour have I spent in the company of the Spitfires, Hurricane, Lancaster, Blenheim, Anson, Oxford and others, not forgetting the collection of wartime USAAF aircraft also housed there. Is there any sight more stirring than the Battle of Britain Memorial Flight airborne in formation?

Strangely, the pride induced in me by wartime exploits of the RAF, offensive and defensive alike, is surpassed by my feelings for an operation which was neither: Operation 'Manna', undertaken during the last few days of the European war to drop food to the starving people of the Netherlands. As I understand it, the operation came about as the result of the efforts of a lone RAF group captain, on the ground with the advancing British Army, who secured a tenuous agreement with the Germans to the effect that, provided the RAF didn't take any offensive action during the food drops, the German gunners wouldn't shoot down the aircraft. To their credit, they did hold their fire.

I probably feel as I do about Operation 'Manna' because I have been privileged to talk to somebody who was there; Mrs Dini Marks (who, with her husband Jaap, we met whilst on holiday on the island of Guernsey and with whom I stayed during one of my cycling holidays to the Netherlands) was a schoolgirl aged about 11 in Den Haag (The Hague) in 1945. Although she remembers clearly the events of those few days, the mere thought of the squadrons of aircraft (mainly Lancasters) appearing at low level out of the western skies and dropping 6,700 tons of food and other essentials leaves her too emotional to speak.

I felt proud to be able to tell Dini that I had done my two years in the RAF. I doubt very much whether sentiments of this sort would be understood by a certain section of today's youth — the unwashed, ill-mannered and inconsiderate yobs responsible for so much of the crime-ridden and lawless society to which I have alluded earlier. I subscribe to the "bring back National Service" call emanating mainly I suppose from those of my generation who experienced it and understand what it was all about. Perhaps military service would no longer be appropriate but I am sure other forms of disciplined public service could be devised. What wouldn't I give to see some of those of whom I write cringing before an enormous SWOman or a fearsome Army Regimental Sergeant Major!

Not for the first time I risk standing accused of tarring all with the same brush; obviously that is not my intention. However, I feel strongly that too much consideration is given these days to the criminal and not enough to the victim and that a taste of discipline for all, at the age of about seventeen or eighteen and of the kind I and my fellows endured, couldn't but do more good than harm. Old-fashioned and politically incorrect are undoubtedly 'sins' for which I risk being pilloried. I will now get down from my soapbox.

Certainly I was sufficiently old-fashioned in the early 1990s to feel moved to apply for the National Service Medal when it became available, upon payment, to all who had performed National Service during the years 1939 to 1960. The Royal British Legion, of which my brother Geof is an active member, had been campaigning for some time for the issue of such a commemorative medal. Whilst it is not an official decoration I nevertheless felt proud to receive my medal, which is numbered 03122.

In *Air Mail*, the journal of the Royal Air Forces Association (RAFA), reference is often made to "the RAF family". I think that just about sums up the spirit of past and present members of the Service. I've read somewhere that, prior to World War II, everybody seemed to know just about everyone else and the Service really felt like one big family. I believe that feeling and spirit continue to this day, a belief fostered just a little on the evening of 28 November 1989 when I was privileged to be in Chelmsford's Chancellor Hall when the RAF Presentation Team attended. Arriving in the first-floor foyer adjacent to the hall itself, I was met by a sea of RAF scarves, ties and blazer badges as well as squadron ties and blazers, not to mention Flying Officer Kite moustaches and the like, crowding the room. The presentation was given by a group captain (a former Tornado pilot) and a young WRAF administrative officer, backed up by one of my own kind — an SAC — operating a projector; very alert he was too: a lone protestor had hardly started asking a question about finance (which turned out to be a very badly received political speech) when an appropriate slide illustrating the financing of the Service appeared, to considerable applause, on the screen. Not all daft, we SACs!

What then are the abiding memories of my two years in 'the mob' which we so derided at the time but of which many of us are now so proud? (With the usual British talent for self-deprecation we wouldn't have admitted it but I am sure we all considered the British armed forces the best, the most professional, in the world and 'the mob' streets ahead of the Navy and the Pongos.)

How about the smell of the smoke from a hundred coke fires standing vertically upon a hundred rudimentary barrack huts at RAF Hednesford on a crystal clear, freezing and windless evening, heralding perhaps the advent of the impending snow so to plague our lives?

Or the first glimpse of the name CHELMSFORD in bold white lettering on a dark blue Great Eastern Railway destination board at dirty, smokey and noisy Liverpool Street station late on a December evening?

Or hundreds of eggs frying together on a cookhouse serving hotplate, to be dished up square shaped, and the attendant hope that someone in filthy whites will have cracked too many for the numbers of hungry erks arriving and you might get two — or even three?

Or the very distinctive aroma of the heavy-duty brown linoleum typical of SHQ and other buildings — or was it the polish? Venturing into the single-storey building housing the reconstituted operations room at former RAF Duxford brings it all back.

Or the sunny, noisy NAAFI canteen at Camp Guynemer with its cheerful international atmosphere and belting juke box, so different on the one hand from a UK NAAFI and on the other from the ambience of the French cafés so close at hand?

Or the 'gash flips', especially the first one, in the Anson when I really began to feel like an airman, and the second, to Nice in the Devon? How could I forget looking down upon the snow-topped Alps?

Or AC1 La Porte, scuttling past my billet at Camp Guynemer in his customary state of self-induced terror, leaping out of his skin at a bellowed "OI, FIRMY!" — victim not for the first time of a concealed aeronautical prankster?

Or the unique and indescribable aura of Paris?

They were great days, not now regretted for one moment; I still have my **small** suitcase but I doubt if they'll need me again.

POSTSCRIPT

As a direct result of my writing this story, not only am I now in touch with the two former colleagues mentioned in Chapter 13 but, thanks largely to the endeavours of those two long-lost friends, contact has also been made with a number of other former AAFCE 'inmates'. Sadly, it was learned that two of those sought had passed away. Efforts to locate the present whereabouts of several more friends are continuing.

Dear reader, if you too found yourself stationed on Camp Guynemer at any time during 1952/53/54/55 and might be interested in regaining contact with old friends, please telephone either David Rogerson on 01703-402846 or the author on 01245-256790.

It is not beyond the bounds of possibility that some sort of reunion might ensue if enough people are interested.

* * *

After the completion of this book I had an opportunity, in July 1996, to visit the sites of RAF Hednesford and RAF Norton. From talking to local people I was able to establish that Hednesford closed in 1956, thereafter being used for a time to accommodate Hungarian refugees, while Norton remained unused after closing in 1965.

As envisaged in Chapter 5, the Hednesford site has been incorporated into Cannock Chase Country Park. It is now accessible only on foot or horseback and is largely wooded, many trees thirty or more feet in height. No evidence of any buildings could be found during my brief visit. The site of the main gate and the road pattern are clear from remaining tarmac, the roadways as I recall them considerably reduced in width. The main camp road is now an avenue of substantial silver birch. It was not easy to reconcile birdsong and the gentle stirring of treetops with screeching DIs and the crashing of boots. The nearby visitor centre houses a small exhibition on the military history of the site and I was able to make an appropriate entry in the book held therein to record visits by former 'inmates' at the RAF station.

Access to the Norton site is gained from Lightwood Lane, off the dual-carriageway Sheffield Ring Road. Incredibly, many buildings remained for some years although it was clear that the guardroom, SHQ and the airmen's billets had been demolished long before my visit. I was told that an incursion by gypsies (who found the electricity still connected and working!) resulted after their eviction in the demolition of most of the remaining buildings and the erection of the substantial soil and concrete post barrier blocking the main gateway. Two rows of back-to-back garages remain, along with sick quarters, the officers' mess and a building termed a 'store block' by one informant. However, a local resident told me this building housed 'convalescent' or 'problem' aircrew during World War II. If this is so, they would have been 'students' attending the Aircrew Refresher Centre mentioned in Chapter 6, to which misdeeds, operational or otherwise, by aircrew of all ranks could result in their committal for short periods.

Norton is at present used by an off-road driving school. Supermarket chains have coveted the site and there is much local agitation about such a large area of derelict land going to waste. Apparently the local authority's intention is that it should house a hospital. The concrete bases of most buildings remain; from those bases the sizes of the buildings and the distances between them, as well as the widths of the roadways, appear smaller than I remember them, an echo of my feelings at Hednesford the previous day. I recall the NAAFI floor being described at a CO's Conference as possibly not suitable for dancing but someone — the S Ad O I think — suggesting that if airmen wanted to dance they'd dance on "any bloody floor". A small portion of that floor came into my possession during my visit; I probably walked, and possibly even danced, upon this remnant 43 years earlier.

* * *

Meanwhile, in France, the section of road passing between the two portions of Camp Guynemer has been re-named Rue des Archives and the HQ side of the site now appears to house the *Centre des Archives interministérielles*, the archives of France.

ABBREVIATIONS

AAFCE	Allied Air Forces Central Europe
ACOS	Assistant Chief of Staff
AC1	Aircraftman First Class
AC2	Aircraftman Second Class
ADC	Aide-de-Camp
Adj	Adjutant
AFC	Air Force Cross
AFS	Auxiliary Fire Service
AG	Air Gunner
AMWD	Air Ministry Works Directorate
AOC	Air Officer Commanding
AP	Air Policeman [US]
ARP	Air Raid Precautions
ATC	Air Training Corps
BBC	British Broadcasting Corporation
BEA	British European Airways
BFPO	British Forces Post Office
CB	Companion of the Order of the Bath
CBE	Commander of the Order of the British Empire
CID	Criminal Investigation Department
C-in-C	Commander-in-Chief
CO	Commanding Officer
Cpl	Corporal
DFC	Distinguished Flying Cross
DI	Drill Instructor
DSO	Companion of the Distinguished Service Order
DSS	Department of Social Security
FA	Football Association
FAF	French Air Force
Fg Off	Flying Officer
Flt Lt	Flight Lieutenant
Flt Sgt	Flight Sergeant
GPO	General Post Office
GRSS	Ground Radio Servicing Squadron
HMV	His Master's Voice
hp	Horse power
HQ	Headquarters
HRH	His Royal Highness
KBE	Knight Commander of the Order of the British Empire
KCB	Knight Commander of the Order of the Bath
KD	Khaki Drill
LAC	Leading Aircraftman
LACW	Leading Aircraftwoman

L/Bdr	Lance-bombardier
LNER	London and North Eastern Railway
MBE	Member of the Order of the British Empire
MO	Medical Officer
MPS	Member of the Pharmaceutical Society
MT	Motor Transport
NAAFI	Navy, Army and Air Force Institutes
NATO	North Atlantic Treaty Organisation
NCO	Non-commissioned Officer
NHS	National Health Service
NS	National Service
OBE	Officer of the Order of the British Empire
OHMS	On Her Majesty's Service
PBX	Private Branch Exchange [Switchboard]
PDU	Personnel Despatch Unit
Plt Off	Pilot Officer
POM	Potential Officer Material
PORs	Personnel Occurrence Reports
POSB	Post Office Savings Bank
POW	Prisoner of War
PSO	Personal Staff Officer
PT	Physical Training
Pte	Private
PTI	Physical Training Instructor
PX	Post Exchange
RAF	Royal Air Force
RAFA	Royal Air Forces Association
RASC	Royal Army Service Corps
RCAF	Royal Canadian Air Force
RNAF	Royal Netherlands Air Force
rpm	Revolutions per minute
RSM	Regimental Sergeant Major
RTO	Railway Transportation (or Traffic) Office(r)
SAC	Senior Aircraftman
S Ad O	Senior Administration Officer
SD	Service Dress
Sgt	Sergeant
SHAPE	Supreme Headquarters Allied Powers Europe
SHQ	Station Headquarters
SNCF	Société Nationale des Chemins de Fer Français
S of RT	School of Recruit Training
SP	Service Policeman
Sqn Ldr	Squadron Leader
SROs	Station Routine Orders
SWO	Station Warrant Officer
TABT	Typhoid Para Tetanus [Inoculation]
TAF	Tactical Air Force

TNT	Trinitrotoluene [High explosive]
UK	United Kingdom
US	United States
USA	United States of America
USAAF	United States Army Air Force
USAF	United States Air Force
USSR	Union of Soviet Socialist Republics
u/t	Under training
VC	Victoria Cross
VE	Victory in Europe
VIP	Very Important Person
VJ	Victory over Japan
WAAF	Women's Auxiliary Air Force
Wg Cdr	Wing Commander
W/O	Warrant Officer
WRAF	Women's Royal Air Force
WRVS	Women's Royal Voluntary Service
WVS	Women's Voluntary Service

BIBLIOGRAPHY

Arthur, Max, *There Shall Be Wings*; Hodder and Stoughton Ltd., (1993).

Bowyer, Chaz, *History of the RAF*; Hamlyn, (1977).

Currie, Davison and Ogley, *The Essex Weather Book*; Froglets
Publications Ltd., (1992).

Deighton, Len, *Battle of Britain*; Jonathan Cape Ltd., (1980).

Embry, Air Chief Marshal Sir Basil E., *Mission Completed*;
Methuen & Co., Ltd., (1957).

Forty, George, *Called Up (A National Service Scrapbook)*;
Ian Allan Ltd., (1980).

Freeman, Roger A., *Airfields of the Eighth Then and Now*; Battle of
Britain Prints International Ltd.

Hamlin, John F., *Stand By Yer Beds!*; GMS Enterprises, (1995).

Hastings, Max, *Bomber Command*; Michael Joseph Ltd., (1979).

Hough, Richard and Richards, Denis, *The Battle of Britain: the Jubilee
History*; Hodder & Stoughton Ltd., (1989).

Kinsey, Gordon, *Bawdsey — Birth of the Beam*; Terence
Dalton Ltd., (1983).

Longmate, Norman, *The Bombers*; Arrow Books Ltd., (1988).

Robertson, Bruce, *The RAF: a Pictorial History*; Robert Hale Ltd., (1978).

Royle, Trevor, *The Best Years of Their Lives*; Michael Joseph Ltd., (1986).

Wilmut, Roger and Grafton, Jimmy, *The Goon Show Companion*; Sphere
Books Ltd., (1977).